# Where There is Evil

Sandra Brown was educated at Coatbridge High School, Hamilton College and the Open University, which awarded her an Honours Degree in 1978 and a Masters in Education in 1996. A Primary Deputy Headteacher, then a Senior Lecturer in Further Education, she is the author of a number of articles. Recently she has worked for a children's charity in Scotland, which has involved her in a wide range of issues affecting children and their parents, including child protection.

She believes that dangerous sex offenders, with very few exceptions, should be detained for life, and argues that it is time, in this country, that we review how such people are dealt with by the authorities. Where there is compelling evidence of a pattern of sexual deviance, she calls for juries to be fully informed of the defendant's history.

*Where There is Evil* is her first book.

Sandra Brown

# *Where There is Evil*

*To Sheena*

*Best Wishes*

*from*

*Sandra*

PAN BOOKS

First published 1998 by Macmillan

This edition published 1999 by Pan Books
an imprint of Pan Macmillan Ltd
Pan Macmillan, 20 New Wharf Road, London N1 9RR
Basingstoke and Oxford
Associated companies throughout the world
www.panmacmillan.com

ISBN 0 330 36757 9

9

A CIP catalogue record for this book is available from
the British Library.

Phototypeset by Intype, London Ltd
Printed and bound in Great Britain by
Mackays of Chatham plc, Chatham, Kent

*Dedicated to the memories of
my mother Mary Milne Frew
and of
Mary McCall Anderson
(Moira)*

# Acknowledgements

Space does not allow me to fully recognize all individual sources of support who contributed to the writing of this book. I would like to mention some specifically, however, whose names may not appear within, and to whom I am indebted. First, three hugely enthusiastic professionals, who have dedicated time and energy: Georgina Morley at Macmillan, who now swaps nursing my project for motherhood, Hazel Orme, who has edited my work with great sensitivity, and my agent Sarah Leigh, who has demonstrated her belief in what I was doing from the day she first read my manuscript. My thanks also go to Mark Lucas and John Boothe for early advice, and to Jimmy Boyle and Tim Corrie for their insight.

On a personal level, I can never thank my husband, Ronnie, or our children, Ross and Lauren, enough for their unshakeable faith that I would get there – even if it has taken five years. My gratitude to great friends who have given such stalwart support in that period – Madelene Thompson, who whisked me to Paris for a weekend break, Margaret Clark, who inspired confidence in my ability to use language by reading into the small hours through an 'unputdownable' weekend, and above all to my college buddies, our little group, all still teaching new generations of children – Janet McGill, June Porte, Liz Bruce, Irene McIntosh and Barbara McKechnie.

Special thanks must go to former colleagues who cared (they know who they are); to my long-standing friends, Irene and Sheila, who have always been there for me; to Barbara Jordan and Jean Kendal; Gillian Grainger, for her wise advice; to Irene Hamilton, my neighbour and friend for her helpful suggestions; and to Maureen Berti, from San Jose, who stressed by phone and Internet: 'The only alternative to perseverance is failure.' I am deeply grateful too for the endorsement and love shown by Christine and Bob Lawrie, who showed me that the power of prayer works; and for the positive strength of my courageous friend, Linda Moyes of Pitlochry, who read screeds of writing when she had much harder battles to fight than me.

Finally, my gratitude goes to Elizabeth Taylor Nimmo, Janet Anderson Hart in Sydney, and her cousin Moreen McLaggan of Anstruther, Fife; they shared their memories of Moira, and also my view that even one person speaking out can make a difference.

Edinburgh, November 1997

Men and women make their own history, but they do not make it just as they please; they do not make it under circumstances chosen by themselves, but under circumstances directly encountered, given and transmitted from the past. The tradition of all the dead generations weighs like a nightmare on the brain of the living.

Karl Marx

# Prologue

At the start of a bitterly cold February in 1992, my routine as a wife and mother living in the suburbs of Edinburgh and working in nearby West Lothian as a senior lecturer in childcare in a demanding college post was disrupted. I was sent on a week's management course, which included assertiveness training. What I learnt triggered off a series of events that have affected my entire life. Before I returned to West Lothian College, I had an experience that altered the direction of my life irrevocably.

It also affected my husband, my teenage son and my ten-year-old daughter. It almost destroyed relationships within the rest of my large extended family, dividing me from my mother and brothers. It led to me instigating a major criminal investigation in the Strathclyde region of Scotland, which involved reopening files almost forty years old.

Later, I was in and out of police stations, procurators' offices and I met leading politicians. Strangers saluted my courage and told me they would not have had the strength to do what I was doing. Others, including some relatives, called me a bitch hell-bent on revenge. A tiny handful of members of my church supported me with their prayers,

1

while people from my past showed open hostility. Some said I needed psychiatric help.

All of this resulted from a single conversation I had with my father on 7 February 1992, when we met and spoke for the first time in twenty-seven years.

# Coatbridge, Lanarkshire, Scotland

I was a child in the 1950s, when there was a distinct sense of right and wrong. It was a golden age of innocence when respect for elders was insisted upon, the postman put the letters in your hand, and my grandmother pulled down the blinds in the house when a neighbour had died or when a funeral was going past. We lived life at a slower pace, and knew no one who suffered from stress. Indeed, we had never heard of such a thing.

I ran happily to fetch what we called the 'messages' from gloomy shops with sawdust floors. Assistants brought you items from the shelf; the butter was patted briskly into shape and the cheese neatly severed from the block with wire. The money was whisked on a series of pulleys to the girl in her tower-like cash desk and I dreamed of one day having her job, and inscribing copper-plate figures in a huge ledger. We all shopped at the Co-op, although we knew that some people – the toffs – had their shopping delivered by message boys, who wore three-quarter-length aprons, pedalling their sturdy bikes along tree-lined streets to the big houses where tips were likely. Customers were valued then, and honesty rewarded. It seemed as though life would go on like this for ever.

Coatbridge was dominated by its blast furnaces and

had earned itself the nickname the Iron Burgh. The population was primarily working class, and trips abroad were only for the wealthy, and although the community had experienced its share of scandalous events the local newspaper headlines tended to run BUTCHER FINED FOR HAVING TOO MUCH FAT IN MINCE or MAN FINED FOR RIDING BICYCLE WITHOUT LIGHTS.

The community itself appeared to be a safe place to rear a family. We children walked unaccompanied to and from school and the park. We played for hours in streets that had few cars. Indeed, they were such a rarity that the AA man saluted members as they passed him. The minister called regularly to see us and was offered tea in the best china cup with roses on it, and digestive biscuits thick-spread with butter. Nobody we knew bought chocolate ones, which were too expensive for ordinary folk.

The end of innocence came on 23 February 1957. That date was a watershed in my life and in every other Coatbridge child's. Overnight, fear seeped into a small community where it had been thought that everyone knew everyone else. Two families in particular were affected for ever by the tragedy. The repercussions of one little girl's disappearance caused shock waves and disbelief that never entirely subsided.

# Chapter One

I was just eight years old when Moira Anderson vanished from the streets of Coatbridge in a fierce blizzard on 23 February 1957. She was carrying out an errand for her grandmother that involved the shortest of journeys to the Co-op for some butter.

Moira was pretty, with straight fair hair framing an impish face. Everyone who remembers her recalls a child with an answer for everything. Not cheeky, but a renowned tomboy who was full of life, with intelligent blue eyes and a bubbly personality. One of her uncles told the police that Moira 'was a girl who should've been born a boy – she could beat them all at bools [marbles] and she wasn't a great one for dolls or skipping'. The middle child of three girls, her parents Andrew and Marjorie (also known as Maisie) had settled in a sandstone tenement building at 71 Eglinton Street, a stone's throw from Dunbeth Park, the haunt of all the local children, and close to Coatbridge College in nearby Kildonan Street. The tenements were near Dunbeth Avenue, a prestigious address, and a main bus route passed them. The whole Cliftonville area, with its tree-lined streets was, and still is, regarded as a desirable part of the burgh in which to live.

My mother's sister, my aunt Margaret, lived nearby, and my family and I were just a few streets away. I was a frequent visitor to the park, usually with my aunt's off-spring to give her a break, or playing with the girls I knew from school. I often saw Marilyn Twycross; she was part of a little group that included Marjorie, the youngest Anderson girl. I only knew Moira by sight.

Janet, the eldest daughter, was thirteen, and protective of her younger sisters, who bore a striking resemblance to her. People often confused the first two Anderson girls as their appearance was so similar, but they had distinct personalities and different interests. The sisters were close and Moira confided in Janet. A few days before she disappeared, Moira told her that a young man with a knife had stopped her near their gran's home and had asked her to go with him, offering her money. Terrified, she had run away but had told no one except Janet.

The family of Andrew, or 'Sparks', Anderson, a boiler-erman, was well known in the town. They were not well-to-do, but they were respectable. To earn pocket money Moira ran errands for an elderly neighbour called Mrs Bruce, and did other odd jobs for her and for her mother. The coppers she earned were augmented by her part-time job delivering milk each morning, for Rankin's Dairy. Rain or shine, Moira never missed a delivery, although the work involved pushing a heavy handcart of crates full of milk bottles round local streets. She made seven shillings and sixpence each week and picked up generous tips at Christmas. She put her money straight into the school bank each Monday morning, until funds had grown sufficiently for her to transfer them to the Airdrie Savings Bank. Her main expenditure was on swimming on Monday evenings, after which she bought threepence worth of chips and two pickled onions from the chippie at Jackson Street, before catching the Clifton-ville bus home with her sister.

The Andersons had neither car nor television. Andrew was a keen Glasgow Rangers supporter, and he took Moira to matches at Ibrox and at Airdrie when he could afford to. He would say to her as they entered, 'Now, don't listen to the foul language, just shut your ears and concentrate on the game.' The family also had a small holiday cabin in the countryside, where Mrs Anderson liked to send her daughters to put roses in their cheeks. Seaside visits to relatives who lived on the Scottish East Coast were not unusual, even in winter. Janet had been allowed to go that particular February weekend.

That Saturday Moira went to her granny's home in the mid-afternoon, to meet her cousins and their friend. The older girls, Jeannette and Beth Mathieson, were going to take her to the pictures. Her parents had approved the plan: the girls' grandfather was dying in Glasgow Royal Infirmary and they planned to visit him. In the end Moira's mother stayed at home. She had asked Moira to visit her gran, who had Asian flu, before the outing, to check if she needed anything.

When Moira arrived at her grandmother's house in Muiryhall Street, her Uncle Jim, a bachelor who lived with his mother, said that he'd bought fish for their tea but that there was no fat to cook it. He asked Moira to go to the Co-op. She swithered about taking her grandmother's dog Glen with her as she liked to do, but the snow was falling heavily and her uncle told her not to dawdle. He thought if she hurried she would get to the store before it closed at 4.15 p.m.

The Co-op in Laird Street was no distance from Muiryhall Street, and when she set off Moira was warmly dressed in her navy blue school coat and a pixie hat with red bands knitted into it. It was the last time she was ever seen.

That afternoon the streets were deserted, mainly because of the blizzard, but also because, as a contemporary report in the *Scottish Daily Express* read, 'At that time ... the men are at football matches, the women at shops downtown, the kiddies at cinema matinées.' The staff in the Co-op knew Moira well but had told the newspaper's journalist: 'Moira did not come in here on Saturday afternoon.' They were adamant that they had not closed early.

Moira's uncle became angry as he waited for the child to return and the afternoon wore on. 'She said she wouldn't be long!' he complained to the Mathieson girls. He remembered, with some exasperation, how Moira could not resist a challenge to a game of marbles – she was renowned for her skill and had humiliated more than a few male companions, winning their best 'bools' from them with ease. But surely she wouldn't be playing marbles on a day like this. He became increasingly anxious.

Eventually Moira's cousins set off for the Regal where they hoped to spot her in the queue. Their luck was out. Moira wasn't there and the five o'clock show was packed out. They went on to the Theatre Royal in Jackson Street, where they saw a film starring Peter Finch. By that time, they'd given up on Moira.

Later that evening, when Moira's cousins were back at home with their parents, they were astonished when

Moira's father appeared at the door looking for her. He was horrified to hear that his daughter had not been with them. He could not believe that on a journey of five hundred yards, his daughter, who knew the area inside out, could have gone missing. Stunned, he left to tell his wife.

It took time for the news of Moira's disappearance to spread: communications in the fifties were a poor shadow of what we now take for granted. A local search took place, the next day, on the traditional Scottish Sabbath but Monday's *Daily Record* made no mention that the child had vanished. On Tuesday, though, it devoted the centre-spread to the story, and illustrated the route she had followed. There is one sentence in which the reporter who wrote the story unwittingly touched on the key to the mystery: 'Something made Moira change her mind about shopping.' But as the days slipped past the question 'What?' was left unanswered.

A few days later, on 2 March, the family's sick grand-father, James Anderson, died, which doubled their pain. After the funeral, hopes for Moira's safety faded fast, but Mrs Anderson insisted on buying the Monopoly set Moira had said she'd love for her twelfth birthday on 31 March, saying, 'I won't give up hope yet.' But the date, which was also Mothering Sunday that year, came and went and Moira had not appeared for either her present or her birthday tea.

There had been no reconstruction of Moira's journey to the Co-op and no door-to-door inquiry took place. Had the police spoken to the Andersons' neighbours, they would have found that one had been a vital witness. Mrs Twycross was the mother of my playmate Marilyn. She had been trying to clear her path of the heavy snow, and had seen Moira on her way to the Co-op. She had called a greeting. She felt sure the child had shouted back, 'Is the bus away yet?' before she carried on, and Mrs Twycross had scurried back into the warmth of her home. Like others, she expected the police to visit Moira's neighbours but none came round and she dismissed what she had seen.

The *Daily Record*'s report ended with Maisie Anderson's words: 'I know Moira has been taken away against her will – she would never speak to strangers. Everybody knew her. She was such a tomboy, so full of fun and life. She wouldn't go willingly with her birthday so close.'

It had been just after midnight on that Saturday might that Andrew Anderson had contacted the local police station, which was almost opposite my home in Dunbeth Road. He told the officer on duty of his daughter's plans for that afternoon. The managers of half a dozen cinemas were called from their homes in case Moira had been locked in somewhere. Even the Carnegie Library was opened and searched because she was an avid reader who spent lots of time there. The houses of all relatives and friends were checked and double-checked.

As the week progressed with no news, a huge search was mounted. The bin men abandoned their strike to join police on the hunt, scouring back yards, sheds, garages and derelict buildings. The big event of Saturday, an Ayr United v. Airdrie football match at Broomfield, had attracted large crowds, then had been cancelled with the awful weather. Could a football supporter have stopped Moira for directions and abducted her? Andrew was firm that his daughter would never have gone off with a

WHERE THERE IS EVIL

stranger, but as the hunt dragged on he said, 'I fear she has been picked up in a car and taken away somewhere. But Moira never liked leaving the town, even to go into Glasgow. She spent almost all her spare time playing around the house.' But Maisie Anderson insisted again that Moira would not have gone anywhere with a strange man.

Terror built up in the local children. Our mothers promised dire punishments if we played out late without permission. My friends and I walked in pairs to school, and had to bear the ignominy of being collected from the clubs we attended. I gave up Brownies on my mother's insistence but was allowed to carry on with Red Cross classes, which were held much closer to home. We muttered darkly about the injustice of this, but we looked over our shoulders constantly as we avoided former favourite play areas such as the old graveyard in Church Lane, by the school.

Overnight, the freedom of an entire generation of children had been wiped out by a single event.

As the days lengthened, townsfolk continued to surmise what might have happened. Some limelight-seeking individuals invented possibly useful information. One woman near Eglinton Street where the Andersons lived insisted she had heard screeching brakes and had seen a car speed off that afternoon. Police dismissed her theory that Moira had been knocked down and that a panicking motorist had bundled her body into his car when they checked the view from her window. She couldn't have seen or heard what she had described. They explained to her that with the amount of snow that had fallen on the roads it was highly unlikely that any vehicle could have been heard. All the side streets had been treacherous, and very few main roads had remained open on that Saturday.

Other leads took the police nowhere. A family described seeing the missing girl at a Queen's Park funfair on Glasgow's South Side, but the show folk could not corroborate this. A navy blue raincoat belt was found by a railwayman in a marshy area of bog near Coatbridge known as the Moss, but proved not to be Moira's. Most dramatic of all, a girl seen being dragged forcibly into a van at Baillieston, by Coatbridge, that night, turned out to have been a willing hitchhiker.

Suspicion fell on the Anderson family themselves: as police understand it, the majority of victims know their killer. Moira's sister Janet recalls that her uncle Jim was grilled endlessly as he had been the last known person to have spoken to the child. Whispers followed him for many years and Janet feels that the episode blighted his life.

Even Moira's parents found themselves the object of speculation. Fathers of missing children are automatic suspects, and Andrew was conscious of people looking at him askance. Maisie, it was falsely said, had often had to punish Moira. She was lively, more trouble than the other two girls, a handful. Perhaps a family argument had gone too far.

Rumours of a family dispute persisted for several days, and on 5 March, eleven days after Moira had vanished, Coatbridge CID officers were reported by the *Glasgow Herald* to have searched the Andersons' holiday home, but found nothing.

The same officers travelled to Greenock, where an elderly woman insisted she had spotted a girl bearing a resemblance to Moira, and south to Doncaster to interview a lorry driver who thought he had spotted her with two men. Both leads came to nothing.

New lines of inquiry gradually dried up, and what had been front-page news was relegated to inside columns, then odd paragraphs tucked in corners. 'Moira – Still No News', 'Coatbridge Girl Still Untraced', 'Girl Still Missing'.

On 18 May the *Herald* reported that a photo of Moira would appear on television, some three months after she had vanished. The police had been urged to have it broadcast before, but had felt that the BBC would not transmit it as 'It would serve no useful purpose'.

Two days later, when the picture had been shown, it was reported that the television appeal had brought no response.

# Chapter Two

As time dragged by with no news, faith in Coatbridge Burgh Police plummeted. Just days after Moira's disappearance, a dinner was held in honour of the retiring Chief Constable Daniel McLauchlan OBE. The new Chief, Charles McIntosh, was left with a hot potato. In his statement to the *Scotsman* of 26 February, he said that he was in command of the investigation and appealed for witnesses who might have seen Moira on the Saturday to come forward. From their statements, he said, perhaps a complete picture of her movements on the day of her disappearance might emerge. To co-ordinate the inquiry, he promoted Detective Sergeant John F. MacDonald to Uniformed Inspector in charge of the Coatbridge CID.

The *Airdrie and Coatbridge Advertiser* carried a photograph of the new man, and I can remember my father discussing these promotions: we lived opposite the police station and he was on nodding terms with all the officers, who in those days jumped on and off the buses and who had an arrangement with drivers where they expected to travel free. In return, they were prepared to look the other way when problems arose regarding the staff of Baxter's Bus Service.

Whether it was because of the turmoil of McLauchlan's

departure, McIntosh's arrival, or MacDonald's promotion, or whether the announcement in the middle of the search for Moira that the Chief Constable for Lanarkshire was coming to visit the local force, there is no doubt that the search for the missing child became unco-ordinated. In 1993, a former police officer, now living in Canada, telephoned the Scottish *Sunday Mail* to say he recalled how disillusioned he had been by his time spent with the Coatbridge Burgh Police. Contrary to what was being said in the newspapers at the time about areas being searched two and three times, he had felt uneasy then and for years afterwards about the attitude of some of those in charge. Superiors, he said, were more concerned about getting offices spick and span and ensuring filing cabinets were up to date because of the impending visit of the highest-ranking officer in the county. A distinct lack of urgency had been shown about Moira, and he had overheard several men shrug off her disappearance with the words, 'Och, the lassie's likely had a row wi' her mammy and went off. She'll turn up soon enough.' The group of officers he had been with were told not to search anywhere beyond the town boundary.

Furthermore, egos were bruised, when because of lack of headway and the Andersons' view that the local police were not experienced in dealing with missing persons, the Glasgow CID joined the case. They were not overwhelmed by help. They briefly linked Peter Manuel, who went down in criminal history as Scotland's most infamous serial killer, to Moira, and her name was mentioned when he conducted his own defence at his trial in May 1958. Manuel indicated that two detectives had said to him after an identification parade that they were going to pin eight murders on him, including 'the little girl who disappeared in Coatbridge last year'. But they had to rule out Manuel: he had been in prison at the time of Moira's disappearance, completing a stretch for breaking into Hamilton colliery. He might have been in the clear about Moira, but he went on to gain further notoriety as the last person hanged in Scotland.

Other members of the public share the view that the search was fragmented and lacked foresight. A local man commented in 1993 that he never understood why the Monkland Canal, which went right through the town, had not been dragged. At the time the official line was that it was too choked and overgrown with weeds, and because of Suez the petrol crisis was uppermost in the minds of the authorities.

Also in 1993, William McDonald of Glenboig made a statement to those who reopened Moira's file, saying how astounded he had been to see land infilled at Coltswood, only a mile from Moira's home, that spring. 'I couldn't believe my eyes to see quarrying and infill work going on when a local child had just gone missing.'

Others have commented that they were amazed that no door-to-door interviewing took place, not even around Muiryhall Street, where Moira's grandmother lived. A relative of mine, who has stayed in neighbouring Albion Street all his life, said, 'We always expected police to call because our household had three single men, all of them in different age groups, but it just never happened.'

The local police had made the naïve assumption that people would come forward automatically with any relevant information, but they were mistaken. Members of the public thought progress was being made when it was not.

They felt sure that any local deviants would be undergoing thorough checking.

The only 'local' suspect whose movements were thoroughly checked was Ian Simpson, who was mentally handicapped, from Mitchell Street, near Kirkwood. His sister, by sheer coincidence, lived almost next door to the Co-op to which Moira had been sent.

In the 1990s Inspector John F. MacDonald revealed that Simpson was always his number one suspect, but he had a cast-iron alibi. He had been away with the Territorial Army that weekend, and his sister insisted he had been nowhere near her home in Laird Street. He was allowed to go free. However, he was eventually taken to Carstairs, the state psychiatric hospital, after hitching a lift from a Leeds man whom he murdered and buried in a lay-by in the Scottish mountains. Taking the victim's car, he picked up a foreign student and murdered him, too, dumping the body in a forest near Dumfries. He was in Carstairs from 1962 till February 1976, when he was hacked to death with a staff member and a police officer during a break-out by fellow inmates.

The *Airdrie and Coatbridge Advertiser*, published weekly on Saturdays in 1957, summarized the events of the first week, stressing the concern being shown throughout the district: 'Moira's name is mentioned in shops, buses, public houses, in fact everywhere that people gather ... all wish to help, yet all feel helpless in their ability to do so.' Seldom, they reported, in the history of the Monklands had there been such a poignant human drama, and Mrs Anderson had the sympathy of countless mothers. All of Scotland was in shock. The paper described the 'sightings' in Greenock and Doncaster, but it went on to say:

> Coatbridge Police revealed that they had been con-
> tacted by a woman who had seen Moira board a
> Baxter's bus in Alexander Street at 5.15 p.m. on Sat-
> urday. It was bound for Kirkwood [a modern housing
> area on the town's outskirts], and the woman, who
> knows Moira by sight, distinctly remembers smiling
> at the little girl as she smiled back. The police
> managed to trace the conductress of this bus, but she
> has been unable to aid the investigation . . . The bus
> went from Coatdyke Cross via Muiryhall St, Kil-
> donan St, Alexander St, along Sunnyside Road
> towards the main town centre landmark known to
> every local as The Fountain, and then along the Main
> St, down towards Whifflet; its final leg would be via
> School St to the Kirkwood area of Old Monkland.

The mention of the bus's destination made the police concentrate on Ian Simpson's alibi. The Anderson parents
queried why Moira would ever wish to go there. They
explained that they knew no one who lived in that part of
town.

After an appeal only one of six passengers had come
forward. James Inglis had been waiting for the bus and
knew Moira: she had been playing in the snow at the bus
stop when the bus arrived, he said, but he was less sure
that she had boarded it.

One other person reported seeing a child loitering at a
bus stop in Whifflet around teatime. She seemed to be
waiting for someone, they said, scuffing the icy pavement

18

with her feet to keep warm. Their description of her shoes was accurate, but they had not noticed who had picked her up. The buses had stopped because of the weather, but the child appeared to have had an arrangement with someone. She had simply melted away into the night.

Instead of reconstructing the five-minute bus journey to the Whitelaw Fountain in the town centre and then on through Whifflet to the town centre, though, police concentrated their efforts on issuing descriptions of Moira's clothing to all policemen in Greenock, where a search was organized. All ships' crews anchored in port were interviewed to see if they recollected a girl answering Moira's description. None did. Back at Coatbridge, police discounted the bus sightings, and visited schools to question pupils. This met with little success.

When detectives came to my primary school their talk was directed at older children in Primary 4–7. Gartsherrie Academy had a large central hall, and, a Primary 3 child on an errand, my curiosity got the better of me. Clasping the jug I'd been given to fetch water from the cloakroom for painting, I listened. I watched as older pupils shook their heads. Many knew her or, like myself, knew of her, although Moira had been at Coatdyke Primary in Muiry-hall Street. I felt a flash of sympathy go through me when I thought of Marjorie, who was my own age. How awful never to see your big sister again.

Inexplicably the 1957 investigation team failed to interview Moira's best friend, who had spent part of that final day with her. That morning, Moira had visited the Limb Centre in Motherwell with her father. They had returned after 11 a.m. and Moira had popped round to see Elizabeth Taylor with whom she spent most Saturdays at the Regal

19

or Odeon matinées. Elizabeth Taylor Nimmo, now a grandmother, can recall the events of that day vividly. Moira had come round to her house in Dunbeth Avenue, and asked her to come out to play despite the dark sky, which promised bad weather, and an icy wind. Unusually for them, they elected to skip to keep warm and tied one end of a clothes rope to a lamp post, taking turns to twirl it while the other skipped.

Elizabeth Nimmo said, 'The snow started to come on not long after we started the skipping. Funnily enough the morning had been fine, very crisp and bright with no hint of the blizzard coming. It turned into a really terrible day, in fact I'd never seen snow like it. Moira said as soon as she turned up that she would have to go for some messages . . . Then my mother noticed the weather and shouted to me from the window to come in, it was too cold to play. Moira asked if I wanted to go with her, but I wasn't allowed, and that was that. I went into the house and watched some swimming which was on television, which we had then. The last I saw of Moira, she was turning the corner towards her home, obviously popping into her mum before she left for her gran's house.' Elizabeth added, with obvious sorrow, 'Who knows what might have happened if I'd gone with her? Could I have saved her or would the two of us have vanished? It's a question that can never be answered.'

She can still remember how the news was broken to her, and her shock, on the morning after Moira vanished without trace. Usually on Sunday mornings she and Moira went to Band of Hope meetings but that day her father, deeply perturbed, woke her and said, 'Moira didn't come home last night.'

More than thirty years later Elizabeth had her first opportunity to make a formal statement to the police about her friend's disappearance and provided information not previously known.

In April 1993, she gave an interview to the local paper, in which she spoke of the enormity of the tragedy with which the Andersons had had to come to terms. Maisie Anderson, Elizabeth Nimmo said, had died in 1977, never having fully accepted the loss of her child, and Sparks, ironically, died in 1992, a few months after the police were approached to reopen the case. He never knew that there had been a sudden and dramatic development.

'It's very sad,' said Elizabeth. 'Her parents must have gone through hell wondering if she would or wouldn't walk through the door again. And for her sisters, Janet and Marjorie, it must have been hell living with the uncertainty of not knowing whether Moira was alive or dead. I know that her mum believed for years that she was still alive and used to go out looking for her. She even set a place for her daughter at the tea table every night and bought Moira a birthday present each 31st March. I don't believe Moira ran away. She wouldn't have gone willingly with a strange man. Although in those days you could go out and leave your door open, our parents always warned us about speaking to strange men and being offered sweets. For a time I thought she might have been abducted and could still be alive, but not any more.'

Until 1977 many others shared Elizabeth's view. If Moira had still been alive then, she would surely have come to her mother's funeral.

It would be a little longer before the key to the puzzle of Moira's disappearance was unearthed.

# Chapter Three

My mother Mary once told me that in the days following my birth, on 7 January 1949, when she stared into my face, she had a sense of being scrutinized by one of the ancients. A pair of eyes surveyed her that seemed to possess an inner knowledge. 'Everyone told me you'd been here before, Sandra.' She laughed. 'They said you'd probably read all the books and would keep me right. Such a serious wee face!'

My earliest memory is of being held on her lap, and having my little clenched fists prised open by her and her mother, Granny Katie. They were commenting on the length of my fingers.

'I wonder what she'll be when she grows up?' my mother mused.

'Perhaps with these fingers she'll be an artist or play the piano,' said Granny Katie.

To their amusement, I piped up, 'Me gonna read!' and tried to remove my gran's spectacles.

Perhaps this indicated the way in which my relationship with my mother would progress. She discovered that I was a headstrong, independent child who thrived on responsibility. I was often entrusted to keep an eye on my two little brothers while she ran to the Co-op near our first home in Partick Street. Even before their arrival, and before my third birthday, she had found that I was resourceful. One day, the wind slammed the door shut as she hung washing outside. I amazed her by getting up from my nap, toddling down the stairs and stuffing the key, which I pulled from the lock, through the letterbox.

My relationship with my father, though, was fraught with problems. My first memory is of him holding me on the parapet of a bridge overlooking the river Clyde in Glasgow. I was about three. I remember with startling clarity the stark terror I felt when I gazed down at the swirling black water. Despite the knowledge that the arms encircling me were strong ones, I nevertheless felt real mistrust and panicked. Howling with terror, mainly because my father suddenly pretended that he was going to drop me, I was put down. Ever since, I have been frightened of deep running water and heights.

Otherwise my father adored me. I was the first child my mother had borne him who survived and I was named Alexandra after him, although I was always known to everyone as Sandra. He and my mother, Mary Frew, had married, like many others, at the tail end of the war in October 1945. He called himself Sandy, to distinguish himself from his own dad, who was also Alexander Gartshore. My mother, though, always called him Alex.

She had been deeply in love with a young man named Davey Thomson, who was drowned during the war. My father had been a friend of Davey and wrote to her to console her. Later, he suggested that they meet up, since he lived in Bellshill and she in Whifflet, only a couple of miles away.

My mother was from a large family, which was respectable but not wealthy. The eldest child of eight, she was always acutely aware that no matter how bright she was, a wage was needed from her as early as possible. And she *was* bright, but there was no question of her education continuing: she was found a job in Marshall's shoe shop, earning a few welcome shillings a week. Her parents had married at the close of the First World War. Katie Smith hailed from Denny, and went into service at thirteen in the big houses of Glasgow and Paisley. There she met my grandfather, Norman Frew, who worked all his days in the huge iron forges at Beardmore's in Parkhead, Glasgow. He brought her to set up home in Coatbridge, where his father had a profitable grocer's shop. But with eight in the family, they never knew a life in which they could have a holiday.

My father came from a quite different background. He was one of only three children and there was more to go round. By all accounts, though, he did not care about possessions and was a loner, keen to skip tedious hours in the classroom for the bluebell woods of the estate on which he spent his early years. He was a constant source of anxiety to his father, who could never be quite sure where he was. His maternal grandmother was heard to comment that young Alex reminded her of her philandering late husband – out at all hours, fond of females and feckless. To anyone who would listen she said that her worries had ended when she was widowed, 'because then I knew where he was'. My father, she claimed, was a chip off the same block.

Born in 1921, my father's humble beginnings in a cottage on a rambling estate obscure the grand origins

of the family from which he sprang. The Gartshores of
Gartshore have been traced back to the twelfth century
by one of my relatives, Graham. Given lands and their
own charter by a Scottish monarch, for generations they
lived quietly on their estate by Kirkintilloch, a small town
near Glasgow. A brief skirmish with fame came in 1745
when Bonnie Prince Charlie's troops marched through the
town and someone took a potshot at him. Angry at such
audacity, Charles had my father's ancestor, the Laird of
Gartshore, imprisoned to force the guilty party to give
themselves up. According to records in Kirkintilloch
Library, it was only on the intervention of a beautiful lady
in the entourage of the Young Pretender that the Laird
was not hanged.

All went well with the family estate until 1813, when
it passed to Marjorie Gartshore, known as May, who never
married. She left everything to a child named John Murray,
fourth son of the Lord Lieutenant of Scotland, who came
from Edinburgh. No one is quite sure why she did this
and also insisted that he took the name – she had ignored
her Gartshore relatives in the surrounding areas – but
John Murray Gartshore was a disaster. He drank heavily,
gambled away large sums of money, and finally lost Gartshore House and all its land, including pits and
brickworks, on the turn of dice, to a powerful family
of iron and steel magnates, the Bairds of Gartsherrie. They
in turn passed it to a daughter who married Lord
Whitelaw, now a peer in the House of Lords.

While my grandfather accepted this state of affairs with
equanimity, I recall the bitter tone in my father's voice
when the subject came up. He brooded over it, and certainly felt cheated. He always laughed when Grandpa

related that the ultimate irony for Murray was that he had ended up working *for* the Bairds, cleaning out the blast furnaces, and indeed, his end was, perhaps, fitting in that, in a drunken stupor, he fell asleep in a furnace and was cremated accidentally.

Perhaps it was this reversal in family fortunes that led to my father growing up with a chip on his shoulder. My granny's sister, Aunt May, said of him that he seemed to think the world owed him a living: his truanting was a way of flouting authority. Beaten frequently for running off, he shrugged off physical punishment until he stood over six feet tall and could no longer be walloped easily. Aunt May also noticed that my father could slip with extraordinary ease into a fantasy world where he told lies so smoothly that it was only when people checked things out that he was caught. Yet he could charm women effortlessly – but was regarded with some suspicion by most men.

I was the apple of his eye. Long before seat belts were invented, I am told that he would tie me with scarves into the passenger seat of the butcher's van in which he delivered meat. Maybe he did this because I was, perhaps, doubly precious to my mother: she had undergone a major operation to have children, then had conceived, only to have Catherine, her first-born child, survive just six days.

Like many other newly-weds, at the end of the Second World War, my parents had to stay with their parents Katie and Norman, occupying one of their three bedrooms. After my birth, they were given a room and kitchen at 26 Partick Street in the Greenend area of Coatbridge. Here, Norman was born in July 1952, then the youngest of the family, Ian Alexander. I recall his appearance in

26

January 1955 very well, as I was entrusted with many tasks involving the new baby. A photo of Norman and me holding our tiny brother on the settee is one of the few that was taken in that home.

# Chapter Four

The house in Partick Street, long since knocked down, was a tenement building typical of many in Coatbridge. There was communal housing on stair landings, drying greens, which were the hub of all activity for the squads of children, and the wash houses, in which the women chatted as they stretchered out row after row of clothes to flap in the wind. To own a little Acme wringer with two rollers, which you could tighten over your own sink by turning little wing nuts, was the greatest thing my mother could imagine.

All the women were allocated different days to have their 'stretch' of the greens, but everyone coveted Monday as a wash day – it was traditionally thought the best. Certainly no one would have dared hang out the tiniest amount of washing on a Sunday – not even a cloth over the rope many had suspended across their landings. This would have been regarded as scandalous, blasphemous even!

We children were seen and not heard and play was indulged as long as it did not interfere with the Sabbath. I looked enviously at the Catholic children who seemed not only to have more freedom, but did mysterious things with candles and were allowed to have pierced ears. As for the beautiful white Communion dresses the girls I knew got to wear ... it just was too much to bear! The closest I got to one was as a train bearer at my aunt Jean's wedding, where I endured having my blonde curls put into long ringlets purely to gain ownership of a miniature bride's dress in sparkling white. As for earrings, they were a lost cause as far as my mother was concerned: she classed them as items only gypsies or 'bad women' wore.

Those Catholic girls fascinated me and their religion was kept secret: teachers would not answer your questions about it at school. I was allowed to run for messages to the Co-op and there my friend Nessie and I would encounter a little group of them. We occasionally followed them across the road to the swing park in Elm Street, which is still there, though modernized. They were nine or ten years old, and happy to teach younger ones the skills of street play. Two have stayed in my mind, but for different reasons. One, called Jeannie, could twirl with all the dexterity of a trapeze artist, and showed us how to 'tummle yir wulkies', which involved placing your body next to the iron rail at the park entrance, then tumbling over it head first. She loved all animals but her looks were spoiled by an Alsatian someone had tied up outside the Co-op. That incident taught me to be a wary of dogs I did not know, and although Jeannie assured me I should only worry about strays, I knew differently.

The other Catholic girl lived just opposite the Co-op, at 218 Calder Street, and was one of a big family, which I envied. She was called Rena, and her dad, Eddie Costello, worked in the scrap yard and knew my father. Our homes were a stone's throw apart, and she and her pals taught us wee ones to play 'Truth, Dare or Promise', but they only bothered with us if they were bored, and certainly not if any lads were about.

When I was seven, we moved house and lost contact with most of our Partick and Calder Street neighbours, but years later when I was living in Whifflet, next door to Granny Frew, I encountered Rena. It was 1963, I think. I was in my navy High School blazer standing at the bus stop at the top of Ashgrove. A woman with a wee baby was already there waiting for the bus up town, and just before it appeared over the brow of the brae, I felt she was vaguely familiar. As we boarded both of us exchanged greetings with the conductress, and although I sat a few seats forward, when I heard the words, 'Hello, Rena,' I turned my head to look. It was her, chatting away as she perched the wee one on her knee. She still had such a nice smile, though now the make-up was very Dusty Springfield, her blonde hair sprayed stiff with Belair, eyeliner black and tilted up noticeably at the corners, Egyptian-style. She must have been about nineteen, but still looked younger than her age, despite all the Max Factor. I could not catch her eye and was too shy to move near her. Over the brief journey of just two or three stops, the two women exchanged pleasantries, and I learned that our families were once again living close to each other. Her baby was lovely, and beautifully dressed, but while the clippie was cooing at her, Rena was observing the reactions of others to the colour of the little one's skin.

'What are you calling her?' she was asked.

'Mary, after my mother,' Rena replied, 'and she's being christened in St Mary's.'

Before I could smile at her the clippie had helped her off, and they waved a cheery farewell to each other.

I never saw Rena and her child again and never thought of her until one day in the spring of 1994, when the grim events that had occurred in Gloucester, England, began to unfold on the front page of every newspaper. With mounting horror, I realized who Catherine West, Fred West's first wife, had been.

I telephoned my mother and we asked each other how a local girl like that could have lost all contact with her large family. The other news item that had stunned me was that Rena Costello's first little girl was also missing, and suspected dead. But the police were searching for the remains of a child called Charmaine, which couldn't have been the same one. Sadly, it turned out that Rena had named her baby Charmaine Carol Mary.

But I have happy memories of Partick Street, where I became, like Moira Anderson, an incorrigible tomboy. I played from morning till night both in our building – out of sight of my mother – and outside, climbing the dykes that separated Partick Street from Kelvin Street. I whined for baseball boots like the boys and, in despair, my mother relented. I thought nothing of running over the roofs of the wash houses and lowering myself off walls nine or ten feet high. I practically lived in an overflowing neighbouring scrap yard, which belonged to Martin and Black's, the factory renowned for huge wire ropes that were sent round the world to hold up steel suspension bridges. This was our playground, and we thrived on danger. It was all the mothers could do to drag us in after hours of play, especially in the long daylight of Scottish summer evenings. For me, surrender to my mother's yells to come in preceded a thorough scrub at our kitchen sink, but many others were just thrown into a shared bed with two or three other siblings, all equally filthy. Perhaps given a jam 'piece' or sandwich if they were lucky, they had old coats or sacking over them instead of a quilt. These circumstances were quite normal and caused no raised eyebrows in a neighbourhood where no one had a bath or an inside toilet, but instead shared communal outdoor 'cludgies' to which each family had a key.

Despite my bravado in front of the boys I played with, I was terrified to venture to that outside toilet at night. I was petrified by the spiders that scuttled along the white-washed step when you were sitting there, frozen to the spot by the draught blasting under the door and round your bare legs.

In our special playground, a troop of us played hide 'n' seek, kick the can, dodgie ball (a variation on rounders) or devised gang huts of whatever we could find lying around. Long grass and purple-coloured weeds helped with the camouflage needed for games like Tarzan, and also discouraged adults from hunting for us. Sometimes we went on the scrounge for discarded Tizer and Irn-Bru bottles left by workmen from their lunch. We were cute enough to take them to the corner shop for the deposit pennies, which would buy us liquorice or sherbet in a small bag. When we were really feeling adventurous, we went further into the railway yards in the Meadows, where rows and rows of wagons had been shunted on to railway sidings to await goods for transport all over Britain. We would scramble over pyramids of coal in the wagons or slide open their doors to gaze fearfully into gloomy, mys-terious interiors, but the real frisson of excitement came from the knowledge that at any moment we could be caught by the railway police for trespassing. As five- and six-year-olds, we didn't know what this word meant, but everyone ran for their lives as soon as an adult was spotted in the distance.

In the street behind our house, I manoeuvred Cherry Blossom boot-polish tins round hopscotch squares, because cars were few and far between. The milk was delivered by horse and cart and the Co-op man had to be given yellow tokens in exchange for the two daily pints of milk. My father's delivery van was one of the rare vehicles parked by the kerb. The only other I remember belonged to the baker, who came a few times a week and to whom I was sometimes sent for bread, scones and pancakes. In the post-war years, women still regarded it as shaming not to produce their own home baking of Victoria sponges, fairy cakes and Scottish shortbread for guests, and it was unusual to eat bought cakes. I saw it as a treat to be sent for cakes from the van.

Children were not given regular pocket money so if someone was getting married, we hung round the entrance to their close or gate. When the bride emerged, we knew her dad would throw a shower of coppers for luck. With no heed for danger we would all yell, 'Scramble!' and launch ourselves almost under the taxi's back wheels to compete for the spoils. If you met a family taking a baby to its christening, you might have the good fortune to be given a christening 'piece', which was something like a home-baked biscuit with a glinting threepenny bit hidden inside. Granny Katie hid coins in her famous clootie dumplings at Christmas, but as she had twenty grand-children and not much money, it was a real stroke of luck to get one. 'Finder's keepers!' we would yell triumphantly.

Soap was my mother's solution for everything in an

environment where hygiene was poor. It was not uncommon to see a 'rats' flitting', or mass evacuation of the rodents who would abandon housing about to be knocked down, as if some benefactor had tipped them off. My mother's practices with the carbolic did not stop me picking up, to her great shame, ringworm and, later, impetigo. All my long hair was shorn, and lurid gentian violet was painted on my face.

I recall being severely punished once by my mother, who ran the household pretty much single-handedly after my father obtained his PSV licence and started with Baxter's Buses, the local family-run bus company that served Airdrie and Coatbridge. We entertained a number of visitors to afternoon tea one day, and I set the table. I took enormous care with the china dishes and teapot, then filled the sugar bowl. People stirred it into their tea, sipped and suddenly there were grimaces all round the table. It was salt! My mother, last to sit down, had been wondering why there was an awkward silence with no one drinking and was 'black affronted' when she was told why. I got such a row from her, but no wallop as she knew it had been unintentional. I seem to remember that I made amends with a spirited rendition of a then popular song, 'Where Will The Baby's Dimple Be?' in which I did a cutesy Shirley Temple routine.

'Doing a turn,' as it was called, held no problems for me: few people had television and we made our own entertainment. In the large family from which my mother came, everyone performed at family parties. Even the youngest grandchild was expected to dance or say a poem, or tell a little joke. Only my dad never took part, but was always a figure on the sidelines. In photographs, he is always right in the background, mainly because of his height, which rendered him head and shoulders above everyone else. If one word summed him up, it was 'watchful'. He was affable, and went out of his way to be pleasant to his wife's clan, but there was something about him that made me feel he was on his guard, and which set him apart from my jolly uncles. Even before I started school, I sensed this, and as my highly vocal uncles formed a chorus line, and belted out songs like 'Moonlight Bay', I knew that they disliked him. I was too young to realize that this was because of his infidelity to my mother.

My feelings about my father were becoming confused: I loved being twirled upside down by him until I was about five, and started to feel uncomfortable when he flipped me over. When I finally refused to run to him and greet him like this, he was angry with me and found subtle ways to punish me. He thought it funny, if I was 'uppity', to dip a teaspoon in freshly made tea and hold it, red-hot, against my bare arm or leg as I passed him. The blisters, he told my mother, had been caused by me splashing myself with hot tea, I was so careless. I looked at him wordlessly when he made statements like this: it didn't seem possible that my own father could be so mean. When he had me in tears after he had burst a paper bag he had blown up at the back of my head, or when he insisted one Christmas that I got nothing from Santa because I had been naughty, my mother accepted what he said, and did not question his punishments. The culture in which she had always lived did not encourage women to overturn the views of their menfolk. Although she made sure I got some presents later, that particular Christmas morning I found a lump of coal at the end of my bed.

But these punishments were only the start. Later I dreaded the signal that he was really annoyed about something: his hands would go to the large leather belt round his waist, a relic from his Army days, and he would unbuckle it so that the end swung from his hand and the huge brass buckle dangled, to be lashed over bare legs, back and buttocks. Anywhere not easily seen once the victim was dressed.

# Chapter Five

Before we had left Partick Street, in late 1955, I had begun to notice how my father took every opportunity to joke coarsely with young adult women, which had them flushing in embarrassment. Then, to my distress, he would pounce, squeezing at knees and grabbing at suspenders. If they were unable to resist this onslaught, he would grope at their breasts. He might start playfully, holding something they needed just out of reach, and they would end up involved in what seemed harmless horseplay – at first. His physique, of course, ensured that he was the victor unless other men were around or his victim was unusually spirited. It worried me that he would not stop running his hands all over them. He would pin the person to the ground, rubbing his face hard against their skin and declaring loudly that he was just playing a game. Couldn't they take it then? All women liked this game, he said – he called it 'Beardie' – and the yells of outrage from those on whom he inflicted it were often because their chins were left raw. His sheer brute strength ensured that often the woman only put up token resistance or squealed hysterically, which normally brought him to his senses.

This behaviour never occurred around my mother or other men, and he chose his victims with care, making

37

sure that if the woman was married her husband was half his size. In one or two cases, I noticed he did not meet much resistance, and later I realized that he chalked up these conquests as affairs. My mother had had to contend with this from early in their marriage. In her seventies she told me that the first one she had discovered had been the most painful: when she had given birth to the little girl she lost and was still in hospital, my father had taken a nurse to the pictures and then dancing. She confronted him about all the clean underwear and shirts he had gone through in record time and told him that he had been seen, but he denied it. My mother, though, had challenged the nurse, who had admitted it. 'It hit me then what he was like,' my mother said. 'I couldn't believe someone could do that after his wife had gone through a big operation to carry his child. Then I made the mistake of thinking he might change, if he was given responsibilities.'

In Partick Street, however, he went to great lengths to be accepted as a family man. He was at the memorable street party held for Queen Elizabeth's Coronation, where people packed like sardines into our next-door neighbour's house to get a glimpse of the ceremony on a flickering black and white TV set. Afterwards, we ate outside on the drying greens where red, white and blue tables were set under clothes lines draped with streamers. In the weeks before, my father had spent considerable time with hardboard, a hacksaw and nails. He stencilled 'E.R.' and '1953' on the board and adorned it with crêpe paper, surprising my mother with the trouble he had taken.

He fantasized about having a sideline that would make him money and lead to the kind of lifestyle to which he felt he was entitled. He thought of inventing something, and set up the small back bedroom as a workshop, which fast degenerated into a Steptoe-like room full of objects such as radios or clocks, which he was always in the middle of taking apart. My mother gave up trying to tidy this mess and simply closed the door on his domain. I can recall her muttering that she hoped one day they would have a place where he could have a workshop outside.

I started school in January 1954, aged five. I began at Whifflet Primary, in the days when there were two intakes a year. I loved my first day there, and was only slightly disconcerted by someone sitting next to me leaving a steamy puddle directly below our joint desk, which with great empathy I ignored. I came home amazed to have made the discovery that I shared my Christian name with another little girl, Sandra Corbett. Thrilled by all the new experiences I had encountered, I regaled my mother with the letters of the alphabet I had learnt, and tested her thoroughly, checking that she understood.

'I already *know* my ABC,' she explained, with a laugh. 'You're the one that's started school to learn all your letters, and it's going to take a long, long time. I hope you manage to stay at school longer than me – I had to leave at age fourteen even though I got medals, to work in Coatbridge. You won't have to leave early, but you've got to go back tomorrow, young lady, and stick in at your lessons. At this rate, you'll never get up in the morning.'

'I've got to go *back*?' I was horrified. Like many another child before me, the realization that school stretched ahead for years was incomprehensible. I went off to bed in a grumpy mood.

I stayed at Whifflet Primary for a year, but in 1955

two milestones disrupted my scholarly routine. One was the birth of my younger brother, of whose impending arrival I had been told nothing. I was sent on holiday to Granny Jenny's and the first I knew of Ian's birth was after I came home and spotted a cot beside my parent's bed. I was captivated by a tiny hand waving in the air. His birth meant that we needed a bigger home, and this is how we came to be offered what we regarded as a step up in the world, the house at 51 Dunbeth Road, Coatbridge, about a mile and a half from Whifflet.

My mother was thrilled. It was downstairs, instead of upstairs on a landing, it was near all the shops in the town centre, and was opposite the town hall and the police station. The smaller number of people in the building meant the wash houses did not need such a strict rota, and drying greens would be more flexible, a boon for someone with a young baby, but we had inherited yet another shared outside toilet.

Number 51 had a small kitchenette, a living room with two bed recesses and a separate room for my parents. There was even a tiny garden, which my mother enjoyed filling with wallflowers and Virginia stock and Tom Thumbs, teaching me how to plant the tiny seeds.

In our main living space, one bed recess had a double bed fitted into it for the children, while my father set about converting the other to a dining area, with makeshift bench and table.

My father was by now working on the buses: he did shifts with sometimes unsocial hours. To compensate, his wages rose remarkably from sixteen shillings to several pounds per week, which in the 1950s represented good money. So much so, that he began to look out for a family car. Mr Allison, the butcher, had allowed him to use the van at weekends, and my father missed it.

After trying to resurrect one or two old bangers, he purchased a shiny black Baby Austin car from a Mr Cowie, who was retiring from his hairdresser's shop in Coatdyke. We were all excited at the arrival of the new addition to the family – especially me, when my father drove me to my new school.

Gartsherrie Academy was a large, handsome Victorian building, which dominated the top of the highest hill in Coatbridge, vying for position with Mount Zion, the local name for the kirk with its clock that even today presents four slightly varying faces of the hour to the town.

My father now had two main obsessions outside his work: taking things to bits, and his Baby Austin, which became his pride and joy. He lavished all his spare time on it, polishing and cleaning its bodywork, painting the black mudguards, and treating any signs of impending rust. Anyone laying a finger on the gleaming surface of the bonnet or boot was shouted at, and I was horrified when Ian, my little brother, who had just turned two, was soundly beaten for daubing it with white emulsion paint. Children of all ages, but in particular my friends, were attracted to this vehicle like bees to a honey pot, and it was regarded then as a great treat to be taken even a short distance in someone's car.

A car meant outings for all the family. Going off on a day trip, bags stuffed with sandwiches, was a welcome event, especially as going off on a fortnight's break, perhaps 'doon the watter' to Millport or Rothesay, was financially out of the question. In the Baby Austin, we would set off to places like the East Neuk of Fife, particularly the Silver Sands at Aberdour, and Culross, Pittenweem and Burntisland. Our other favourites on the West Coast were Largs and Ayr, and inland, if it was too cool for the seaside, we headed to Loch Lomond, where Balmaha was a well-loved spot.

On these family outings, I have no recollection of my father doing anything other than driving us there and back, and joining in the picnic lunch. He would disappear with his car after he had eaten, leaving us playing and my mother reading or chatting to one of the grannies, whom we often squeezed in. We assumed that he was meeting fellow bus drivers, familiar with the billiard halls and other social haunts popular with those who had brought bus-loads of trippers.

At first I loved it when my new friends who lived around Dunbeth Road came to play and we were offered the chance to go for a short trip by my father. I felt special as they ran to ask their parents if they were allowed to go with Sandra and her daddy. Laughing excitedly, we would all pile in. There was Joy, who lived beside the Maxwell church, which had a drama club for youngsters that she was desperate for me to join. You had to be over seven, so I had a little while to wait, but with her I went to see a show put on by the Maxwell church kids. The two Anderson girls, Moira and her sister Janet, and Moira's pal, Elizabeth Taylor, were all in this club, and Joy and I saw them on stage. We could not wait to be up there singing and dancing too. Joy and I went to Brownies together too. I became friends with two 'sisters', both called Elizabeth. One had long dark ringlets and was called by her full name, the other was fair, with identical ringlets, and known as Beth. They were cousins, in fact, being brought up together. Another pal who sometimes tagged along was Elizabeth Bunting, who lived further down Dunbeth Road, a few doors away. A bubbly redhead, who often had uncontrollable fits of the giggles, she was in my class at Gartsherrie Academy. Elizabeth's father was the manager of our local Co-op store. There were other girls, too, Jean and Beryl, the inspectors' daughters from the police houses.

My father would take me and a group of my friends to local beauty spots, like the lochs at Coatbridge, now a country park. Then there was only a rudimentary car park – used at night by the odd courting couple – a dilapidated toilet block, set among a clump of rhododendron bushes, and paths for walkers. One hot day in 1956, he took some of us away to this remote area. The eldest of us would have been eight or nine, the others just seven. When we got there I was sent for ice creams from a van we had passed. It was a fair distance away and I returned with ice cream cones dripping up my arms to find the doors of the black Baby Austin locked, the windows misted. I could, however, make out that clothing was scattered about inside before everyone got out. What, I puzzled to myself, had been going on? Had he been playing the horrible Beardie game or what?

Once, in the same place, we had all got into the car to escape a shower of rain. I was in the front passenger seat, and my father began a tickling game. As usual, when he gripped my knee and tweaked it, I let out a cry, then laughed as he went for my ribs. Two of my playmates in the back giggled at his antics, then he turned his attention to them. My head swivelled round over my right shoulder, and I saw that while I had got underarm and rib tickling, he was tugging at my friends' knickers and groping at their chests. I turned away, feeling sick. I pulled up my knees and hunched over them, staring straight ahead, trying to ignore the noises. Something told me that what was happening was wrong. Two of my chums had no father figure, so it may be that they thought this was how a loving father behaved. Perhaps they felt reassured by my presence that all was well.

I remember at that same lochside spot, my friends giggled when he played with us in the rhododendron bushes, but it struck me as odd that a grown man would want to join in hide and seek with wee girls. He took turns at coming to look for us, and said he knew good places to hide if anyone wanted to go with him. My confusion grew as I played through that summer, and I found excuses not to be near him. He only laughed at my discomfort.

One day, I was told by Elizabeth, the redhead, that she was not allowed to play with me any more, and no reason was given. Beth and Elizabeth, too, came to say that they were not allowed to play with me any more or to cross the doorstep of 51 Dunbeth Road. 'We're just not to, and we're not allowed to say why,' they murmured in unison, shaking their ringlets disconsolately. Their cheeks were pink.

Aged seven and eight, I could not form my doubts into questions, and something would not *allow* me to talk to anyone, particularly not my mother. However, I worked out ways of keeping my friends clear of my dad. I could not have forseen that Alexander would shift his attention from my friends to young girls he lured into his bus cabin.

His behaviour was witnessed by a number of his colleagues, who might have found it distasteful, but not one reported it to the authorities.

# Chapter Six

From the age of about seven, when my friends were turning away from me, I began to escape into the world of books. If it was too cold to be out playing, I would either be found in the tiny branch library, a few doors down Dunbeth Road, where I exhausted their supply of Enid Blyton and Bobbsey Twins books, or curled up in a corner of the house, my back to the wall and a book inches from my face. 'Get your nose out of that book, you lazy wee bitch!' my father would roar if I shut out his constant demands – he was the type of man who refused to wash a cup, and preferred to leave a row of dirty ones along the mantelpiece for others to deal with. 'It isnae healthy a lassie reading all the time the way ye do. Ye'll end up wi' glasses, then a' the lads will ca' ye Specky – d'ye hear me? Ye'll wear yer eyes oot!'

I would ignore him and my mother would try to pacify him.

'Who d'ye think ye are? Miss High and Mighty, that's you!' he would yell, 'Think ye're better than all of us, don't ye? Well, ye're nut, Miss Prim. Ah'll show ye who's boss round this hoose! Ye'll get ma hand over yer arse in a minute!'

'Leave her alone,' my mother would implore. 'She isn't doing any harm.'

She would step between us, or send me off on some errand until he was setting off on his next shift. The two of us had our own strategies for coping with my father.

Yet he had another side and I can remember him too as a loving father, good-humoured and joking, swinging me up in his arms and calling me his princess. Around my seventh birthday, he took me with a crowd of his mates from Baxter's to see *The Dancing Years on Ice*. The trip to Murrayfield in Edinburgh was exciting enough, but I was entranced by the spectacular show, and returned shining-eyed to Dunbeth Road, describing every moment to my mother and treasuring the special programme he had bought me.

Once or twice I tested the ground with my mother by telling her tentatively that my father 'acted funny' with my friends, but I got nowhere. 'Oh, he's just playing with you all,' she said dismissively. 'He's just a big wean himself. Learn to ignore it.'

That summer of 1956 was warm and my father took me off on a Baxter's outing, while my mother and brothers were at home. It was an all-day excursion to the Trossachs of Scotland, a beautiful area to visit on a sunny day. On the bus, my father indulged in his favourite shenanigans with a group of three or four young women right at the back, while an older conductress I didn't know was requested to take charge of me.

What should have been a glorious day, spent paddling in the river that runs through picturesque Callendar, was spoilt. With my bright blue cotton seersucker dress tucked into my knickers, I surveyed him kissing and cuddling the giggling females. I tried in vain to ignore him, but tears stung my eyes as he spent the afternoon rolling around on the grass, putting his hand up the women's skirts and every so often openly departing into the bushes. Other adults in the large party took pity on me and helped me to catch minnows to put in my jar. In between all the hilarity, they posed for snaps taken with the little box Brownie my father had brought.

My father must have noticed eventually how quiet I had become, for I was suddenly taken to a café in the town for a special treat. I was only slightly cheered by the huge knickerbocker glory, my first, which he put before me.

My father knew I would never tell my mother the brutal truth – that I, her child, knew that he was unfaithful to her. And he knew that she was unlikely to see his faults for herself. She would stick by him through thick and thin. I puzzled over this endlessly. *Why* did she seem to admire him, even look up to him? He was a reliable worker: he provided for his family and was the main breadwinner, though money always had to be augmented by a series of part-time jobs taken by my mother. He was also inordinately proud of being a teetotaller: terrified of losing his PSV licence, which in those days was difficult to obtain, he refused to touch a drop of alcohol, and adhered to this strict code even at Hogmanay. He almost always volunteered to do overtime, would not take even a sip of Grandpa Frew's famous elderberry wine, and refused to venture into a pub.

My mother always regarded his temperance as a major saving grace and she watched in horror as other women tried to cope with men who did not hand over their weekly pay packet on Friday nights, but went straight to the pub and drank every penny before weaving their way home. 'There are worse things,' my mother would say heavily, 'than fancying the wimmin.'

Also, however unsatisfactory other aspects of her marriage were, she was from a family to which you could not return if things were not right. Marriage was seen as irrevocably binding and divorce frowned on as against all the teachings of the Church. 'You've made your bed, now lie on it,' would have been the response of her parents to any complaints. Divorce then was a social stigma, and just as we accepted that the work chosen by young men would be what they did till retirement, so we assumed that marriage would be with one lifelong partner. In the 1950s we knew no one who was divorced, and the word was only associated with Hollywood film stars.

Even my interest in the printed word led to a puzzling and upsetting discovery about my father. I stumbled across magazines belonging to him while I was looking through a cupboard, and wondering about the existence of Father Christmas – I had spotted some Christmas wrapping and, although I knew I should not be doing it, I had started to rummage. Under piles of *Exchange and Mart* I found what I now realize were graphic pornography magazines. They were not like *TitBits* or *Reveille*, which I had seen high up on the shelves in Mrs Linnie's little newsagent shop in St John's Street near the chapel. These magazines showed torture and graphic scenes of women in wartime concentration camps being branded on their naked bodies with hot irons. With a strange mixture of guilt, fascination and shame, I replaced the magazines so that nobody could tell they had been disturbed. Knowing my mother preferred to keep clear of my father's domain, I was positive she knew nothing of them. She even disapproved of me looking at our family medical book, in which there were pull-out pictures of intestines, and information on the mysterious, forbidden human reproductive system. I had learned to study it when she was not around, but this was different. This was yet another matter on which I knew instinctively that it would be better to remain silent.

# Chapter Seven

When I was seven my father was involved in two incidents that eroded any remaining love I had for him.

My mother deemed that I was old enough to take my father his 'piece' – lunch sandwiches – if he was asked to do an extra shift. This meant walking down to the foot of Dunbeth Road, to the bus stop on Main Street at which all the local buses pulled in. I would look for his usual vehicle, the single-decker Cliftonville bus, which was timed to arrive every half-hour, the crews passing each other or meeting up for mealtimes at the terminus. At busy times as many as eight buses an hour might ply this route, which was popular because it took passengers right through the town centre. The final destination varied: my father's bus nearly always went to Kirkwood in Old Monkland, and turned at what was then a quiet, rather desolate spot near the cemetery.

Normally I greeted my father, settled on his bus at the front and chattered to him. Needless to say, my fare was not collected by his clippie, who would sit, if she ever had the chance, on the first seat on the right as you walked up the aisle, so that she could talk to the driver. A little door at waist height separated him from his passengers. People always chatted to the driver and eventually a rule was made, and prominently posted up, warning that it was an offence to engage him in conversation.

One day in 1956, I had gone as usual with my father's sandwiches. My mother decided, because the bus was going to Kirkwood and my dad's aunt May lived just across the road from the terminus, that I should take some flowers to May's old mother, rather than having my own sandwiches with my dad and his clippie. I was quite happy to do this, as Aunt May and Uncle Harry, her husband, had a television set. I knew they would let me watch the after-lunchtime children's programmes, including *The Woodentops*, which I liked.

My aunt greeted me and waved at my father, who was turning his bus and parking it next to another single-decker. She was fairly used to drivers and conductresses who were friends of my father coming to ask if they could fill up their flasks or pop into her bathroom. She made me some tea, then gave me the sad news that the TV repair man had just departed with the set: it had broken down. After some desultory conversation, I tiptoed with the flowers into my great-grandmother's room. She did not stir, and I decided to rejoin my father, who was due for a half-hour break at the terminus.

I boarded his bus by pushing hard on the concertina-style folding door at the front. My arrival was totally unexpected by all four adults who were grouped near the back of the vehicle, sprawled on the side seats. They did not even realize I was walking up the narrow aisle towards them, until I was almost there. My father and his conductress were grappling with each other in a way I had never seen before, while opposite them the driver of the other bus was locked in a passionate embrace with *his* clippie.

In the few seconds I had to register the scene, I noticed that a pair of frilly briefs was hanging out of my father's pocket and the woman's stockings were round her ankles. He was clambering on to the seat just over her, pinning down her wrists with one strong arm. What on earth were they *doing*?

'Their telly's broken so I've come back,' I announced.

In the ensuing scramble, I was aware of my father's furious, scarlet face looking over his right shoulder. He gaped at me. 'Get the hell out of here!' he roared.

I raced back to my aunt's house. When I sobbed out to her what had happened, she pointed upwards to the ceiling where her elderly mother slept and put a finger to her lips. She put her arm round me. 'It wasn't your fault,' she murmured soothingly. 'Just forget it, hen, he'll have forgotten all about it when you go back, you'll see.'

'But what will my mum say? He's bound to tell her,' I spluttered.

'Bet you he won't say.' She looked at me knowingly. 'And maybe best you don't mention it to her either, Sandra. He married a saint when he wed your mum, you know. That's what oor Jenny ma sister aye says, Alex merrit a saint.'

With brisk efficiency, she began to wipe my cheeks with a cold flannel, and said, 'Now, just you forget all about it.'

Perhaps, after the incident at the bus terminus, my father was concerned that I might disclose the relationship he had with his clippie: a brief period followed in which he was pleasant to my mother. He should take her out more often, he mused, Mary needed to get away from the kids a bit. Bemused, my mother pointed out that I was not nearly old enough, at seven, to be left in charge of the two boys. He talked of arranging a babysitter, and although Mary dismissed this as more pie in the sky, he brought a thirteen-year-old girl to our home one day and introduced her as Betty. The young, giggly blonde sister of one of his colleagues, she wished to earn pocket money.

Surprised, but pleased, my mother agreed it would be nice to go to the pictures with her husband and an occasional dance. A deal was struck, and Betty became a regular visitor to Dunbeth Road, always escorted home by my father. I looked forward to her visits, while noting with distaste the way my dad looked at her, particularly when my mother was not in the room. I came to regard her as yet another threat to my mother's happiness, and began to show a distinct coolness towards her, which my father thought uppity.

Betty's visits continued as winter approached, but one Saturday she did not come. My dad, in a jovial mood, handed money ceremoniously to my mother. 'Why don't you take the kids and yourself to the pictures?'

I jumped up and down in great excitement, because *The Wizard of Oz* was showing at the Garden near my granny's, and I loved the story. My mother was pleased by his generosity, and the way in which he helped organize the two younger ones, putting Ian into a pushchair. All smiles, he waved us goodbye, and said he would have a meal fixed up from the chippie nearby for our early-evening return. We set off happily enough, arrived at the cinema, and paid our admission money at the kiosk. All was well during the Wee Picture, and Ian nodded off to sleep. Then the main feature began. While I was entranced with the Munchkins, Norman, who was three years younger than me and not yet at school, began to whimper, at first quietly, then louder.

In vain my mother tried to hush him, glancing round apologetically. Maybe he would have settled down, if the Wicked Witch of the West had not then made her dramatic entrance. Norman's screams of terror filled the cinema and Ian woke up and joined in. My mother dragged us towards the exit, which did not suit me. I chimed in with the howls of protest, as a frantic usherette hurried us into the corridor. Luckily, my mother knew her, and not only did she refund our ticket money, she told my mother that I could see another showing of the picture free.

However, there we all were, turfed out of the cinema much earlier than anticipated. 'Never mind,' my mother said stoically. 'Let's just head home early for our fish and chips. At least that part of your dad's treat you *will* get, Sandra.'

We caught a bus from Whifflet up to Coatbridge. I ran on ahead of mum and reached our back door first. I burst into our small living room and froze. My father was with a little girl of about two, the child of one of our neighbours. She was sitting on our couch, half-dressed, with an expression of bewilderment on her face. Then my mother appeared behind me. An unholy row broke out and we kids were all bundled into the bedroom, and told to keep quiet.

Just before Christmas in 1956, without warning, some men arrived and took our daddy away, witnessed by Norman. For several days, we were all in a daze and people refused to discuss my father's disappearance. I was unable to fathom what on earth he had done now and I was too scared to ask. All I knew was that adults fell silent when

I walked into rooms, whether it was at home, at Granny Katie's in Ashgrove, or Granny Jenny's in Bellshill. Voices dropped to a whisper in my presence, children acted oddly towards me at school and neighbours avoided my mother and huddled in small groups to murmur together. I began to think that whatever had happened must involve me, but I was terrified to know how. Eventually, I could not prevent myself from asking, 'What's happened to my daddy? Where is he gone?'

I confronted my mother and grandmother as they sat sobbing together, and yet apart, in our living room, in which a Christmas tree waited forlornly to be dressed. My mother couldn't look at me, and sobbed all the harder. It was one thing to see her cry, but odd to see Granny Jenny, a big strapping woman who had worked all her life gutting fish and butchering meat, crying her heart out. I was stricken by her face. She blew her nose noisily, then looked at me, her eyes puffed and swollen. She was wearing black from top to toe, and the material reeked of camphor. Had someone died?

'Hospital,' she croaked, 'Yer daddy's been taken awa' tae the hospital, hen. Dinnae ask yer mammy any mair aboot it, she's far too upset the noo. Ye'll be telt all aboot it when ye're a lot bigger.'

I looked at her solemnly and nodded. There was a long silence, punctuated only by the ticking of the clock on the mantelpiece, their whimpers and the occasional movement of great glowing cinders in the fire as logs shifted. My eyes fixed on the firelight, which usually fascinated me with its myriad pictures, and I rolled myself into a little ball, chin perched miserably on my knees. 'Does it mean Santa won't be coming to us this year then?' There were cuddles of reassurance, and I was told that this year would be a bit different, but Santa would not forget where we stayed. The subject had been changed, but neither woman ever voluntarily told me where my father was.

Reluctantly, I accepted what I was told. One day in the summer of 1957, I asked my grandfather as we picked sweet peas together, confidentially, 'Why can't I visit my daddy in hospital?'

He looked at me quickly, then carried on cutting the twisted tendrils. 'There are some hospitals children aren't allowed to visit – d'you mind when Gran and I took ye on the train to see someone at Hartwood?'

I nodded, all ears. My dad's father was chief boilerman then at Bellshill Maternity near where they stayed, and I reasoned that he must know about these things.

'Well, it's a mental hospital – you and William had to play outside, remember? This is the same. Your dad's in a mental home. They wouldn't let you in, Sandra.'

I absorbed this answer and suppressed more questions. I did remember the visit to some relative. It had stuck in my mind because, as we played in the grounds of the hospital, my cousin and I had seen some patients shovelling snow. As one bent perspiring over a spade, heaving the glistening heaps into the front of a wheelbarrow, another was busy tipping snow out of the back. This had greatly appealed to the humour of two five-years-olds, but we were also slightly fearful of these souls who had been labelled 'daft', and we ran off as they approached us.

For many years, I accepted that my father's absence had been due to mental illness – which then carried such a stigma it could not be discussed.

# Chapter Eight

In all families there are unspoken agreements about what may and may not be discussed. People live with the worry that in a moment of unguarded confidence, a dreadful secret might be disclosed that could never be recanted, and that might shatter the family.

In 1957, children were kept in ignorance of sexual matters and few of us had effective strategies to deal with flashers, or someone touching us inappropriately on the bus or at the pictures. Then people avoided discussing sex with their children, through embarrassment. Facts had to be gleaned from playground pals, who were mines of misinformation. I was so naïve about the monthly cycle that when my best friend at primary, Carol Fairley, told me with a giggle one day that she had a period, I said in all innocence: 'I've got one too – bet mine's better than yours! I've made a great pattern.'

Her shocked face puzzled me till it dawned on her that I had thought she'd said 'peerie'. (We were very proud of these small wooden toys which we spun on the ground using a special whipping cord. They would birl for ages, depending on the skill of the player, and I had discovered from some older girls the trick of colouring circular bands of rainbow chalk on the surface, so that a really good shot produced a wonderful, mesmerizing kaleidoscopic blur of vivid hues.) Then she dissolved into giggles, until she realized she had a chance to show off her superior knowledge of what I could shortly expect to happen to me each month.

Although my father made a brief reappearance shortly after my eighth birthday, on 7 January 1957, I was told by my mother that he would be going away again. She spoke in tones of misery, so I knew that I would not see him for a long time. This filled me with a mixture of relief and shame that I could not have explained to anyone, even if I could have found someone willing to listen.

When he disappeared again, it was spring, and by that time the search for Moira was in full swing.

What do I recall of the actual weekend of her disappearance? When my mother and I discussed it, many years later, our memories dovetailed together in the jigsaw of events. It had been a landmark for us both, and for quite different reasons.

My mother said that my father had had an early rise that day, to take the miners to the Annathill colliery, then had been home mid-morning before going out after lunch to do a two until ten shift. She told me that she could recall that weekend in some detail because her parents had had a visitor from Australia. Grandpa Frew's sister, Auntie Cis, who had emigrated years before, had come for a reunion. A family gathering was held on Saturday evening at Ashgrove to celebrate her arrival, and my mother was annoyed that my father had not arranged for someone to swap with him, particularly when he had already done an early-morning shift. She organized us to attend the party, then had to call it off anyway; like many others in the town, I had succumbed to Asian flu, which was sweeping Scotland.

It was the first time I had ever been ill with a high fever, and I remember it well. It was not until Sunday, on cotton-wool legs, that I went unsteadily to my grandmother's, having been off school all week. I was delighted to be given pretty handkerchiefs embroidered with kangaroos, from the Australian guest of honour. My mother told them I'd been put straight to bed with the younger ones, the night before, in the recess bed in the wall. At ten o'clock, she had debated whether to send for the doctor as my temperature was sky high, and she kept looking for my father parking his car in our yard.

There was no sign of him, but she found that once she had sponged me with a flannel and water I was a bit better. Worried by his non-appearance when the snow had been so bad earlier, she decided not to go to bed but to keep an eye on me while she made some vegetable soup for the Sunday.

It was nearly midnight before my father's car drew up outside in the yard, and he let himself in. She told him about me and reminded him to go next day to say hello to her aunt. Then she offered him some soup. He said he was tired, and she noticed he did look exhausted, but the weather had caused mayhem.

On Sunday, my father got up early and took the sandwiches she had wrapped in the waxed paper she saved from the loaves of bread we got at the Co-op. He went to work, saying he'd be back mid-afternoon. I arose looking much better, but my mother decided against going to church. After lunch, she thought I was well enough to go to Coat's Sunday School, five minutes from our home, and she sent me off with Norman. As it was after three, she expected to see my father, but again he was delayed and she thought he must have gone to see Aunt Cis. When the door opened at last, it wasn't my father but her sister-in-law, my aunt Betty, who, like Aunt Margaret, stayed in Alexander Street just over the hill. She was breathless with hurrying, and frozen, her legs mottled with purple and blue from the cold.

'You've no idea what's going on at our place!' She threw herself on the couch and told my mother that men were combing the streets looking for a child, who had vanished the day before. 'There's men everywhere, all checking our closes and coal cellars, and even the bins. They don't have any idea what's happened to this wee lassie at all. Isn't it terrible?'

My mother agreed. 'Who is it?'

'Someone told me it's one of Andra Anderson's lassies, the middle one,' her sister-in-law announced, self-importantly. 'Moira, I think she's called, but I could be wrong. He works in the creamery beside me at the Red Bridge. I hear he's worried out of his mind, poor man. If she's run off after an argument, and caused all this fuss with the polis getting involved, then I bet he'll kill her when he gets hold of the wee besom.'

When we kids returned, it was to find them tutting in disapproval over their tea. My mother asked me if I knew the missing girl. I said I knew her wee sister, Marjorie.

'Och, she's bound to turn up,' my aunt Betty rolled her eyes heavenward, 'and I wouldn't like to be in her shoes when she does. She'll be for it!'

'No, no, it's her folks I feel heart sorry for,' my mother murmured. 'They'll forgive her anything, as long as she's all right – you know what it's like when kids get you up to high doh like that. She's probably shut in somewhere, from playing hide 'n' seek. She'll probably have just curled up and gone to sleep. You're right, she'll show up, large as life, and wonder what all the fuss was about.'

But the days of searching turned into weeks. Aunt Cis left us, and though we never again met, her diary of the visit still exists with these events meticulously noted.

My father went off the scene again, the first of many prolonged absences, and our lives settled into a hard-working, yet uneventful routine without him, but as my mother took on the role of a single parent I was given responsibility for things that today I would not dream of asking my young daughter to do.

As well as helping to parent my brothers, I went cleaning with my mother, at Falconer and Prentice's, the quantity surveyors' offices, in nearby Church Street, opposite the side door of Woolworths. This made up part of the wages we sorely missed from my dad's income. In those days, there was no income support or any single-parent benefit. On some occasions I went at dusk to these offices on my own to clean them though I was not yet ten years old.

I thought the lives of my friends uneventful compared to mine. They went home from school to meals laid on by mothers who did not have to go out to work – then, the norm was for women to be at home. I do not recall any of my pals doing char work as I did. Yet while my mother treated me in some ways as an adult and confidante, she also protected me from what she saw as information that would taint me.

On one horrifying occasion I was attacked and assaulted in Dunbeth Road. My aunt Margaret was ill and my mother sent me to her house with some fish one evening. I trotted off, to walk a five-minute journey, one year on from Moira's disappearance. Although it was dark, it was not late, just around teatime. Near the high school, a young man suddenly leaped out at me. I was knocked off my feet and I landed on my back. My hood slid down over my eyes and I could not get a good look at him, but I was overcome by two things: a horrible smell of Woodbines, and an excruciating pain after his hand shot under my skirt. I was gasping for air, while he muttered obscenities, and already I could feel a giant bump forming on the back of my skull where it had hit the ground. A sense of outrage shot through me and I let out a yell. A light came on in the porch of a big house, and the man ran off, but not before aiming a savage kick at me.

Despite the noise, no one appeared. Shakily, I got to my feet and picked up my battered parcel. My uncle opened his door to a small, dishevelled girl, scraped and bruised, with blood tricking down over one knee-high school stocking. It was a good half-hour before they could calm me down with the obligatory cup of tea.

'You'll be OK, Sandra,' my aunt murmured soothingly, after I had blurted out what had happened. 'Your uncle Archie will walk back with you and make sure he isn't still about, and he'll speak to your mum.'

We duly went home together, passing the police station, and my uncle and mother spoke in whispers as I got ready for bed. I waited for my mother to ask me what had happened. Instead, she gave me a cuddle, a hot-water bottle, and reminded me to say my prayers. She assured me that we would talk about everything later, when I felt better, then gave me a quick goodnight kiss. Adult voices droned as I drifted into sleep.

I was sent to school the next day as if nothing untoward had occurred. I was too humiliated to mention it to any of my chums, and my mother did not discuss it with me. What should have been reported by her as an indecent assault on a child was swept under the carpet, as if by not confronting it my mother could convince herself that her child remained untouched.

When my father returned from his long absence, his attitude towards me had taken a turn for the worse. While he had been gone I had grown, and I had my tenth birthday just after he reappeared. I withdrew again and, though I was not a naughty child, the beatings started, ostensibly 'to knock the cheek' out of me. My mother kept us as separate as possible. As she had gathered some self-esteem from the way she had coped during his absence, she asserted herself more than she had before and several times she intervened when he beat me black and blue.

'They may have beaten you up where you were,' she yelled at him once, in front of me, 'but don't you lift a finger to my weans without good reason!'

I noticed the antagonistic looks that passed between them with satisfaction.

'Keep out of his way, Sandra! Don't annoy him or give him cheek,' she hissed at me, and mostly I complied with this, but she could not always be around. I wouldn't answer my father when he used endearments, I refused to kiss him goodnight, and I ignored his rules in preference to my mother's, which we had got used to during his absence. I would even curl my lip in contempt at him and not bother to disguise it, which caused dreadful ructions.

One beating he gave me was so bad that I ran away, my lip split from a blow which, uncharacteristically, had been delivered to my face, where others might notice it. I wandered for hours, left Dunbeth Park when the gate was locked at sunset, and trailed around the streets till dawn found me almost back home, sitting on the stone steps of the town hall. I must have nodded off, for the next thing I remember is a kindly policeman with a torch picking me up and carrying me round the corner to the station. There he examined my face, made me a cup of Cadbury's hot chocolate and asked what ailed me.

I dissolved into tears. 'My dad's a great big bully, an' he thumps me for nuthin'.' I heard myself get the words out, before a huge wave of guilt swept over me. This was an overwhelming betrayal, although I owed my dad no favours. But what of my mother? Hadn't she enough to cope with, without me giving her extra trouble? She must be worried sick about me. 'Maybe I deserved it. I'll have to go back, I s'pose,' I added flatly, looking at the floor. 'They'll be angry, though.'

He regarded me sympathetically, and handed me a chocolate biscuit, a big treat. I was torn between wanting to stay in front of his one-bar electric fire, and heading for home. I gave him my name and address, as requested, and he scrawled them in his wee notebook, rather than in the gigantic ledger on the surface of the mahogany counter. I wriggled down reluctantly from the chair.

'But you're just round the corner!' He smiled at me. 'I'll walk you round, will I?'

He must have seen how my face changed as my father, dressed immaculately in his uniform, came to our back door. Of my mother, there was no sign, but my father stood there, a smirk on his face that I couldn't understand. Smiles passed between him and the friendly policeman as I hovered uncertainly on the step.

'Think we have some lost property here.' The young cop spoke in amiable tones.

'You've saved me the bother of coming to the station,' said my parent affably, placing a hand on my shoulder that told me my nocturnal adventure was over. 'In you come, young lady, you've had your mum up the pole with worry.'

'Bit of a tiff, then?' The young officer's voice lost none of its friendliness. 'The lassie's got a split lip there, but nothing too serious.'

'Och, just a bit of a dust-up, that's all,' replied my dad soothingly. 'Nothing I can't handle. Just you let me deal with it, officer.'

I was pushed into the living room, while both of them spoke about kids these days, and then the younger man departed with a wave. I realized with sickening accuracy that there was no way the younger guy could confront the six-footer standing on our step. They had recognized each other by sight, and the cop was just one of many who jumped on and off my dad's bus: he would dismiss what he had seen.

My parents thought that a good way to patch up their marriage was to take a family holiday. Our trip to the small seaside resort of Montrose, however, was an unmitigated disaster. Not only was the weather bad, but several times my mother ended up in tears. I never knew what had been said when we called in to see relatives who lived near Banchory, and have tea with them, but when someone referred to an acquaintance called Betty she dissolved into sobs.

Our holiday home, in a back street of Montrose, was Spartan, with meters that had to be fed regularly with shillings to give gas for heating or hot water. The elderly couple who let part of their home did not appreciate young children, and expected us all to be out for the greater part of the day, rain or shine. We ventured out of town on a number of day trips, all of which seemed to begin with accusations by my father about how long it took my mother to organize the children and the food, and to end in rows over directions to various places like Brechin and Stonehaven, and silences. Just as bad were the looks of hatred I received in the driver's mirror when I suggested we stopped, or played one more game of I Spy for the sake of the two smaller ones.

There were no books to speak of at our lodgings except The Pilgrim's Progress, which I devoured in a day. The one outing voted a success was to the lighthouse at nearby Scurdie Ness, where my brothers and I had the chance to run about and explore without being told to be quiet.

On the last evening, a Friday, our landlords encouraged my mother to take me to their Kingdom Hall, where they thought we would have ample entertainment to round off our holiday. For once, the rain was not lashing down, and we set out, with much muttering from me because Ian and Norman were being taken to the fair by my father.

Its twinkly lights were inviting and in vain I pleaded with my mother to change our plans. I reminded her of the pocket money I had left, but she was adamant that Mr and Mrs Young, our hosts, would be on the look-out for us at their religious meeting and she never broke a promise.

The hall was full of people with damp macs and umbrellas, who all sang heartily from Sankey hymnbooks to an out-of-tune piano. Afterwards, over cups of tea and wonderful Scottish home baking, they shook their heads mournfully about the weather: 'Na, it cannae last . . .'

I was thrilled when my mother agreed that as it wasn't late we could walk down to the fairground and meet the others before going home, perhaps getting some fish and chips on the way. I had a go on a few hoopla stalls, but we couldn't spot my father and brothers. My mother smiled tolerantly as I picked up a fluffy gonk I'd won, and agreed I could spend a few more coppers at the next stall, where you could win a coconut by knocking down cans. But she was too distracted to enjoy herself watching me. 'Perhaps they've headed home already,' she said anxiously. 'Oh, well, come on, Sandra, we should, too. Remember we'll have all the packing tomorrow.'

I pulled a face but I tried not to show how disappointed I was that my dad was not there to take me on the ghost train or the dodgems, or to buy me a ride on the waltzers. When we got into our lodgings, however, there was no sign of the rest of the family. We ate our fish suppers, washed up and cleared the table, and started to think about bed. My mother was worried. 'Where on earth can he be?' she demanded, as she ordered me into my baby-doll pyjamas, bought specially for the holiday. I shrugged and snuggled down with a *Reader's Digest*. The

WHERE THERE IS EVIL

minutes ticked by, and my mother paced up and down on the well-worn lino. Then she started to pile things into cases. Just when I was rubbing my eyes, and checking that it really was after midnight on the Baby Ben clock, and she was muttering about going to the police station, we heard a key turn in the lock. My father was carrying one child, who was fast asleep, and wheeling another in his pushchair.

My parents hissed angrily at each other as she demanded to know his movements. It transpired that my father had met a woman at the fair and, according to him, she had invited herself and the children to her home for supper.

'You've been sitting with some woman while I've been worried sick about these weans. How could you?' my mother asked.

'She was a very *nice* wummin.' My father smirked. 'She took to me right away, and she was good to Norman and Ian.' Then he added, 'And tae me.'

My mother smacked him across the face and marched off to bed.

The atmosphere in our car going home next day could have been cut with a knife, and as we left Montrose behind I knew it was somewhere I would never wish to see again.

# Chapter Nine

In November 1959, a kindly town councillor had listened to my mother's plea to be relocated near her parents during her husband's absence, and we were installed at 9 Ash-grove, directly above my grandparents in number 11, with adjoining gardens on a large corner plot. Perhaps my mother felt that such close proximity to his father-in-law would ensure that my father changed his ways when he came home, but this was not to be. My grandfather detested him, and deplored his sexual conduct, but his policy was to avoid him, while exerting a strong patriarchal influence on the rest of his large family.

My grandfather's principles and values were drummed into me: no matter how glorious the weather, playing outside on a Sunday was off-limits, and even a game of snap was forbidden. It never crossed my mother's mind to question why we had to adhere to the rigid code of discipline laid down by her father.

Religion had also played a strong part in the life of the Anderson family. After Moira's tragic disappearance, her two sisters continued to attend Band of Hope meetings, which Moira had loved. Janet never came to terms with the fact that one evening she had rushed Moira home when the younger girl had wanted to learn about becoming

a missionary. It would keep, she said, but shortly afterwards Moira vanished.

I started at Coatbridge High School in August 1961
and my workload increased dramatically. As my mother
and her sister helped me to cover all of my books and
jotters with wallpaper samples, they agreed that I needed
the privacy of my own room and a good part of Sunday to
myself to get my homework completed to a good standard.

Although my mother was delighted that I had won a
place to the town's élite senior high school, kitting me
out in its uniform gave her nightmares. A navy blazer
represented a major investment, and a leather briefcase was
out of the question. Hand-me-downs came to the rescue
once again: the blazer came with elbow patches and the
white shirts, for boys, had to be adapted. I transformed
them to short-sleeved blouses, over which I could wear
the navy V-neck sweater with a gold neck edge that
Granny Frew had knitted.

The ignominy of having to start at secondary school
without the case I needed for books filled me with far
more apprehension than facing algebra, logarithms, Latin
and French for the first time. Also I shrank from the gaze
of the terrifying rector, James Cooper, who had been feared
by generations of local schoolchildren mainly because of
his height, which was six foot ten.

As I embarked on my secondary school career, where
I made friends who have lasted ever since, my father
embarked on a string of affairs with various young women,
some of whom were strangers and some of whom were
known to my mother. There was Norma, sister of one of
his driver pals, several bus conductresses, mostly single,
then a long line of women who were all married, including

a Lily and a Rose. Occasionally my mother took me with her to confront the current woman. One stands out. Taken off school for the day, and cringing with embarrassment, I was marched up a garden path in the Townhead area of Coatbridge, to the door of a thunderstruck woman named Cora, whose husband worked away from home. My mother delivered a furious tirade and declared that Alexander was married, and should be left well alone. Not only that, he was also the father of three children and *this* was the eldest, at which I was pushed forward to underline the potential jeopardizing of a family. The raised voices attracted a small interested crowd of neighbours, mainly women, slyly nudging each other and uniformly folding their arms across their chests.

That afternoon, Cora told us that she and my father had been planning to run off to England together but her husband had been informed of this anonymously and arrived on the scene threatening to throttle my father. It was agreed that the affair must end with no further contact. Later, Mary told me of one other ultimatum she had made: 'I want him away from Baxter's Buses, Sandra,' she said. 'For two good reasons.'

First, the environment supplied him with an endless rota of female conductresses and opportunities for affairs. Second, she was convinced he was being influenced by a driver she regarded as a shady character, a small, powerfully built man, with whom he had struck up a friendship. The other man had a reputation for being quick with his fists, and I too, detested him, having noticed how terrified his quiet little wife and his young son were when he was around.

My mother was sure that if our family left Coatbridge,

she could leave the past behind and start afresh with my father. With this in mind, she wrote to his young brother, who lived in Leicester, to see if he could help. Uncle Robbie was the antithesis of my dad. An ex-Marine, his language could be colourful and his temper flared up quickly, but he shared none of my father's sexual traits, and was a man of integrity. He had done well for himself, and was manager of the city's sewage works. Although his wife had reservations about my father going to live with them initially, and had no time for his extra-marital exploits, Robbie agreed that he would find Alex work, which he did as a security man at the sewage plant. My father was to establish himself in the post, which was reasonably paid, and once he had found a house, my mother would join him and send for us when funds allowed. My brothers, still both at primary school, were quite excited by all this.

My father was keen to leave Coatbridge, and left to the relief of his own parents and my mother's, who all found him difficult to cope with. However, no sooner had my mother arrived to visit him than Uncle Robbie had a catastrophic falling out with his brother. He had been given a copy of the telephone bill for the plant, and had spotted a series of long-distance calls to Coatbridge. In those days, bills were not itemized but, knowing we were not on the phone, Robbie tackled my dad and discovered that the affair with Cora was not over. The house he had found was to share with her, not us.

My uncle hit the roof. He had to pay for the private calls himself and then to dismiss his own brother. My father had caused him such humiliation that he ordered him out of his home, and said he would have no more to do with him. He sat my mother down and gently explained why he would provide no further help with the planned move, as she sat sobbing, and my dad packed, to my aunt's undisguised relief. 'I'll always have a lot of time for you and the kids, Mary, and I'll help you ones any way I can,' Robbie told her, 'but I wash my hands of oor Alex. That big bastard had better no' show his face over my doorstep again or I'll let him have it. I know how strong your Christian duty is, but if I were you, I'd think about divorce and get shot of him.'

But my mother simply followed my father back to Lanarkshire.

The first thing I insisted on in our new home, at 9 Ashgrove, was that not only did I have a bedroom to myself, but that a lock was put on the door. No one questioned why I wanted it, and when any friends expressed surprise, I explained it was to keep my little brothers out. The other great advantage about living next door to my grandmother was that I could spend a great deal of time in her house. If ever I found myself alone with my dad, I made a beeline for downstairs or made excuses not to open my bedroom door.

I was careful now about whom I brought home. Two chums I played with were different in maturity and appearance. Barbara had been raised in a strict, religious background. She was small, fiercely intelligent with glasses. The other girl, whom I shall call Ellen, was much taller, heavier, more physically developed than either Barbara or me and more wordly wise too. The three of us had little pocket money, but Barbara and I noticed that Ellen pleaded poverty regularly, but then acquired funds out of the blue, treating us when the ice cream van came and occasionally being what we called 'flush'. My father looked out for her comings and goings and Ellen warmed to any sign of affection.

I liked the teenage Ellen. We shared a love of reading and would sometimes go to the cinema together. One night, when we were fourteen, Ellen and I sat mesmerized through the first of the James Bond films, at the Odeon in Coatbridge, and missed the last bus to Whifflet. Shrugging off the mile and a half walk, we queued for chips, then set off on foot, chatting with two young lads faced with the same journey – we were pretty pleased to have their company on the dark road. Before we arrived in Whifflet main street, we were on first-name terms and arm in arm. Near Tennents Works, the boy beside me nudged me and pointed to a small black car that was going along slowly just behind a blonde woman, who was hurrying away. 'These weirdos make ye sick, eh?' he muttered, putting his arm round me protectively. 'Ye know whit they call 'em, don't ye?'

I shrugged nervously. I had a sick feeling in my stomach as I saw the woman shake her fist angrily at the driver of the car, who sped off. I knew who it was.

'Kerb crawlers, that's what,' my escort went on knowledgeably. 'Jist as well you ones are wi' me and ma mate, though I think that wummin's got rid o' him.'

To push it out of my mind, I began to chat animatedly to him while Ellen and her new-found friend strolled behind us. In Whifflet, we agreed to split up, since Ellen lived in Shawhead. Waving goodbye, my escort and I went on towards my house. Just before we got to my street, a car drew up with a screech of brakes, and out jumped a menacing figure. My companion gave an almighty start as my father yelled at him. Letting go of my arm, he took off like a harrier, not stopping to find out what it was all about, and I almost laughed as I saw him bound athletically over the six-foot fence at the back of St Mary's school, and disappear into the night. 'Just what the hell are you up to, Miss?' my dad shouted. 'I'll leather your hide for ye! Get in the car this minute, you little bitch!'

I did so silently, fully expecting him to lash out at me with his fists. Instead he peered at me in the gloom, and muttered something about how inconsiderate I was to worry my mother, who, he said, had sent him out looking for me. 'Who was that little runt?' he demanded, as he parked our car.

I explained how our journey had come about, and I said I had spotted his vehicle on the viaduct. 'It must have been when you were searching for me,' I said sardonically, looking him right in the eye. 'Too bad you missed us then. I'll let Mum know I'm fine.'

'No, no,' he glowered at me, 'there's no need, I'll tell her. She'll be in her bed now anyway, so just leave it. We'll say no more about it.'

That incident alerted me to danger: my father would have beaten up the young man if he had had the chance, and he had looked almost pathologically jealous. I realized I would have to think of other strategies to deter him from coming anywhere near me.

Protection came in the form of my friendship with Irene. We started to go around together in the second year of high school, and shared the usual teenage interests that occupy all adolescents. We haunted the local church halls on a Saturday night; where for the princely entry fee of one and sixpence you could dance all evening to top-ten hits and learn the Locomotion, the Hitchhiker and the Twist, while sipping nothing more dangerous than Coke and lemonade. We became part of a group that circulated round churches and Scout halls, where pairs of girls could dance to their hearts' content, often in large groups round a pile of handbags, till duos of bashful young males tapped them on the shoulders.

Irene lived several miles away, and when we went out together I often stayed at her home. We adorned our bedroom walls with posters of the Fab Four cut from a magazine called *208*. Irene's older sister, Elizabeth, tolerated the chatter of two youngsters late into the night, and their parents liked me – so much so that when they went on holiday I was taken with them several summers on the trot, and consigned my memories of Montrose to the holiday-from-hell album I placed in a bottom drawer. Irene's father taught me to swim and dive in places like Bournemouth and Scarborough and effectively took the place of my own father. He encouraged us to cycle everywhere, and to go off youth-hostelling all round Scotland. I can still feel the warm breeze in my hair as we cycled through the pass of Killiecrankie, singing 'The House of the Rising Sun' and sipping lurid Creamola Foam.

It was through Irene that I met my first real boyfriend, John Somerville, who lived in Muirhead, another small village near her home. She had gone out with him first, and knew his family well, so I had no qualms about him and we went out together happily for almost three years. Although I was only fifteen, John was an athletically built eighteen-year-old, who ran at county level and who could have played football professionally. He was striking, with broad shoulders, piercing blue eyes that crinkled when he smiled, and fair hair.

My father could not ignore his fitness and strength: he was a motor mechanic in Fagan's garage near my home in Whifflet and thought nothing of removing car engines single-handed. He and John detested each other on sight, which did not surprise me, and I now realize that John was the physical tower of strength I needed to support me. My father no longer dared beat me whenever he liked, as he knew his behaviour would not go unchallenged.

Granny Katie was a rock of strength too and staunchly championed everything I did. When she met John she brushed aside my mother's concerns about a lad courting me when I was still so young. Granny had only a few years left, and died of cancer at Christmas in 1966. Her death was a great blow to Mary in what was yet another turbulent period in her life caused by my father.

# Chapter Ten

When my father ran off from Coatbridge in 1965, my mother decided that she was going to see a solicitor about a divorce. Everyone held their breath to see if she would change her mind. She did not.

Still somewhat bemused, as well as in a state of deep relief, I told the tale of his hasty departure to one of my friends at high school as we perched together on art stools and worked on life drawings for our Higher art examinations. Myra Readings was a cool, fair, beautiful girl whose home in Alexander Street I often visited after school before catching the Cliftonville bus to Ashgrove. Her parents seemed to have such a warm, stable relationship and, as an only child, she came from a lovely home and seemed to have everything anyone could possibly want. Now she shot me a look of undisguised horror, when I described how my father had vanished with his clippie, Pat Hanlon, who was half his age.

'They've run away together completely out of the blue? My God!'

Myra's shocked tone caught the attention of several heads which turned with great curiosity towards us, and red-faced, I motioned her to keep her voice down.

'Well, I don't think it *was* out of the blue for the two

of them, really. They dumped a brown paper parcel behind our front door,' I whispered. 'Later, it turned out to be their bus uniforms, folded with their badges and hats, all wrapped up to be handed in to Baxter's bus depot.'

'So it was planned!' Myra's huge blue eyes rounded in astonishment.

I thought of the journey my mother and I had made to Gartlea bus station in Airdrie to return these items. We'd crossed the yard and entered the gloom of the depot, and were shown into a filthy office for the use of the inspectors, whom my father loathed (he called them 'wankers with watches' when he spotted them loitering at bus stops), and my mother handed over the parcel with a muffled explanation, then sat beside me. The man to whom she entrusted it went off to see about any due pay. We knew that my father's time sheet would be in. It was the only paperwork he ever did.

My mother was petrified that no money would be forthcoming, even though common sense told her that, traditionally, there would be what was known as lying-in money and some holiday pay. When the man returned, he doffed his peaked cap and cleared his throat, obviously finding his task difficult. 'I'm very, very sorry to hear what's happened to you, Mrs Gartshore,' he sighed, 'and Mr Baxter is very vexed to hear your news, too. He says if there is anything he can do to help your . . . predicament, just let him know.'

My mother's eyes were downcast as she nodded disconsolately, but I saw relief in them as he offered her a brown wages packet before he ushered us out. It was only when we got home to Whifflet that she allowed me to open it at our kitchen table. When I tried to ask questions, she said, 'Now, now, then,' as if she was trying to calm a restive young animal. I pulled out a long strip of typed information on greaseproof paper, which was folded con-certina-style with some notes, mainly fivers. These she sorted into piles for different household requirements, and then she put the lying-in cash into an old biscuit tin, saying with weary conviction: 'We'll need this kept aside, for as sure as God's my judge, he'll not send us any support, neither for me, nor any of his three weans.'

'So what happened then?' Myra's voice brought me out of my reverie. She almost fell off her seat in astonishment when I revealed that, at the end of her tether, my mother had hit my dad over the head with a frying pan. Myra had never met my mother, but knew Alexander Gartshore from the bus that passed her door. She was aware that he was six foot four, while his wife was small.

'She hit *him*?' Myra's huge blue eyes were like saucers. 'My God! Why?'

'She came home from the Women's Guild at the church at half past nine one night, and there he was, canoodling in his Cortina, right at our gate, with this girl, and they weren't bothered who saw them. When my mum realized what was going on and pulled the car door open, he told her they were going off to Leeds, just like that, and wanted to take my wee brother Ian with the two of them,' I explained, quite matter-of-fact, and trying to ignore Myra's stricken face. 'So my mum ran into the house and tried to stop him packing while the female waited in the car. She was so furious with him, she must have seen red, and she walloped him with the frying pan, right over the head. But he didn't belt her back.'

'And did Ian go with them?' Myra knew that I was

fond of both of my brothers, but I was particularly protective of Ian, who was only nine. I shook my head.

'No, thank goodness. And it's good riddance to bad rubbish, as far as I'm concerned. We're better off without him.'

'I'm glad you're not going to lose your wee brother, too, but I can't imagine how you can say you won't miss your dad, Sandra – I'd hate it if mine went away, I know I'd miss him so much. You're bound to, you know.'

If only you knew, I thought to myself.

But I was unprepared for the depression into which my mother slumped in the autumn of 1965. I constantly felt I had to keep her spirits up. I would cajole her, with remarks like, 'We're doing just fine, Mum. We're far better off without him. We'll manage, just wait and see. You've got me, haven't you?'

Her eyes would blur with tears, though she nodded in agreement. I knew, although she could not say it to me, that she missed him and needed him, and that angered me, for I knew there was no future with such a man and that tears were pointless. Once or twice, when the months were slipping by and his return looked more and more unlikely, she made remarks that cast him in a good light. She pointed out to me one evening as I toasted some bread on a long fork and held it near a roaring fire, where I was drying my hair, 'You know, it was your dad, Sandra, that got me this grate, just after we moved here. I've always liked it. Don't you miss him?'

A yawn froze in my tonsils.

She spoke again in the same wistful tone. 'I know you hate it when I mention his name, but he *does* have good points, he really does . . . I can remember telling him when we looked round here that I'd love a new fireplace and grate, and the very next week he stopped his bus to let me know he'd won the sweepstake at work. "Just you go and pick any grate you fancy, Mary." Those were his very words. "I want us to be comfortable in this house." He handed me the lot when he got it, and ye know, a lot of men wouldn't have done that. They'd have blown half of it on drink, but not your dad. I got my fireplace and grate, jist as he promised.'

She looked at me beseechingly, but I would not meet her eyes. There was no chance of me ever feeling comfortable in any house I shared with my father. I could never tell her that one of my last memories of my dad was a weird incident that had occurred in church of all places.

Just weeks before he left my father, hardly a regular churchgoer, happened to sit beside me. As it was a warm late-summer day, I had on a navy mini-dress, bought with money from my sixteenth birthday, with a neat white Peter Pan collar, and a cardigan over it. Granny Katie had admired my new navy blue high heels with their white piping and my matching shoulder bag, and had made remarks about me being sweet sixteen. I hurried round to the little kirk with a spring in my step, and my newly washed fair hair bouncing on my shoulders. My mood changed the moment my father settled beside me, and he smirked as I wriggled along to my left to make more room – in vain, the pew was packed that day. I was stuck with him.

Smiling sardonically, because he knew I hated him being in such close proximity, he deliberately cast his eye over all the women sitting in the rows in front of us, with the air of an experienced cattleman at a sale of bloodstock.

When the service began, I felt claustrophobic, and more and more aware of my breathing. During the sermon, I could swear that I could hear my own blood rushing through my ears, and my heart pounding as if I was running a marathon. It seemed so loud to me that I was amazed no one else could hear it. What was causing such panic? I couldn't be sure at first whether it was being hemmed in by rows of people in a warm atmosphere, or whether it was the air of malevolence I felt coming from my own father. I suddenly realized that his eyes were boring through my dress, observing every movement of my thighs. The service seemed endless, and I was stuck to my seat with terror, unable even to close my eyes in prayer.

I knew that day, beyond doubt, that given the glimmer of an opportunity, my father would ravish me without compunction. Little wonder, then, that I dismissed my mother's nostalgic longings for him with exasperation.

I was determined that we would survive without a main breadwinner in our home, but financially, things became difficult, and even minor items became major expenditures. As funds grew scarce, it looked likely that I would have to abandon my plans to go on into higher education and seek employment. I swallowed my pride and went to see Mr Cooper, still an awe-inspiring figure though I was now a fifth-year prefect.

That interview in his office, in the spring of 1966, when I stammered my way through my explanation for asking to see him, is vivid in my mind. It was practically unheard of for a pupil to go to his room without a summons from him. I told him something of our circumstances, and of the pressure on me to leave school and go to work. His brows knitted together.

'So, you see, sir, my mum's been left with three of us to bring up. I don't *want* to leave school, Mr Cooper, but it might come to that, and my gran who lives in Bellshill, well, she says she can get me a good job in Woolworths there, if she can just speak to someone she knows—'

'How old are you, my dear?' he interrupted, in his booming voice, and his big bushy silvery eyebrows stopped frowning.

'Seventeen just a few weeks ago,' I took a deep breath. 'I could leave at Easter, sir, but I'd like either to go to art school or to be a teacher, and for that I'd need my Highers ... but I'm helping out my mum as much as I can just now—'

'In what way?' he interjected.

'I work on Saturdays, in Glasgow, in a record shop, till six, and in the evenings I go cleaning offices with my mum, but we're really struggling, and this week it's been difficult even to get enough to cover my bus fares to school, never mind lunches.'

'Hasn't your mother applied for free school meals for you and your brothers?'

'Definitely not, sir, she'd be far too embarrassed to do that ... She wouldn't want any of us singled out for free dinners. She has her pride.'

'Tell me about your Saturday job and what that involves.'

I told him I earned seventeen and sixpence for working all day in Paterson's, a large music shop in Buchanan Street. I had got the job, selling long-play records down in the bowels of the store, through my friend Irene, who had persuaded the eagle-eyed, austere manageress to interview me. Irene sold singles and EPs. Our camaraderie was the one thing that kept me going.

The rector rose and crossed to the window, his black gown flapping behind him. 'Slave labour,' he grunted at last. 'Seventeen and sixpence is unacceptable in your present position for what your work is, if what you tell me is true. It won't do.'

I gazed at him silently, so curious I had forgotten to be nervous.

'I shall speak to the Carnegie Library Committee, of which I am a member this year, and propose that a position is found for you on Saturdays and over holidays, at a decent rate of pay, and to cut down on the number of expenses you are currently paying for travel, etc. Do you like books, my dear?'

I couldn't believe my ears. Did I like books? I assured him I had had my ticket to the adult section of the main library in Coatbridge before I reached the official age, because I had exhausted the supply in the junior section. 'Books – they're the most important thing of all, sir. I'd love to work there.'

'I make no promises, but I have high hopes for you, and I will do my best. Meanwhile, I will make arrangements for you to be given school dinner tickets in the normal manner, but your mother is not required to pay for them. Please tell her that. And one other thing, I think you should consider primary teaching as a very suitable career, Sandra. Say to her I said so. Now, back to class.'

I was so excited I could hardly breathe, and had to squeak out my thanks as he showed me gruffly to the door. I returned, walking on air, to my English class. I was desperate to rush home and tell my mother that perhaps, after all, I did not need to think of Woolworths, and could ignore Granny Jenny's remarks that it was not worth while to keep a girl on at school: 'They just go on tae huv weans, so it's a waste o' time.'

My mother was delighted, and I heaved a sigh of relief. Mr Cooper indeed used his influence and I gave up travelling to Glasgow on Saturdays to work instead in the Carnegie Library, where I loved my part-time work in the children's, then the adult section, for some four years. I picked up the necessary Highers to train as a teacher.

I parted from John to concentrate on my studies and found college life suited me. Mr Cooper's interest in my career continued and he played matchmaker unwittingly, too: the library was where I met a handsome fellow student delivering Christmas mail, who later became my husband.

# Chapter Eleven

As adulthood beckoned it seemed to me that the best way to cope with the past was to bury the rotten memories and avoid any connection with my dad. I tried to deny the influence he had had on me or that I bore any resemblance to him. I was furious when Granny Jenny had remarked that all three of his children had inherited his height but I also had his nose. I spent weeks studying my reflection in Granny Katie's triple dressing table mirror and was convinced that Granny Jenny might be right, but would never have given her the satisfaction of saying so.

Many people found it remarkable that my mother had not turned against Granny Jenny for her son's treatment of his first family but they got on well and my mother stressed, 'It's not Jenny's fault that her son Alex turned out so feckless . . . she's done nothing to us, and she's still your gran.'

Jenny was proud that she had been born in the same year as the Queen Mother. We were close, though this was more through my efforts than hers, and we never shared the almost psychic relationship I had with Granny Katie, to whom I related my dreams. Like Joe Gargery's wife in *Great Expectations*, Jenny wore a rubber apron, to which pins and brooches were stuck and her chest bristled with jagged objects that ruled out cuddles. Her lively sense of humour hid the fact that she did not find it easy to show affection to children or young adults.

When I enrolled as a student at Hamilton College of Education in 1967 and found I was entitled to the maximum student grant, it did not occur to me to spend the first cheque I received, which was for the largest amount of money my mother and I had ever seen. My mother presented it at the bank, and we solemnly halved it between us so that I could go and purchase my books. She could not believe that the huge sum I had received would be available each term. She was over the moon. I couldn't tell her that many of my peers were well-to-do young women, who regarded their grants as pin money for their exclusive use. The three hundred students in my year contained a sprinkling of privately educated girls from privileged backgrounds, several of whom even drove to college in smart little sport cars. I was finally on the same planet as some of the St Clare's types from my childhood comics, and now I knew I had little in common with them.

The lecturers I related to best were the ones who clearly identified with a strong working-class background, and who encouraged my growing interest in writing. My memories of student days are warm primarily because I did not have to worry about my father's presence. I had spare cash, and did not have to borrow make-up and tights from Irene, who had gone to study languages at university.

My mother followed every aspect of my college career with interest and pleasure, and no one could have been prouder than she when I graduated in 1970 with a teaching diploma that received merit in academic subjects. After the ceremony, when I emerged a fully fledged teacher, she reflected that education was the key to making something of your life. 'There are times I wish I'd never married,' she said thoughtfully, 'when I look back and think what a waste, and I know I wanted to be a teacher, or a writer . . .' Then her face softened. 'But if I hadn't married, then I wouldn't have had you ones.'

It is only now that I can acknowledge publicly the amount of support she gave me. There was much about her to admire: she had found great courage and strength in the face of hardship during my childhood, and yet she could also retrieve a sense of fun when she was with children. She made her own childhood sound magical to me, as we lay in bed and laughed about all the adventures and scrapes her brothers got into. Her own spirit and determination shone through in the stories. Over the years, I told them to the primary children I taught and then to my own two children, Ross and Lauren.

She sized up all the lads I brought home after my first serious relationship with John, and she was anxious about my eventual choice of partner. It was important to me that she approved of Ronnie, the man I married at the age of twenty-three. I have put total faith in him, and throughout our marriage we have shared similar values and beliefs. He has shown me, through our children, how special fatherhood can be. Thankfully, he made a good impression on my mother.

Ronnie and I set a wedding date in October 1971, and we saved hard, putting away almost every penny from my assistant teacher's salary of forty pounds a month, which was what I received when I started my first post, ten pounds of which went to my mother for my board. I had been employed on graduation by my old primary-school head teacher, Mr Allan. Ronnie put his meagre wage as a graduate civil engineer straight into a joint bank account. We knew, without ever discussing it, that the only way we could have a family wedding 'do' was to pay for it ourselves.

He also knew, intuitively, that there were elements of my childhood I did not feel able to discuss with him. He had never met my father although our families lived near each other. His parents seemed to like me, and I respected them. The ugly parts of my past remained locked inside me.

It felt strange to be back at the school I had attended so many years ago, but I enjoyed teaching. The staff at Gartsherrie Academy still contained some of the old guard, but happily they were held in affection and were more than helpful to the new raw recruits. Miss Pringle, the delightful infant teacher, dedicated to educating children since a whole generation of young men had not returned from the First World War, was still there; so was Miss McLean, a real character, whose sisters owned the most amazing drapery shop in the town, renowned as a surrealistic labyrinth of underwear and hosiery you could get lost in. I renewed a childhood friendship, too: Fiona, a long-ago playmate from Dunbeth Park, was in the next-door classroom, to my delight.

After our engagement, I heard Granny Jenny and my mother discuss Ronnie approvingly and knew what was coming next. Jenny's bottom lip trembled and she said to my mother, 'He should give away his only lass.' I flatly refused to consider sending my father an invitation.

My mother agreed, and said to her mother-in-law:

'Sandra and Ronnie are paying for everything themselves, so it's up to them who they invite. I'm divorced from Alex, now, and it's certainly up to the bride who gives her away, Jenny, she can ask whoever she wants.'

When I got married Uncle Robbie gave me away in church. He was delighted to help out, and brought all his family. They no longer lived in Leicester but had settled on Canvey Island.

'Stupid bastard,' was his pithy comment when he saw me in my wedding dress, and we got into the limousine. 'He'll live to regret what he left behind him.'

For the first three years of our married life, my husband and I lived fifteen floors up in one of the new high-rise tower blocks that suddenly dominated the landscape in Coatbridge, just a stone's throw from my old home in Dunbeth Road, which had been demolished in the mid-sixties. We joked about our penthouse with its panoramic view. Our town had its very own version of American skycrapers. From my lofty vantage point, I could see that, despite the coming of the high flats, the old games had not disappeared completely: girls still thumped balls off the walls of the flats, and when I visited the basement launderette, I was pleased to see an occasional game of peever going on.

Everywhere I had lived as a child, my mother always worried about 'rough elements'. It never seemed to occur to her that the worst influence I ever came across was my father. I also noticed that these 'skyscraper weans' did not venture far from their homes: the lessons of 1957 had not been forgotten.

People still discussed the mystery of Moira Anderson. The whispers and pointing fingers had been hard for the Anderson family when some malicious tongue started a rumour that Mandy Rice-Davies, the call-girl involved in the Profumo scandal of the sixties, was none other than Moira. A likeness, they said, had been spotted, and the next thing was the 'story' broke in the press, causing the family more heartbreak when the tabloids asked if Moira could be one of many runaways from the north who lost their identity deliberately in London, only to surface years later under an assumed name. Most townsfolk, though, thought that Moira's tender age, her background, and the way in which she had disappeared did not match that of a runaway in search of the bright lights. Foul play, they agreed, had been the cause.

Change was in the air not only in the town, with familiar landmarks vanishing overnight, but also in the classroom: in February 1971 we switched to the metric system and the joy of decimals. My brothers married and my mother found the house in Ashgrove too large. She flitted round the corner to School Street, and one of her brothers, Bobby, who had been abroad for many years and was also divorced, moved in. It was company for her, and the arrangement suited them both.

The Anderson girls married and moved away, perhaps feeling they could never have a normal life when the disappearance of their sister was still the focus of speculation in the town. Janet emigrated to Australia, and Marjorie moved away to England.

On the face of it, I was happy and I found marriage liberating. I enjoyed the years of primary teaching before we started our own family in 1978. For a young woman in her twenties, though, my health was not perfect. From puberty, I had suffered crops of severe mouth ulcers, which appeared two dozen or more at a time. I was never free of them for long. I was referred to the Glasgow dental hospital, where I was examined by consultants, dental hygienists and others to attempt to analyse the cause, but to no avail. Pregnancies made little difference, which disappointed those who said hormones were to blame, vitamins did not help, and blood tests showed up no abnormalities. For many years I had to cope with mouthwashes and, during very bad spells, doses of steroids.

It was a mystery, they said, in someone who otherwise seemed perfectly normal. But although I used to believe that if feelings are not expressed outwardly, they disappear, now I know better. As a child, I had been required to file away horrific memories.

The more painful they are, the more poisonous they become within our system. After many years of pain, homeopathic medicine, where the whole person is examined, helped me. The ulcers reduced to manageable levels. Recently, I have even been ulcer-free, and able to enjoy the bliss of eating whatever I wish. Significantly, the homeopathic treatment coincided with a long spell of counselling when, with specialist help, I was able at last to speak of the secrets I had buried deep within me. I was made aware of how much our emotions and memories are tied into the nervous system and how stress can manifest itself.

When my grandfather died, my father was traced by the police for his dad's funeral, and arrived at the last minute. Ronnie and I had a glimpse of him getting into the funeral car. It was the first time my husband had seen him, for I had never shown him any photographs. I refused to sit anywhere near him. Ronnie and I sat with my mother at the opposite end of the room, and I would not look in my father's direction. He spoke briefly to my brothers, which had me seething with anger but, wisely, he knew to avoid me.

Granny Jenny had moved to a tiny sheltered house in Bellshill. My mother phoned her every day, and I visited regularly. I said nothing when I noticed that pictures I had given her of my family disappeared. I guessed she had sent them to Leeds. As she reached her nineties, and eventually Alexander was her last living child, she sometimes became pensive. Robbie, her favourite, she mourned openly, but once she discussed Alexander. She pondered on the terrible things he had done. When I looked at her quizzically, she added hastily, 'I'm just meaning the awful things he pit your mammy through, hen. He pit ye all through hell, and me and Grandpa, tae, God rest his soul. Aye, he wis certainly awfy stupid.'

Renowned for her sense of humour, that day she was depressed. 'Wicked, wicked,' she repeated to me, 'but all of us love our ain. Ye can't help lovin' you and yours, even when ye know they've—' She broke off and wiped her eyes. She motioned me closer to her chair.

'Even when they've what?' But whatever she had been about to confide, she had thought better of it.

Her bright blue eyes dropped from mine. 'Och, leave it.' She waved me away dismissively. 'Sometimes ye're better tae pit things behind ye, and not stir it all back up. Mak me a cuppa tea, Sandra, hen.'

I decided she had meant the way my father had jettisoned all responsibility for his first family.

Meanwhile, Ronnie and I saved until we could buy our own home, a feat unheard of in the generation before ours; raising our children in middle-class bungalows rather than the tenements or council houses familiar to our parents. I enjoyed the early years of parenthood but although I would not say I smothered my children when they were small, I found it hard not to over-protect them. I could barely let them out of my sight when they were little, and I was always on the alert. I told myself it was normal for a young mother to check constantly who was hanging around the school gates, or who was speaking to kids. I told myself this was uppermost in my mind because of my primary-school training, from the years of being responsible for large groups of children. I just couldn't get out of the habit, that was all.

The day came when I realized the truth about my reluctance to leave my children with other adults. I had returned to full-time work and was now a lecturer in child education in a college. 'Auntie' Rosie, our childminder, had my complete trust, and was adored by both of our two children. Her home was just yards from ours, the arrangement suited everyone beautifully. However, that day when I arrived to collect Lauren, nobody was there. I was told that Rosie had had to go to the dental hospital for emergency treatment; they wouldn't be long. I was thunderstruck when Rosie told me later that she had been longer than expected at the clinic, and Ally, her husband, had spent the afternoon with Lauren across the road at the Chambers Street museum. I started to shake. I blurted out, in a complete panic, that I had only met Ally once or twice, and I heard myself ask: 'Ally has been checked out by the social work department, too, hasn't he? He doesn't have any kind of criminal record?'

Many months later, when I was able to speak to Rosie about my past, she said that although she'd been offended at the time, what I had said was clearly understandable.

Today, I still insist on knowing where my children are. There is no question of my daughter going off anywhere alone, not even for a country walk. It is, many people say, a sad reflection on the way society has gone. I don't agree. The dangers were there before, but they went unrecognized, and now at least, while we know we cannot wrap children in cotton wool, we can give them mechanisms for self-protection, explain to them that their bodies are their own and that nobody has the right to touch them.

# Chapter Twelve

In 1992 life was going well for me. I had a good marriage, two children who seemed popular and well adjusted at their schools in a pleasant suburb of Edinburgh, and I'd an interesting job. My teaching career had taken a step forward in 1989, when I'd been promoted to senior lecturer, then shortly afterwards to section head. While this brought much more in the way of administration, I enjoyed it, and attempted to keep a balance between the work I often brought home and the demands of my role as a mother and wife.

After a long, difficult spell, however, when I filled in for almost two years for someone senior to me who was on sick leave, I jumped at the chance of a full week's training in management skills, between 3 and 7 February. The seaside hotel venue was in Portobello, close enough to Edinburgh should any family emergency occur. I had a distinct sense that if anything was to go wrong in the family, it was bound to happen when I was away for any length of time.

Sure enough, it did, but it was not to do with Ross and Lauren. My mother told me when I rang her that my grandmother was ill, and likely to be taken into hospital. Worried, I called Jenny on the Tuesday of the course, and assured her that if she had to go into hospital, it would be like the other two recent occasions when her cast-iron constitution had astonished doctors and she had quickly been discharged. I reminded her to eat, and joked that my mother and I marvelled at her appetite: she was the only woman we knew, I said, who could eat a pot of mince and tatties by herself. Although she laughed, I detected a note of resignation in her voice, as if she knew she wouldn't come home this time.

'Och, Ah think that's me,' she said, quite unsentimentally. 'We've all got tae go sooner or later, and Ah've had a long life, Sandra. If Ah go intae hospital, Ah dinnae want them pittin' me on thae drip things tae keep me goin'. That wid jist scunner me. Ah've lived lang enough.'

'Don't say that, Gran,' I pleaded. 'You still get a lot out of life, and you always know what's going on in the world, not like a lot of old biddies—'

'Och, Ah know that,' she said flatly, 'but Ah hate hospitals, and it's time Ah went. Thanks for phoning, hen, I'm glad ye did, so I can say cheerio.'

Later, my mother told me that Granny Jenny's sense of humour had been intact until the last. She died in Law Hospital, in the early hours of the Friday morning when my course was due to finish. I received an early-morning phone call from Ronnie and, through my tears, arranged that I would go to Coatbridge and Bellshill later that day to take my mother to Granny Jenny's home and discuss what must be done.

Ronnie, though, was unaware that my father had been contacted by the police in Leeds and had already come north. Travelling up by train, he had met up with my cousin, William, and William's fiancée, Lily. All three were now installed in Granny Jenny's tiny house. Later, I discovered that my father had been unhappy to find that one of my brothers had been appointed by her as the executor of her will. In other words, she had excluded her only surviving child. He was shocked to discover her bank book had the joint signature of my brother Norman. He would be the one to sort out her financial affairs.

That Friday morning, 7 February 1992, I struggled to concentrate on the final sessions of the management course. The week had been something of an emotional roller-coaster for everyone involved. There had been role-play exercises and discussions requiring deep soul-searching, which many of the two dozen or so participants had found as gruelling as I had. Nearly all of us had been tearful at one point or another, including several men.

Jeanie, the course leader who had come from Bristol, had given us an interpersonal skills exercise mid-week, which had caused me some problems. With a partner, we had to compare the messages given to us by our parents from an early age. I was stunned at the negative ones I had picked up when I studied the topics of politics, money, relationships, sex, employment, etc. When I looked at the conflicting messages I had received from my parents in my own childhood, I could not understand what had made them think that they had had anything in common when they first met.

From my mother, I had learnt that: to get anywhere you had to work hard; you had to save the pennies so that the pounds could look after themselves; you had to go to church regularly; sex before marriage was not only out of the question, it could not be discussed. My father's philosophies were the opposite: a girl staying on at school was pointless ('a good job' in a factory or shop could always be fixed up by speaking to someone he knew); money was something to spend when it was available, and saving it was none of his business – housekeeping, budgeting and childcare were women's responsibilities; church was not necessary unless you had an ulterior motive; and sex was there for the taking whenever and with whom you liked.

Deep within myself, I had acknowledged my memories but knew I had sealed that cupboard long ago.

Only once had it been forced open, just a chink. In 1981, when I was thirty-six, Ronnie and I had gone to live in Pitlochry, in the Scottish Highlands, not long after Lauren's birth. Ronnie's job had taken us there for two years. They were happy years for me: I taught art locally in a private school, helped run the playgroup and participated in the thriving amateur drama club. Also, I had done something I had wanted to do for years. I had saved money of my own, and decided I would use it to change the one thing I disliked about myself. I underwent surgery in Glasgow at Bon Secours clinic to have my father's inheritance removed. When asked what I wanted in place of my own nose, the consultant glanced up when I said, 'Just one that's *different.*'

I was pleased with the result, and surprised that virtually nobody noticed what I had done, not even close family members. I rarely gave it a thought afterwards, but no longer cared if photographs caught me in full profile, as one wedding snap had.

During the exceptional summers of 1982 and 1983, I immersed myself in community drama festivals, and took the children for swimming and picnics in the loveliest of spots. The small town felt so safe that even in the depths of winter I could return home from babysitting in the early hours and walk back alone through the little wood near our home at the golf course. I could marvel at its beauty without once feeling fear. Childhood anxieties of being attacked were remote, and I would join with others in agreeing that Pitlochry was typical of communities thirty years ago. It was in a kind of time warp. I was in a place where everyone knew everyone else, and where folk felt able to let their children play where they liked in the knowledge that they would come to no harm.

Suddenly a bombshell dropped. It was during a panto put on in Pitlochry Town Hall when I was taking the part of principal boy in *Aladdin* that I happened to encounter a former neighbour from Coatbridge. 'I remember you, Sandra!' she remarked at the after-show party. 'And I remember your dad particularly well. Big, tall, handsome bus driver with dark hair, right?'

I nodded politely as I passed round food for my friends Ian and Linda. I was about to explain that my parents had divorced in the late sixties when she added, 'He'd a wee black car, hadn't he, and was a great one for the ladies! But I always felt sorry about what happened to him, you know.'

I frowned. She went on to tell me that my father, who I had always thought was in hospital between 1957 and 1959, had been in prison. According to her, he had been sentenced for the rape of a thirteen-year-old girl, my parents' babysitter. As the woman chatted, I attempted to act normally, but I felt sick. In fact, I needed a brandy, a drink I rarely touch.

Suddenly it registered with the woman that her revelation had come as a shock to me. 'I thought you knew,' was all she could say. 'You couldn't miss it at the time, it was in all the papers.'

'I'd only be eight,' I muttered. 'I never knew.'

Cringing with humiliation, I felt I could not discuss it with my husband. Why not just pretend it had never been said? The discovery, however, preyed on my mind and I resolved to speak to my mother. I was devastated. How could she, to whom I was so close, hide something so important all these years? I remembered how adults had whispered or stopped talking when I entered rooms. I had always felt that my father's absence when I was between the ages of eight and ten had been something shameful. I had been right.

I tackled my mother about the length of time I'd been kept in the dark. I told her how upsetting it had been to learn the truth in my thirties from a near stranger. The information, she reluctantly confirmed, was correct. My father had served a prison sentence in Saughton, Edinburgh. There had been no long hospital stay. I noticed, however, that she was defensive of her actions and protective of my father's behaviour. 'I was only trying to shield you,' she said stonily, and then broke down. 'I thought it was the right thing to do at the time. Then I always just kept putting it off. But it wasn't rape. The girl was a teenager who was very promiscuous – she was round all the drivers. Alex was the one who happened to get caught. She was a wee tart.'

Her last phrase was delivered with a venom most unlike her. It hit me that she blamed the child involved. Astonished, I pointed out that the girl had only been thirteen and my father thirty-six: was she seriously trying to say he had been led astray? I was not satisfied with the scant details she provided, and later I resolved that I would find out more about the events that had led to his arrest in December 1956, just before my eighth birthday.

But the opportunity to question her further did not arise easily.

After my initial shock at the conversation I'd had with the woman, I found I was able to put it out of my thoughts, but only for a short time. In my dreams, disturbing images and memories began to surface. I forced them back: lots of people know someone who's been in prison, I argued inwardly, it's something I'll have to learn to live with. I knew, however, that I could not reveal to anyone asking me outright why he had served his sentence. 'I just won't tell people what it was *for*,' I resolved.

I tried to talk to Granny Jenny who wouldn't even look me in the eye. 'All I'm gonnae say, Sandra, is it's long past, and I hate talkin' aboot it, for Ah believe it jist aboot killed his father. Sanny wis never the same after yer dad – after whit happened. Yer grandfaither wis a different kind o' man a' thegither. The one thing Ah can say aboot Sanny is he died as he lived. *He* never harmed a soul, but he always said yer daddy killed—'

She stopped as if terrified she had said too much. Lauren, toddling into the room, distracted me briefly as I placed the guard in front of the blazing fire I had just fuelled. Then she went on: 'Yer daddy killed all Sanny's love for him. That's all Ah wis meaning.'

She refused to say any more on the subject. But I was chilled.

On the sunny, clear morning of my grandmother's death, Jeanie, the management-course leader, noticed a profound change in me and had coffee with me at break time. She had heard I'd suffered a family bereavement and comforted me. We chatted about the assertiveness training which had formed part of the course, and I found myself telling her that a man at work, older than myself, used subtle ways to undermine my authority. I found him difficult to handle. She looked at me obliquely.

'Women who have encountered very early rejection from their opposite sex parent often have problems needing to be liked by males. They go through life effectively seeking male approval,' she commented, and suggested some strategies to try with the man at work. I explained that my father had, indeed, gone off in my early years and had returned only to abandon us again. Jeanie said that she could empathize with this. In some ways, she told me, I was a young version of herself. We had had similar events to cope with in our lives, and she too, had had to deal with problems that stemmed from childhood. I told her I loathed my father for the things he had done. 'Don't underestimate the father–daughter thing,' she said, 'and how powerful that relationship is for the first seven years or so. It's the very first one you have with the opposite sex. Out of curiosity, when did you last speak to him? Have you ever told him how you feel?'

I explained that for twenty-seven years I had felt unwilling to exchange a single word with him. I was frightened of the consequences.

'What would you say to him if you were to meet him today? Role-play it with me,' said Jeanie. I unloaded a lot of anger in the exercise, choosing my words with care. I felt better for it and promised that, should the opportunity arise to tell my dad what I really thought of him, I would grab it.

The opportunity arose that very evening.

I picked up my mother to go to Granny Jenny's. I knew that because of her blindness, caused by diabetes, she could not see how upset and dishevelled I was, but I gasped when she said in the car, 'By the way, I think you should know your father's here at Gran's. He and your cousin William, and his fiancée, they're all here until the funeral on Tuesday.'

Accelerating, I said grimly, 'Actually, it's going to suit me just fine, Mum. I want to have a word with him on my own.'

There was silence while she absorbed this. As soon as we arrived, she began to organize tea for everyone. William and Lily were blowing up an air bed in the living room, as my father had taken the one small bedroom that had been Gran's. He hovered, watching me expectantly with a half-smile. He did not look like a man of almost seventy-one. He was still a man it was hard to ignore.

'I'd like to speak to you in private.' My words were terse, and everyone else studied the floor with interest. He ushered me through to the bedroom, still nodding and smiling. We sat inches apart on the bed, him on the window side, I nearer the door. I was nervous, but adrenaline was pumping through me, and the anger I had expressed in the role-play with Jeanie came back in its rehearsed phrases. Fate had played me the most incredible hand, and I was determined not to cry or lose control. I inhaled deeply, and began.

He drew back, visibly shaken and unprepared for the unrelenting tirade I unleashed.

He muttered, 'Once you're a black sheep, you're always a black sheep.'

I could tell by his manner that he had been wrong-footed by my attack. He tried to get a word in edgeways, making the excuse that his mother had always preferred Robbie, his young brother, to him. He had always felt neglected, and so he was the one who got into scrapes.

'Scrapes?' I cried in disgust, my flesh crawling as he tried to pat my hand. 'Is that what you call going to prison for sexual offences and serving a sentence?'

He caught his breath, and his eyes flickered oddly in the light. I told him how I had learned the truth about his 'hospitalization'. He looked away.

'I thought you knew about that,' he said slowly. 'Your mam should've told you. Her name was Betty, but you won't remember her.'

'But I do,' I retorted angrily. 'She'd fair hair and lots of freckles and she giggled all the time. She came to babysit.'

His eyes narrowed. There was something strange about them, I realized. They were like grey, flinty pebbles now, remote and filled with anger. But they no longer instilled in me the fear of long ago, I noted triumphantly.

'No one gave me the chance of turning over a new leaf,' he said. 'Not one.'

'That's not true!' I burst out. 'My mother told me when you got out of jail both of you got down on your knees in front of the minister and prayed for a fresh start. You promised you'd change your ways.'

'I tried tae,' he said heavily, looking at his hands, 'but not everyone would forgive me and let me start again. Your gran forgave me, and your mam, but my father never ever did.'

There was a silence between us now. I thought it an odd thing to say. According to my mother, her father-in-law had been a tower of strength, organizing petitions with my father's workmates to send to the trial judge to persuade him that the events with the babysitter had been out of character, and getting church people to write saying that my father was a pillar of the community.

'*Why* wouldn't your father forgive you?' I quizzed him several times. I was not prepared to let go now, not when I seemed to have him on a hook.

Another long silence followed.

'He wouldn't forgive me for the Moira Anderson thing.'

My head shot up. Had I heard him correctly? He was looking bleakly out of the window now, where snow had started to swirl past.

A sudden bizarre image of my father and the Scottish soprano much beloved of Hogmanay television offerings and *The White Heather Club* audiences, with her nostalgic duets with Kenneth McKellar, popped into my head. Was he telling me they'd had some kind of illicit affair?

Then he went on: 'I was charged about the babysitter, then I got out on bail. You won't remember this, it was all a long time ago. It was away back in 1957. My father wouldn't forgive me for Moira Anderson. You won't remember her either – you were too wee.'

My heart raced and my throat closed painfully. I did not want to hear any more.

I forced out, 'You're wrong. I *do* remember her.'

'Grandpa was always convinced I'd done it. He said to me tae tell the polis where I'd put the wee lassie.'

My father's fingers were now working at the fabric of

the candlewick bedspread. He stared unseeingly at the snow, which was flashing past the window, the flakes strangely orange in the neon street light, for all the world like phosphorus. Was it my imagination or was the room darkening? Some instinct told me that I must imprint every detail of this weird conversation on my brain.

Terror wrenched at me, and I cried, 'But why on earth would Grandpa even *connect* you to Moira Anderson? What could possibly make him think you were responsible?'

Those cold eyes shifted away again and silence fell. Finally, he said: 'I told him I had nothing to do with her, but I was the driver of the bus the day she went missing. I told Grandpa I didn't even know her, but she got on my bus, in all the snow. I was the last tae speak tae her. I was the last person tae see her . . .'

His voice trailed away and my heart lurched. My mind finished the end of the sentence, which he could not bring himself to say, as tears ran down his face.

*Alive.*

# Chapter Thirteen

As I drove shakily east towards Edinburgh on the M8, which that evening was reduced to one lane, blinding blasts of snow tried to claim the few patches of visible road. My mind was in turmoil. With a kaleidoscope of snowflakes dashing against my windscreen, it seemed as if I was venturing through a tunnel of whirling elements with no clear view ahead. This image has stayed with me, and it sums up the state of mind I was in during the days following the conversation I had had with my father.

Over and over, even when I was asleep, I heard the words he had used, like an interminable tape-recording. Two assurances he had given me before we had left Granny Jenny's bedroom kept echoing through my brain. I had frantically demanded to know if he'd been interviewed when Moira disappeared. 'Oh, aye, I wis.' He nodded quickly. 'I telt them the same as Grandpa. I didn't even know her.'

These two statements disturbed me because I knew he was lying. I didn't know how I could feel so sure of it, but my conviction that my father and Moira had known each other was overwhelming.

In the meantime, there was the funeral to get through,

but before that I managed to pull myself together enough to telephone Aunt Margaret, my mother's sister.

'Margaret, I expect you know my father's back on the scene at the moment, which has been very upsetting for us all. Never mind having to cope with bereavement.' She made the normal expressions of condolence at the other end of the line. 'I don't want to ask my mum about this, but I wondered if you would know. Was my father ever interviewed regarding Moira Anderson going missing in 1957?'

I was astonished when, after a short silence, my aunt said categorically, 'Oh, yes, that's right, he was. In fact I was there at the time. He came in when I was visiting your mum in Dunbeth Road, and I can remember him saying, "Now, don't put my tea out, Mary, I have to go round to the police station to be interviewed." '

I chewed my lip, and said, 'What else do you remember about it?'

'Well, your mum was shattered. I can tell you Mary hit the roof. She said, "Whit's happened now?" because, of course, he was already in all this bother and out on bail.' There was a delicate pause. 'D'you know, Sandra, about all that?'

'I do now,' I said wryly. 'So, let's get this right, you're absolutely sure he was interviewed? When was this?'

'It was a Monday, the week after she disappeared. We were living in Alexander Street, just round the corner from her home, and I remember all the men searching in the back closes. He said to us that he was being seen because during the week some woman had said Moira got on his bus. She'd thought she'd heard the driver say, "Hello, Moira." He was going round to explain to them that it was another girl that he'd actually spoken to that day – a different Moira, a Moira Liddell, who gave all the drivers sweeties, and the lady must have been mistaken ... Anyway, your mum was in a state, and I waited with her till he came back about an hour later.'

Mentally I pictured the scene, reminding myself that my father had had only to walk round the corner to the local station. It would never have occurred to either woman, as one sister comforted the other, to check on his actual movements. As far as they were concerned, when Alexander Gartshore returned to say that all was well, they accepted that he had been through a full police interview and had not been detained. Both women shared a family trait of always seeing the best in others and would go to great lengths to defend an underdog. I could almost see the relief on their faces when he returned, his tale seemingly checked out.

Not only had he convinced them but there was also every chance that if his name were to arise in the investigation they would staunchly defend him and spread the word that he had already been questioned. I shook my head at my father's sheer audacity. I was quite unprepared, however, for my aunt's next revelation, when I outlined the weird conversation he and I had had. She murmured that my grandfather had indeed had problems in believing that his son, already bailed for sexual offences involving a young girl, had had nothing to do with Moira's disappearance. When he heard that Alexander had been driving the bus on which she was alleged to have travelled, he and Jenny had journeyed from their home in Bellshill to Coatbridge to confront him.

Ignoring my father's protests, my grandpa had produced a crowbar and proceeded to pull up floorboards in the kitchen of 51 Dunbeth Road. He was aware that his son had recently renovated the scullery and had purchased new flooring from the ironmongers, Nelson and Clelland, who traded in the town's main street. He also knew that the sink units had been replaced, and he pulled out everything to check behind the new ones, ripping out the false panelling.

My father had been furious. I later heard from my mother that he kept repeating in greatly affronted tones, 'You surely don't think I did away wi' her, do ye?'

My grandfather's search of the whole house, including the large walk-in cupboard in my parents' bedroom which doubled as a workshop, was fruitless. He sat, head in hands, and said grimly, 'You're in enough trouble as it is. God knows I don't want further shame brought on our family's good name, but I'm convinced you're involved in this. You tell the polis where ye pit that wee lassie, Alex.'

But my father stuck to his story that the police had seen him, and the child he'd been seen talking to was not the one for whom everyone was now searching. (Later I found that my grandfather had not restricted himself to our home, but had searched anywhere that someone could conceivably hide a small girl's body. He had insisted on checking the boots of my dad's bus and car.)

'As if I would do such a thing,' my father complained afterwards. 'What kind of man do they think I am, saying I'd lay a finger on anybody? Jist because I'm in bother for the other thing, they're wantin' to pin this on to me, too. My father's right out of order doin' what he's done, and I've telt him all I know, but he still won't believe me, so what can I do? You know I'd never harm any wean, Mary.'

When my mother recounted this conversation to me, years after it had taken place, I felt like saying to her that if the police had spoken to me at the time, and I'd just been a bit older, I would have let them know he was more than capable of harming young children. Moira's appearance, slim, boyish, with an exceptionally striking smile, I could have told them, was a type much admired by a predatory, unscrupulous male like my dad. Her outgoing personality would have drawn him to her like a magnet, as he liked liveliness in a child.

My grandmother's funeral took place on a damp February day in 1992, with a service in Bellshill where she had lived all her life, followed by her cremation at Daldowie near Calderpark Zoo on the south side of Glasgow. Strangely, the crematorium route was lined with policemen who were organizing themselves for the funeral of a respected colleague.

Afterwards we gathered for what we Scots call the 'purvey' – tea, sandwiches, sausage rolls and cakes – in the little hall back at Granny Jenny's sheltered-housing complex. I travelled there with my friend Irene. As soon as we were alone she sensed that something was amiss. She was horrified when I related my father's history.

'I'm sure he *must* have been interviewed at the time, Sandra,' she protested. 'They brought in the Glasgow CID, didn't they? It was in all the papers, and they always round up the local suspects when these things happen.'

'What if they missed him somehow?'

'Surely that's not possible. If he was out on bail they'd be keeping an eye on him?'

I was relieved to hear a tiny question creep into Irene's voice. 'I'm not convinced he was interviewed, don't ask

114

me why, but I'm not. What I do know is that I've got to decide whether I need to find out or not.'

The meal in the pensioners' hall passed without incident. My father sat with his son, another Alex Gartshore and a previously unseen stepbrother, at one end of the room, while I sat at the other with Irene, my mother and my own family. The Canvey Island relatives were in the middle, with my brothers and their wives, and also William, the cousin who had travelled up from Leeds with his fiancée Lily. The only real communication between myself and my father at the table was to pass up photographs that Ronnie and I had taken of Granny Jenny enjoying herself on Christmas Day at the large Victorian house my brothers had bought some years ago, and divided between them. There she was, large as life, laughing and joking in her wheelchair and presiding over Ian and Annette's white lace-covered festive table. When three photos were put side by side, you could see all sixteen or so happy faces in the glow of flickering Christmas candlelight. A warmer family scene could not be imagined.

For Alexander Gartshore, here was evidence that the wife and three children he had abandoned in 1965 had not only survived without him but had prospered.

I noticed that the photographs made a deep impression on my father, the reason for which I understood later when I gathered that he was living in a tower-block flat that could in no way be described as the lap of luxury.

As we left, my father suddenly planted an awkward kiss right on my lips, then pecked my mother's cheek. While we were recovering from this belated display of affection, we were bundled into cars to travel the few miles between Bellshill and Coatbridge.

I was more puzzled that William and Lily had moved out of Gran's home to my brother Norman's. Lily was in a highly emotional state, weeping profusely, which I thought peculiar since she hadn't known Granny Jenny very well.

I was aghast when she told me that my dad had made persistent sexual advances towards her. She said, 'William gave 'im a talking to, but it were no good – he wouldn't give over at all, acted as if it were all a big joke and I were making a fuss about nothing.'

'Why didn't William just thump him one so he got the message?' I asked.

'Well, he is his uncle,' she sobbed through her tears, 'but I couldn't stand much more of it, and then the final straw was when he comes into our room wanting to sleep in beside us—'

My jaw dropped and so, nearly, did the teapot.

'It were the sound of your gran's zimmer. He said he could 'ear these ghostly sounds in 'er bedroom, and he were frightened to sleep all by himself. We told him it were just the wind or the plumbing but he was certain it were 'er.'

William had told him to get lost, and they left the house at the first opportunity.

Later, I decided to speak to my brothers and their wives about what Lily had said and the awful dilemma in which I now found myself. Shock registered on all the faces looking back at me as I said we *had* to do something about this man. No one was safe from him. No women and no female children.

Both my brothers sat as if turned to stone.

I broke down when I explained how our conversation had ended, and told them my deepest suspicions, that our father was responsible for the disappearance of Moira Anderson.

The reactions round the table varied from incredulity to bewilderment to open hostility at the very idea. At first, Ian showed utter disbelief. His voice rose. 'You can't ask me to believe that our father calmly drove around in his bus after doing something as horrendous as that – nobody could carry on doing their job quite normally as if nothing had happened.'

It was like a kick in the stomach, but I understood how he felt. I, too, had wanted it all to go away and be a bad dream.

I pointed out to Ian that criminals *do* go about their business after they have committed offences and they do not have a label tattooed on their foreheads saying THIEF or RAPIST, but I could see that I was asking him and Norman to think the unthinkable.

One of my sisters-in-law asked me furiously, 'What do you hope to gain from opening all of this up again after all these years? Her family have probably forgotten all about it by now. Why upset everyone?'

'What do you mean?' I gasped. 'Her family's never known what happened to her – we can't just sweep this under the carpet as though it was never said. I can't accept that what you've just said is true. You would never *ever* get over your child disappearing. What if it were Michelle or Lauren?'

I was so aware that we *had* our children, but the Andersons' little girl had disappeared for ever. My reference to Michelle and Lauren had a sobering effect on everybody: the thought of either of them going missing and never coming home was unbearable. I could see Norman nod in agreement.

He and Ian then remembered that my father had said some odd things in the past few days. They had felt obliged to let him accompany them on all the various duties that have to be performed after a death. He had sat in the car and seemed a little confused about landmarks, they agreed, not recalling that the Coatbridge Hotel was near Drumpellier golf course. It was likely, they said to me, that all this stuff he'd said about Moira Anderson could be put down to senility.

I pointed out that some confusion about landmarks after a gap of almost thirty years was not unreasonable, and that as someone who had taught umpteen courses for Lothian Region's social work department on dementia to carers who deal with clients with Alzheimer's disease, I was clear that my father was *not* a sufferer. In vain I tried to get through to the shocked group round the table that the truth would have to be confronted and exposed. One sister-in-law rounded on me, 'It's all right for you. You don't live here any more! You changed your name to Brown and now you live in Edinburgh. We have to live here, not you. Everyone knows Norrie and Ian because they drive taxis. We have to think about our kids going to school, everybody looking at them. You've made up your mind that he's guilty, and that's it. You've absolutely no proof and he's *told* you he's been interviewed for it. Leave it well alone.'

'There's things I know about him that you don't,' I said at last, very slowly. 'I can't see why you're this upset when he wasn't *your* dad, and you never knew him, but I want to find out if he was actually interviewed. I don't think he was, somehow, and I'm sure he knew her. He slipped through the net at the time. Not only did he serve a sentence in Saughton in Edinburgh for the girl who was the babysitter, he's responsible for Moira Anderson and managed to get away with it.'

# Chapter Fourteen

The day after the funeral, my father and his son had gone. All that was left to show that he had been there was a letter in which he apologized for their 'shabby behaviour' in not staying to help. This is how I came to obtain my father's address in Leeds.

Once again, he had disappeared out of my life as suddenly as he had come, as usual leaving a trail of havoc, but this time I was far more able to deal with it. I told Ronnie the details of the conversation and my father's behaviour with Lily but I could not bring myself to talk to my mother. Ronnie told me that whatever I decided to do he would support me all the way.

The next few months were a nightmare of pain and confusion, and the only thing that kept me based in reality was work. I drove back and forth to the college campus in Livingston as if on automatic pilot. I felt that my demeanour there was normal, my breathing unhurried, but, of course, many colleagues noticed a difference in me, but put it down to sudden bereavement, knowing that I had been close to my grandmother.

Then, my concentration deteriorated. I had a car accident and my handbag was stolen from my office, with the family snaps we had taken at Christmas. While I could pull myself together enough to phone banks and let our minister, George Grubb, know that a set of church and Sunday-school keys were missing, I could not cope with the loss of those irreplaceable photos and their negatives. I was inconsolable, but would not listen to my husband's advice to take some time off work. I couldn't sleep, I lost weight and I was irritable with Ross and Lauren. My inability to concentrate, particularly when driving, became frightening. I would drive through to the Scottish Vocational Council's headquarters in Glasgow, where I was one of a small national team developing a new childcare course, and realize I had driven over forty miles on motorways without registering one landmark or road sign. I would find I hadn't checked the petrol indicator. The situation couldn't go on.

I made an appointment with our doctor, Brian Venters. By the time I was called, I was like a wet rag. I couldn't think straight, I couldn't look at anyone and, even worse, when he asked me cheerily what he could do for me, I burst into tears. Not a word emerged as he gently asked me what was wrong. It was as if the most enormous stone was lodged in my throat. Twenty minutes passed, in which I attempted to speak several times. Nothing came out. Just when I was positive that our GP would suggest I stop wasting his and everyone else's time, I blurted out that it was to do with my father. Another five minutes of racking sobs followed. Then, somehow, I managed to disclose some of what I had seen my father do when I was a child, of what had happened to my friends. He closed his eyes. I told him of my father's sentence and how I had only found out at the age of thirty-six. I explained how my grandmother's death had brought my father on the scene again and, haltingly, repeated the conversation where he had linked himself to Moira. When I stopped, Brian swore under his breath and said, 'I see people in here regularly, Sandra, whose families have been destroyed by child abuse, but this bastard takes the biscuit. Obviously you're in a state because as well as your grandmother's death – and it sounds to me as if she was the glue holding you all together to some extent – you're also having to deal with making a decision about what you're going to do about this disclosure he's made. Right?'

I agreed, and explained about my sleepless nights. 'I can help with the sleep getting back to normal,' he stated firmly, 'not through medication, just through some relaxation exercises I can show you. But also you need some very good counselling, someone to listen to all that has happened to you, including your early childhood, and I know just the person. Ashley is her name and she'll come to your home.'

Easter 1992 came and went, and so did the first of our sessions, but even before I met Ashley, a tiny, neat little person with bright eyes and silver blonde hair, I had already taken a further step on the road down which I was being slowly drawn. I had told my husband I was certain that I should take the information I had to the police and have my dad's claims checked out. I could not live with keeping such things to myself, where they would lodge in my conscience for ever. I was aware of the huge weight of responsibility involved in going to the police, and knew the likely negative reaction of my family. Ronnie and I had talked it through and I was clear that, while there was a risk of relatives being shattered by my disclosure, other lives might finally heal.

I wondered about speaking to a long-standing friend, Billy McCloy. Now a police inspector, he had become a leading member of Coatbridge and Airdrie Operatic Society, the amateur club in which I had been involved for some ten years. He'd married Fiona, who had been at Gartsherrie Academy with me both as pupil and teacher. I'd known Billy since he had joined the police, and we had attended each other's weddings.

Billy and I met at his home. An Airdrie boy, he knew much of the background to Moira Anderson's disappearance. We agreed, however that neither of us could recall a bus ever being involved in the case. That crucial sighting had been overlooked by both police and public in 1957.

I told Billy I needed him to check if Alexander Gartshore had or had not been interviewed in 1957. I implored him to go through the records without anyone else's knowledge. Slowly Billy explained that it wasn't as simple as I thought: records from the fifties would not be to hand. He would need a reason as to why he wanted to trawl through them. I asked him to check the police computer files to discover if my father had been in any further trouble down south in the seventies and eighties. He groaned. 'Sandra, it's more than my job's worth to do that. The best thing is for me to speak to someone you can trust who's based here in Airdrie, and they'll visit you in Edinburgh, take a statement, and *that* way you'll find out what you need to know, but I can assure you, if what you're saying is right, there's no way they'll have missed your dad at the time. He's *bound* to have been interviewed.'

I agreed. A few days later, Billy's colleague rang me and made arrangements to visit my home. I organized the children to go on a holiday treat that day to the newly opened leisure centre in Coatbridge. They had just gone off, full of excitement, when two plain-clothes policeman arrived. One was thick set, dour and gruff-looking, older than his buddy, while the other was handsome and noticeably fit, probably around my own age, with a lively, intelligent face. The voice on the phone had been friendly, but my heart sank slightly as they stood on the step, grim-faced. Their handshakes, though, were firm and positive. Both men settled in our family room at the back of the house and I made us a cup of tea before the interview began. Jim McEwan introduced himself as Detective Inspector, and indicated that his companion was Bobby Glenn.

Jim outlined a little of what he had gleaned from Billy McCloy, then leaned forward and tapped a large box file which he had carried in with him. My heart gave an enormous leap, as I saw a slightly dusty but still legible label marked 'Moira Anderson Enquiry, 1957'.

'What I can tell you categorically before we take a formal statement, Sandra, is that we have combed through the original investigation files which you see here, and there is absolutely no trace of an Alexander Gartshore ever being interviewed at that time or later. *No trace*. What I can do is show you that, indeed, contrary to what a large number of people seem to recall about this girl's disappearance, there is a confirmed sighting of her, in fact, several of her being on a local-service bus after the time given out by the officers then carrying out the inquiry, who did not choose to make this public at the time. It hardly featured in the press. I think you may be interested to read this page.'

He passed me the bulky file with its yellowing entries. Nearly forty years on, I read James Inglis' statement that she was the child to whom he spoke – he knew all three sisters and was unlikely to have confused Moira with Janet, despite their resemblance. Janet, in any case, was away from her home. The incident had stuck in his mind because while he had been sheltering in a doorway opposite the bus stop she, a typical child, had played in the snow.

For reasons best known to themselves, MacDonald and McIntosh dismissed Inglis, and made no attempt to interview the bus driver; they also put aside the statement of the woman although she was clear that Moira had not only boarded the bus, but might have sat at the front near the driver to speak to him. She herself had walked much further up the middle aisle of the bus and had sat near a side door at the back, by which she later left. She said she could not be sure where the little girl got off, but had the impression that she was still there when she disembarked. Her statement was not fully investigated, although she was a policeman's wife, from Irvine Crescent, near Moira's granny.

The investigating officers did not choose to reveal publicly that a third local witness had spotted Moira boarding the bus. An old lady who lived over Molly Gardiner's sweet shop in Alexander Street had been peering at the white-out conditions, and had noticed a little girl playing among the lock-up garages. As the woman reflected wryly that children rarely feel the cold, she noticed the girl fall over with quite a bump, then pick herself up and rub her bottom. Then she spent some time searching among the thick snow as if she had lost something. She checked through her pockets and bag as if, this witness concluded, she had dropped money, perhaps her bus fare, for she seemed to have been looking out for the local bus. Moments later it pulled in at the stop opposite the woman's home. When the bus departed, the small group of passengers had all got on and the child was no longer there. She was sure the kiddie had got on it with everyone else. I read the statement of a policeman's wife, Mrs Chalmers, who had exchanged a smile on the bus with Moira.

I looked up at Jim in amazement. 'My father floored me with what he told me about driving his bus that day and being the last to speak to her. I was only eight but I don't recall all this about her getting on a bus at all. Everyone just said she'd disappeared in the blizzard. Why on earth did they not act on this? Surely, if they had a policeman's wife making such a clear statement...'

'That goes for nothing,' put in Bobby Glenn bleakly.

'Are all these witnesses dead?' I swept my hand down the page.

'Only the young guy is still alive,' Jim glanced at me briefly, 'and he's a pensioner now. However, we've already been to see him. I've told him the way we're treating this investigation is as if it happened yesterday. He stands by every word he said, and the statements of the other witnesses will be treated with respect even if they're no longer with us.'

I realized that Jim was saying that my conversation with my father, as related to Billy McCloy, was being treated very seriously. In a strange way, while it petrified me, that knowledge provided a little comfort. It was clear that these two detectives did not regard me as some deluded woman wasting police time. They believed what I was saying.

'Read on,' said Jim, pointing to the bottom section of the page. This part indicated that whoever had taken the statements from the two bus passengers had gone to the bus station to see the crew. I read with some disbelief the perfunctory words: 'The driver indicated that neither he nor the conductress were aware of any child answering Moira's description.'

As I read out this sentence, we all shook our heads. Not only had the unknown interviewer not bothered speaking to the female companion of the bus driver, he had not checked that he had the correct crew. He had not even asked the man he had questioned for his name.

But at least one mystery had been solved: my father had never been questioned about Moira. I'd been right to trust my instincts.

Suddenly Jim asked, 'Was your dad in the Freemasons, by any chance?'

Alexander had, indeed, been a member, I told him, but how active I couldn't say. Though I was aware of rumours of corruption linking the police and freemasonry, I dismissed it as a reason for others protecting him. Much later, I discovered from a reliable source that my dad's lodge was composed of 90 per cent of policemen.

'Now,' Jim said, 'I think, Sandra, you'd better start at the very beginning. Tell me about your earliest memories of your dad.'

# Chapter Fifteen

The two detectives listened to what I disclosed that day. They absorbed my words, and occasionally asked questions, treating me with great sensitivity. Some of my memories were not sharply defined, while others were vivid in appalling detail. Psychologists have recognized a phenomenon they refer to as forty-year syndrome, found usually in survivors of the Holocaust: the subject denies painful truths for many years in the interests of their own survival and mental well-being. Reality emerges four decades or so later, when the person is secure in their own self-esteem and in the path they have chosen to follow. Something triggers the images that accompany the memories in the form of flashbacks which register on the inner screen of the brain. For me, the trigger had been the conversation with my dad.

I was relieved that these men were also in their middle years, and that, like me, they could recall the era of Forbidden Subjects.

Tellingly, each could remember exactly what he had been doing on the weekend that the news had broken about Moira's disappearance. Jim thought that people of our parents' generation, colleagues, friends, ex-neighbours, would remember my father well from that time. He was anxious to start gathering a detailed picture of him.

'So does this mean you're reopening the inquiry?' I asked, as Jim started to gather his papers together.

He looked at me. 'This inquiry's never been closed, but despite the length of time involved, which convinces me foul play occurred, it has never, for some reason, been upgraded to a murder investigation. It remains a missing-person file.'

I gave him my father's address, and arranged to look out photographs of my father in 1957 from old family albums. I asked when Jim intended to see him: I was fearful of the consequences of that, as my dad would know who had spoken to the police and I remembered my eldest step-brother's scowling face at Granny Jenny's funeral.

Jim reassured me that he would not be going to Leeds until he was very sure of all the facts, and that he would warn me before he went. I also asked him not to approach my mother: I had said nothing to her of contacting the police, because of her health and her advancing years. Jim said that if he needed to talk to her he would be in touch with me first.

Jim contacted me again a few days later, and I arranged to see him at his base, which was the police station in the Wellwynd in Airdrie. As I waited for him in the small reception area, I wondered if the pleasant, open-faced young cop at the counter had any idea why I was there. He had taken my name, said that DI McEwan was caught up on police business, and that I would have to wait a short while.

When Jim appeared, he swept me through to his office where I stopped dead. The room was sparsely furnished, with a mahogany desk in the centre, and a tall metal cupboard opposite. Pinned up beside a large-scale map of Coatbridge Burgh from the 1950s were two black and white photographs. One was the familiar haunting head-and-shoulders portrait of Moira, eyes crinkling with laughter at the school photographer who had taken it, fair hair swept to one side with a slide, hands folded into the crooks of her arms on her school desk. The other was of a heavily jowled man in his sixties, whose eyes gazed straight ahead with a penetrating stare. My father.

Jim asked, 'Can you identify for me, Sandra, that that *is* your dad?'

My mouth was dry as I nodded. 'Is that a mug shot?' I stammered. 'When was it taken?'

'Yeah, it is. Taken mid-eighties, I think.' Jim gazed back at me steadily. 'Down south.'

He would not tell me what offences had been committed.

Then he showed me a copy of the newspaper article from April 1957, in which my father's rape case had been reported. I noticed that the sexual offences against Betty the babysitter were said to have happened over a two-month period, but I knew that they had gone on for longer than that. My father's solicitor attempted to cast responsibility for all the incidents on the girl.

Although the girl is now only 14, she is mature. After the first incident took place, and despite the girl's youth, Gartshore was in her power for fear that she would betray him to his wife. In my opinion, the girl had simply become a menace to Gartshore, and he should have ordered her out of the house, never to show her face again. Instead of that he allowed the offences to continue.

All the blandishments of a young woman were used by her when she came to Gartshore's house. In cases of indecency towards young girls, the accused person often lures them away to lonely and isolated spots. But the accused in this place did nothing like that. The offences were committed in his own home, where he lived happily with his wife and three young children until the appearance of this girl.

He had argued that my father had a good war record, was a good father, and had been a churchgoer all his life. He had learnt a bitter lesson, but wished to avoid prison. If he was sent there, his wife might leave him, his home might be broken up, his children would suffer and he would emerge 'an embittered member of society'.

But Sheriff Young, who had heard the case, sentenced my father to eighteen months' imprisonment, saying he 'had heard nothing said that minimizes the serious crime of which you are guilty'.

Jim told me that he had recently interviewed Betty. She had said that she had *not* been promiscuous and had been forced into sexual intercourse on the first occasion by my father. It had been rape, and he had given her money to keep quiet about it. She had met him over a six-month period, mainly in Dunbeth Park where Moira and her chums had played, and after the first time, intercourse had taken place by mutual consent, but never, she insisted, in my home.

I could imagine how the article must have upset both my sets of grandparents. My schoolteacher, purple-rinsed

Miss Marshall, must have known that my father was serving a prison sentence for sexual offences against a girl just a few years older than her charges. It seemed unlikely to me, given the relatively small population in our area of thirty thousand or so, that anyone could have missed the newsprint devoted to my father's trial.

Jim agreed, and said, 'Which makes it all the odder that our friend in Stornoway, ex-Inspector John F. MacDonald, seemed to have no recollection that your dad was ever in any kind of bother. He remembered him, including the unusual surname, and was able to give us a description of him. In fact, he was very shocked by what we revealed. He said, "But it couldn't have been him. He stopped his bus for all the old ladies, and dropped them at their gates . . . and the kiddies all gave him sweets." He was one hundred per cent clear that your dad never figured as a suspect at the time. He was convinced it was the handicapped guy, Ian Simpson.'

I could see that Jim could not fathom either why the man in charge at the time could know my father by sight yet not his history, given that he had made local headlines and been sentenced: 'I know hindsight's a wonderful thing, but I just can't think what these guys were doing that they let your dad slip through the net.'

My father had been arrested and questioned in December 1956, and charged with 'Having carnal knowledge of a minor and other offences of a sexual nature' on 23 January 1957. Between Christmas and New Year, my grandfather Gartshore had raised bail money to get his son home and had pressured the Baxter family to allow him to have his job back until the case came to trial in the spring. At the end of January my dad had resumed his seat at the front of the Cliftonville bus, which passed Moira's door.

Three weeks later, she disappeared. My father was sentenced to prison in April 1957. That summer, when townsfolk were wondering at the lack of headway in the local investigation, my father had been out of sight in one of Her Majesty's institutions.

I asked myself why MacDonald had been reluctant to accept the help of the Glasgow CID. Why had he not wanted to screen Moira's photograph on television? Why had he not disclosed that the policeman's wife, Mrs Chalmers, had not been the sole witness to the bus sighting?

Everything seemed to point to my father having been missed from the round-up of suspects either through sheer ineptitude or because someone in John F. MacDonald's force had protected him.

# Chapter Sixteen

My next meeting with Jim McEwan took place at Bathgate police station. On 30 April 1992 the reception area was plastered with dramatic posters of a missing fifteen-year-old girl. The face of Vicky Hamilton, who had disappeared on 10 February 1991, stared down at us from the walls. She had vanished from the main square of Bathgate, as mysteriously as Moira had from another small town thirty-five years before, when there was eight inches of snow on the ground. She too, has never been seen again.

Disposal of a body in such bad weather conditions is difficult: snowstorms and frozen ground make it impossible to dig a makeshift grave. Jim and I had discussed this when I pointed out the route my father's bus had usually taken, where the terminii had been located. I'd shown him my father's favourite haunts and other familiar places. We agreed that if he had killed Moira it was unlikely that he had travelled any great distance that night, given the road conditions and fear of being seen. We felt that, if we had had to get rid of a body, we would have chosen old mine workings or water.

Unfortunately, Coatbridge is riddled with old colliery workings, abandoned pits, lochs and ponds in surrounding marshland, not to mention the Monkland Canal; it had gone right through the town in the fifties. I told Jim of one memory I had from about age four or five, when my dad took me on a long walk one Sunday to a small loch, where some swans were gliding about in the reeds. Now named Clyde Calders nature reserve, and visible today to passing M8 motorists, my dad had told me it was called Dick's Pond. He had known it from boyhood. 'Aye, Sandra, I used tae play here,' he said, showing me how to select a small pebble and skim it across the surface of the water. 'Come on, you have a go at this!' I asked him why we couldn't see the stones come back up, and he explained: 'Ye see out there? Ah knew a laddie when ah wis wee, who went swimming out in the middle there. He got drownt. He wisnae ever found again. Ye see, underneath there's a big old mine shaft that goes richt doon. Naebody kens how far doon it goes, but they never goat him. Pit a body oot there, and naebody wid ever find it, it's sae deep, hen. If ever ah wanted rid o' somethin', that's where I'd pit it.'

Jim told me that he had spoken with the West Yorkshire police, who had provided further information. The offences that had brought my father to the attention of officers south of the border had related to deception and trying to obtain a mortgage under false pretences. I breathed a huge sigh of relief – then thought, so what if he's been in jail for other things, and not child molesting, he's probably still adept at getting away with that. Jim went on, 'Look, they're very interested in what we're telling them, but your dad's name doesn't show up on their list of known paedophiles. He's only known to them for these offences.'

'So what's new?' I asked. 'They just don't know about him, that's all.'

'Well,' Jim said, 'Leeds has one of the biggest known rings of paedophiles in Britain, but he's not known to them through complaints of perversion.'

We stood up to leave, and Jim said he'd be in touch. Over the next few months we spoke regularly on the telephone but could not meet again until July.

Meanwhile, Jim had told me that he would need to speak to my brothers. Although they were three and six years younger than me, and the period in our lives in which Jim was most interested was 1957, when they had been tiny, he had to interview them. He also said that he was keen to know if my father had had any contact with other young female relatives. I was horrified at the very idea. 'Well, no. I've no sisters, and all my cousins who are female are all much younger than me,' I said. 'It was my friends he molested, not any of my relatives – they would be too wee, and besides, I would have known if anything had ever happened. Something would have been said.'

'These things are often hushed up in families. We may even be making assumptions that only female children attract him – many paedophiles don't discriminate.' Then he asked the question that was repeated by countless others over the following months.

'Are you absolutely sure, Sandra, that nothing happened to you? I have to ask it. It's just that when abuse is uncovered like this, it's rare to find that all the offences take place *outside* the family circle.'

Although my instincts told me I had not been one of my father's victims, I was terrified that perhaps this memory might still be lurking in my subconscious.

I decided to convene a meeting with my brothers. We got together at Ian's house, and discussed our different memories of our father, recalling in particular how he had gone off to Leeds. We seemed like witnesses of an accident, victims who had seen the same build-up and the same event simultaneously, but who all had personal images of it. Ian had been pulled in and out of the car parked at our door by my parents. He had witnessed not only the row between our parents, over the presence of Pat Hanlon in the car, but also our mother hitting back with the frying pan. She had fought like a tigress and won.

Norman had shared my father's interest in cars and the two had been close, but he too felt bitter about the way we had been abandoned. He was the only one of us who was upset when he never received a birthday or Christmas card, and the only one to visit my father in Leeds, in an attempt, perhaps, to mend bridges. He went only once and would not discuss what had happened there. Norman remembered how I had tried to keep myself and my friends out of my father's way, and how I'd insisted on a bedroom door I could lock from an early age. Both my brothers swore that their father had never molested them. Physical beatings, yes, sexual overtures, definitely not.

But I still needed to talk to my cousins.

# Chapter Seventeen

Before we set off to the United States for a family holiday
with our friends Janet and John McGill and their children,
I saw Ashley several times for counselling. She felt the
holiday would do me the world of good, as long as I got a
balance of rest and sightseeing. She was right and everyone
ensured that, for two weeks, the worry took a back seat,
and I relaxed.

Janet and John knew of the chain of events unfolding
in my life. Janet told me that she had heard years before
from a relative that my father was well known to all of
the half-dozen Coatbridge cinema owners as a perpetual
nuisance, someone who sat next to children or young
women and pestered them. He had been asked to leave a
number of times. Most women moved to avoid him, but
many children sat frozen with shame and did not know
how to react. Janet had never felt it appropriate to tell me
until now.

Before we went away, I drew up from our extensive
family tree a list of all my cousins from the huge clan on
my mother's side, concentrating on the girls. I dismissed
those who had gone to live abroad, which left six, all much
younger than me, three sets of sisters. The eldest would
have been fourteen or so when my father left Coatbridge,

the youngest only three or four. I shall call my three sets of cousins A and B, C and D, E and F.

Before I approached any of them, I phoned an aunt I felt I could trust for advice. I was convinced that nothing could have happened to her daughters, both lovely, well-adjusted young women, whom I adored. But as soon as I broached the matter, there was an awkward silence. I repeated that I couldn't say why I needed to know but for the sake of my health I did. Finally, she said I should speak privately to C, the elder of her girls. She would say no more, and hung up.

I was stunned. I had looked after C as a child, and I have always felt close to her. I rang my cousin and asked to see her right away. She told me to come to her home.

She and her husband were shocked by the terrible state I was in when I arrived. After some tea, I stumbled through an explanation, and although C was upset, she was relieved that I was not about to tell her I was leaving my husband – she and her partner could think of no other reason why I should be so distraught!

When I asked if my father had ever made sexual advances towards her when she was little, she looked at me directly and said, 'Yes, it's true. When I was six. Did my mother tell you what happened? I've had some counselling about it, which has helped, in the last little while, but I've never been able to say anything to you about it because he was your dad.

'It was a beautiful warm day, some time in the summer of 1962. My little sister and I were both in similar outfits, little cotton dresses, with matching bolero-style sleeveless jackets, so it must have been scorching. So good, that we were taken to visit Granny Frew, and were able to have afternoon tea in the back garden at Ashgrove. A rug was put out, and while the adults sat in deck chairs, we'd our own little picnic, then we went off to play. Your mum was there, and mine, and they both were enjoying chatting in the sunshine to wee Katie. You weren't there, or your brothers, but your dad was working in his garage.'

Grandpa Frew had had a hut that screened off the area where the picnic was being held from my parents' garden. That land ran to one side of our home, and formed a large triangle dominated in the centre by the garage my mother had had built for my father's exclusive use. Within months Alexander had filled this garage with all his usual junk.

'I don't know what he actually shouted to get my attention from the front garden, where D and I were playing. She was only four years old then, so I really was expected to keep a close eye on her and make sure she didn't venture on to the road. But he used some kind of pretext to lure me into the garage, perhaps it was an offer of sweets, I don't know. I recall he was sitting, not where the garage doors were open, but up near the top, beyond his black car, with its bonnet up. He'd something on his knee which he was fixing. I wasn't keen to go further up into the gloomier part of the place, but whatever he said, it must have been persuasive. As I passed his car and approached him, I felt something wasn't right, and I hesitated. I remember he said: "C'mere, hen, there's something Ah want ye tae hold for me here." Well, I couldn't see what exactly he was doing, and it was drummed into us to be polite, so I stepped closer. I was a pretty helpful wee girl, and it would look bad to say no, but I didn't like him. I saw that it was one of those old one-bar electric fires that he had across his knees, with a flex hanging over on to the floor. He'd on these navy blue work overalls over his own clothes. I didn't know why he was inside his garage on such a nice day. Anyway, I was really quite close to him by now, almost within arm's reach, when I stopped dead. He had this really weird expression on his face, a funny look that I just didn't trust. He said, "Come on, hen, I want you to hold this for me. Come on, haud it jist for a minute, that's all ye've to do. It's a cable."

'Well, I could see that what he was pointing to, something big and white and sticking right out of those overalls, wasn't anything electrical, but it sure as heck gave me one almighty shock! I was rooted to the spot, and staring with such incredulity, I could describe his underwear for you right down to the last detail. But I couldn't think what to do – I don't know what your dad would have tried next, though I had nightmares afterwards about that. Strangely, it was D who really saved the situation. She'd followed just at the back of me, all curiosity, to see what Uncle Alex wanted me to do, and as I stood there, transfixed, I suddenly felt her at my elbow, peering round and trying to see what he was showing me. I just panicked, because I knew I must protect her, though I couldn't have said exactly from what. I backed away, turned abruptly and said, "*Run!*" and grabbed her hand, and we rushed out.'

I was incredulous that my father could have done such a thing while a tea party was in full swing just yards away. His cunning was frightening too, for of course he had been smart enough to leave the doors of his garage standing open: any passer-by could have glanced in his direction, but the car bonnet obscured a perfect view. This outwardly normal scene meant that if he was accused of anything by a child, he could claim that their imagination was overactive, and protest that no one would dream of exposing himself where he could be so easily seen.

'I got my little sister back to where my mother was, and she saw we were both very upset. I whispered to her that my uncle Alex was doing bad things. She took me inside right away, and I was categorically told never to repeat such an accusation.'

Jim McEwan had been absolutely correct about denial within families.

'I wasn't believed. I was told to stop telling such lies, and we were taken home.'

Despite my aunt's apparent refusal to believe that anything sinister had occurred, she ensured that for the next few years contact between her daughters and my father was minimal.

Yet because her mother had been so adamant that C had told lies about my father, when later, aged eight, she was indecently assaulted by a neighbour, she said nothing, but attempted to avoid her attacker. Shortly afterwards this same teenage boy came to babysit for her parents. Eventually, they noticed how his visits terrified her and he was asked to stop coming, but not before the damage had been done.

My cousin told me that she had had counselling, which had helped, and that she was fund-raising for Childline in Scotland: she wanted to channel the anger she felt at what had happened into something positive. 'There are far too many people out there saying, "Child abuse? What's all the fuss about?" Or they say the figures are overestimated, denying they've ever come across it. Or they kid themselves that these sordid events only happen in poor families, which is rubbish. I'm a classic example of a child who spoke up, but wasn't believed. I wasn't a naughty kiddie who told whoppers, but it was easier for my mother to deny everything I said that day and call her own daughter a liar, rather than raise the alarm. It was hushed up, as it often is, and not confronted. Well, I'm not prepared to hush it up any longer.'

Her courage was infectious and I told her why I was asking questions about my father.

When I got home I had a phone call from C's husband. She had told him of the hostility I was facing from some family members, who hated the idea of public exposure. 'Ignore these people,' he said flatly. 'If it was their child who was abused, or their daughter who had gone missing, it would be a different story. Bottom line is, Sandra, you have to live with the fact that your dad spoke to you, and I agree you could not dismiss what was said and just get on with your life as if nothing had happened. I have real respect for what you've done, and if they can't give you support, then they are not worth bothering about. Those who are right behind you, like ourselves, are the ones who count, so don't give the doubters the time of day.'

His unexpected midnight call really lifted my spirits. There was no way I wanted to cause a split within the larger extended family, which was important to me, but my professional role involved teaching courses on child protection and my integrity would not allow me to ignore what my father had told me.


As soon as I returned from holiday, I telephoned my aunt again, and demanded to know why, given my father's history and, in 1959, that he had then recently emerged from prison for sexual offences, she had allowed her children anywhere near him.

'I thought it might have all been a mistake with the babysitter [Betty], and that maybe he'd learned his lesson,' she said. 'And he was their uncle, married to your mum. They always thought the world of their aunt Mary, so I never thought for one minute he'd try anything with my two.'

'Then why on earth did you ignore what C told you?' I asked.

Several seconds passed while she fished about for answers. Then she said, 'I had to stop it right there. My husband would've killed him if he'd got any inkling about what your dad had done. There would have been terrible trouble in the family, and I couldn't have that on my conscience.'

I marvelled at her logic. Where had the need come from to protect such a man? Why had her loyalty to her own two daughters not come first?

Then my aunt told me the real reason she had not gone straight to the police when this incident occurred. 'You don't know, Sandra, what it was like. I couldn't have put your mum through any more pain. She'd been to hell and back, with people talking and whispering, and everything in the papers. Then she got the house beside your gran, and she seemed to be getting back on her feet. When he got out, we all felt he deserved another chance, and your mum's such a Christian soul, she gave it. I felt I had to protect her. She didn't deserve more pain. And it's all in the past now, anyway, no need to bring it all up. Some things are better left alone.'

'In this case, we can't do that,' I said gently. 'It may

not have been reported then, but it will have to be now.' As calmly as I could, I explained about the investigation and what had triggered it off. The silence at the other end was deafening.

It would be up to C and D, now grown women, I explained, as to whether they made a statement to the police, but her daughters had information that Jim McEwan would be interested to hear. Any evidence that proved I was correct about my father's pattern of behaviour might aid the investigation into the murder of Moira Anderson.

'Oh, my God! You're not saying he's responsible for that!' she screeched.

'I'm having to try not to think about that,' I replied grimly, 'but when I said a moment ago that my dad spoke to me about Moira, and I went to the police with information he gave me, I didn't mean that he was just a witness they had missed at the time. The reason I reported the matter, after nights of no sleep, is because I believe he witnessed her death. And that's because *he* took her life in 1957.'

# Chapter Eighteen

As the leaves started to turn in our garden, there were days when I felt crippled by anxiety, shame and insecurity. Fear of what lay ahead paralysed me, although I continued to work feverishly. It seemed important to have some areas of my life still under control and functioning, so I threw myself into the Master in Education I had embarked on just before my world disintegrated. I met other new students and prepared for my own first exam.

Jim had now interviewed a number of people: some ex-colleagues in the police and some of my father's former workmates. Most seemed, he joked, to be suffering from the disease of the three wise monkeys: they had seen nothing, heard nothing, and were prepared to say nothing, but some of his probing, he felt, was beginning to prove fruitful. I explained what had happened to one set of cousins. I knew it was imperative that I spoke to the other four, but fear gripped me as to what I might find.

I reflected on the wall of silence Jim had encountered from those we had felt would be able to help. Some of the former Baxter's employees were now silver-haired grandparents but the clippies who had been involved in or had observed my father's affairs were reluctant to admit to any part in it. They were wary of what their families would

146

think. Drivers refused to comment in front of their spouses on the wide-scale philandering that had gone on.

This selective amnesia was apparent, too, in the ranks of retired policemen. Though not all were unwilling to be interviewed, Jim's officers were meeting surprising resistance: some former policemen seemed uneasy that this case was being put under a spotlight once more.

One retired policeman, though, Alex Imrie, made a damning statement: 'Complaints were made on numerous occasions about Alexander Gartshore. Very often these were in the vicinity of Dunbeth Park, in particular the bushes there. His exceptional height gave him away. He was long suspected of being a flasher within the park, and in other areas, but this was not able to be proved.' Significantly he added, 'He was never interviewed regarding Moira Anderson.'

The unexpected stonewalling Jim encountered made my desire all the stronger to discover the truth as to what had happened to Moira.

I decided to attempt to speak to my cousin B. Her mother was seriously ill in hospital and I suggested I accompanied her to see how my aunt was doing. We would have a few minutes of privacy in her car. She agreed and we set off. B is an attractive woman, with glossy black hair and striking features. She chatted nineteen to the dozen until I asked, 'I know this is kind of out of the blue, and I don't want it to upset you, but can I ask . . . did my father ever make any sexual advances to you when you were little?'

The question had a dramatic effect. B's knuckles tightened on the steering wheel, and she almost drove through a red light near Monklands Hospital. I was struck by the closed expression that came down like a shutter on her face.

'What a thing to ask!' She tried to regain her composure as she swung her saloon into the car park, checking her driving mirror several times, and avoiding my eye.

'I don't want to upset you or A,' I apologized, 'not when your mum is so ill. But I wouldn't ask if I didn't have to. It's vital. I can explain why I need to know later, but please tell me, did anything – anything at all – ever happen?'

Still she avoided my eyes. Finally, she answered in a strangled tone, 'Your dad, he was . . . I mean it was so long ago . . . he was over-friendly, that's all I want to say.' Then she repeated, 'Just over-friendly.'

Before I could ask her anything else, she swung her legs out of the car, and was off, rushing towards the main entrance so that I had to hurry to catch up. As we strode along the corridors, she pleaded with me not to say anything to her sister, who was grief-stricken about their mother. I promised.

Now that I had discovered another of my father's victims, I knew there must be more.

Meanwhile, I had been telephoned by another relative. She had heard a rumour in the family, but could not accept it was true. Had I really sparked off some criminal investigation into my own father which involved murder?

Yes, I had. She demanded to know what had caused me to go to the police. Wearily, I told her. 'You should have ignored what your dad said, he's your own flesh and blood, no matter whit he's done. He'll be an old confused man by now!' she cried.

I explained that seventy-one was no great age, and that he was pretty sharp.

'It's years since I saw him last, and I never want to see him again,' she said. 'But this information you've taken to the polis – it's dangerous, the work o' the devil. You should've kidded on you never heard him say what he did. There's nae need for all of this to come up again, what good's it going to do?' There followed a string of invective, the main gist of which was that I would live to regret the steps I had taken and had carried out what she considered to be a betrayal of the whole family.

'This will kill your mammy, and you'll be responsible, if you take this any further. D'you hear me? You don't know what ye're getting yerself into, and all yer family tae! They've tae haud up their heads in Coatbridge. This cannae go any further.'

'It already has.'

'Listen, ye wee bitch from hell, whit about yer mammy? This'll kill her, as God's ma judge.'

'I'd never do anything to hurt my mother!' I roared, then took a deep breath. 'Look, I love my mum, but if anyone's hurt her it's that bastard down in Leeds and I've got enough on my mind right now, without you adding your twopence worth. Just remember, the damage was done a long time ago, but not by me.'

I paused for a second in an attempt to control my anger and my language.

'There are people who could have tipped off the police about my dad years ago, and what he got up to, and that includes you. The truth's got to come out, whether it's going to upset folk or not. I've given a number of names to the detective in charge, and they'll be coming to see you, so save your criticism for them. If they'd done their job properly thirty-five years ago, none of this would've happened.'

There was silence and then she declared she would never agree to being interviewed about her memories of Alexander. She point blank refused, she said, and nobody would make her. They would have to drag her, kicking and screaming, before they'd get anything. (In fact, she was seen by the police later and made a revealing statement.) I was still shaking with fury, when she rang off with the parting shot: 'Mark my words, if a' the family turn their backs on ye, ye've only yerself tae blame.'

She left me with a horrible sense that whatever I did, I was going to incur somebody's wrath.

Another attack was more subtle. My mother's sister asked me how I was getting on with my counsellor and I told her that Ashley was probably single-handedly responsible for keeping my life in one piece. While Ronnie and the children were supportive, what was happening to me was outside their experience. 'She's great. We're meeting weekly just now, and I'm finding it a godsend.' I added, 'Isn't it silly that I was a bit resistant to her at the start because she was a psychiatric nurse? I said if anyone needs a psychiatrist, it's my dad!'

'Don't you think, though, Sandra, that it's possibly all in your mind?' Aunt Margaret chose her words with care. 'You always had a very fertile imagination as a child, you know. Isn't it possible you're confused about what your dad said? Do you not think maybe you've made a mistake, and that's why you're having psychiatric help.'

I almost laughed out loud at the absurdity of what she had said. It would have been easier for some of my relatives to hear I was insane than to confront the truth. I refused to be daunted, though, and arranged a meeting with my cousins at B's home.

It was a difficult evening. We had last met at A and B's mother's funeral and they were still in the rawest stages of bereavement.

Only F was not there. Her sister said that she could hardly remember my father, being only three or four when he left, so I imagined that her absence would not matter. I talked at length of what I had been through in the past nine months, while those who had had no inkling sat motionless, drinks untouched. When I spoke of my past and my dad's history there were shudders of horror and tears.

When I had finished, I wiped my eyes, and said, 'I'm pretty sure he never came near me, but for weeks now I've been having flashbacks, remembering the things I saw him do to my friends, the womanizing, the lies. I can't tell when I'm going to have them, they just happen, and I'm right there going through the experience again, feeling the same horrible feelings, even smelling the smells – it's awful. It's one thing to know your dad's a sadistic brute who thought nothing of walloping you with the buckle end of his leather belt, but it's quite another to realize that he is the most awful liar, that he's a paedophile who's molested kiddies all his days, and that there's one victim, at least, who didn't escape with her life. That's why, hard as it is o discuss, I must know about *you*.'

C and D told of what had gone on in the garage at Ashgrove. Then A said, 'Neither of us escaped him, either.' She and her sister, she told us, had not realized for a long time that they were both victims. The campaign my father had waged against them had been sustained over several years.

A is a slim woman, with high cheekbones, dramatic brown eyes, like her sister, and an infectious laugh. Now, she was trembling as she told us how B had related to her our conversation in the car, and how they had decided to talk to me. 'What's the point of keeping it quiet now, even after all this time?' Just as you're remembering flashbacks, Sandra, I have had to contend with incidents that involved your dad – some triggered by even the simplest things. My husband played a joke on me once and left me in the dark, with a bare light bulb swinging about. I was petrified, without being able to think why, then I realized. Your dad pushed me into the cupboard he worked in at your house in Dunbeth Road. I was molested by him there, on more than one occasion, for he was very sly – he's adept at winning over kiddies. Let's face it, we weren't well off in those days, and it was such a novelty to know someone with a car. All the kids were attracted, and I know I was flattered when I was just seven or eight, it made you feel special if he took you somewhere. It seemed so grown-up. Like a fool, I went with him. Then you got into this situation you didn't know how to cope with at that age. You were in his power, and of course, he was so devious. He made it look as if he was a nice man, taking kids out when he knew our parents couldn't afford a car – it was as if he was taking us off their hands, so it didn't ever occur to my family to question what my uncle was actually doing. He thought it all out carefully and only built up gradually.

'I eventually learned how to avoid him, although that was tricky, because we were often sent to our granny

*Right:* My father in 1943, aged twenty-one.

*Below:* My parents with our Partick Street neighbours on Coronation Day, 1953. Mary, my mother, is seated second from the left, and my granny Katie is standing on the far right. My father is standing centre, back row, his handiwork on display.

*Opposite:* Christmas, 1953, at Ashgrove, the home of my maternal grandparents, Kate and Norman Frew, with just some of their twenty-one grandchildren. Almost four, I am cheekily welcoming my father who has just stuck his head round the door. He was still a heroic figure to me at this point.

*Above:* Four generations in the family, taken in February, 1956, when my father's brother Robbie married. I am sitting between my granny Jenny and her mother, in front of my father Alexander, with detested stiff 'aeroplane' bow, on edge in all senses.

The Anderson girls taken around Moira's eleventh birthday in 1956. From left to right: Janet, Marjorie and Moira. This is the last photo of the three sisters taken together. (*Mrs Janet Hart*)

Me, aged seven, autumn 1956 at Gartsherrie Academy, Coatbridge.

The last portrait of Moira, taken at Coatdyke Primary, two months before her disappearance. This photo was shown on television in May 1957 and used extensively by the media. *(Mrs Janet Hart)*

Some of the Baxter buses' staff at a social occasion.
My dad and his colleague Cliff are the two tallest drivers, with
Alexander on the right. Several of the other drivers were
often in our home in Dunbeth Road.

Coatbridge Fountain, heart of the town centre, as it was in my childhood. The Regal cinema was Moira's planned destination on the day she vanished and still exists in the nineties as a bingo hall. *(From* Old Coatbridge *by Campbell McCutcheon, Richard Stenlake Publishing, Ochiltree)*

Witchwood Pond, in the Townhead area of Coatbridge.
The extent of the marshland around the sizeable area of water can be
seen from this angle. The tower block had not been built in 1957.
*(Airdrie and Coatbridge Advertiser)*

Frew's, and he'd try all sorts of ruses with pocket money and extra sweets. I told my mother when I reached my early teens, but I knew she found it hard to believe, and would never have let such a terrible shameful thing reach her husband's ears. She told me I'd to forget it, and then he left, anyway.

'He took away all my innocence. It was wicked, he touched me everywhere, so really it was everything except actual penetration. I was so wee, and he was such a huge man, the tallest we knew. Maybe that's why he didn't do that, I don't know. But it's affected my whole life since. Even the smallest thing can trigger off a memory. One of my children got a job, and when he brought home his work clothes for me to wash, I almost had a heart attack – they were exactly like the navy blue ones your dad wore, Sandra, with buttons right up.'

A described to us how the abuse in her childhood had caused her to suffer severe depressions, and had interfered with her ability to enjoy relationships. She had questioned her own ability to relate to anyone sexually. After her marriage, although she knew she had married the right man, her fits of depression worsened with her two pregnancies, and she began to feel suicidal. She had been taken into a psychiatric hospital, where it was recognized that she had a phobia about anyone touching her body, but the root of the problem was never diagnosed. She, too, had walled up her awful memories. But A went on, 'The one good thing that has come out of all of this being brought to light is that I now *know* why I've had all these problems. It makes sense with hindsight, and it's clear I'm not going crazy. It's made me realize that the healthiest thing is to be upfront and honest with your family and kids – there are no secrets in our home. And that's why I told B that there's no point in covering up what happened to her.'

It was her sister's turn to speak. 'I have been a victim all my life,' she said quietly. 'There was a horrible old man I knew, and there was your dad, Sandra. The first one was a ghastly neighbour who would grope at you, but your dad was something else. No way at the hospital could I have told you what he did, but he abused me from when I was seven or so until I was ten, I think. I remember the first time. I hadn't a clue, being so wee, I just went along with it. But I knew something wasn't right, and I ran to the back green where Granny Frew was hanging out her sheets. I can still see those lines of washing flapping away, and her getting angry with me. I was told to stop making it up. Another time I tried to tell her what was happening to me whenever I went out to play, she just wheesht me to be quiet, then took me inside as if I'd fallen. I got a cuddle and a biscuit.'

A and B agreed that this had happened on several occasions. Much as all of us had adored our grandmother, we had no answer as to why she had concealed the truth when her son-in-law was picking off his victims one by one from the ranks of her own granddaughters.

'Mostly, I would just go rigid all over when it happened,' B continued, 'whether it was in his car or his bedroom. He even assaulted me there one time your mum sent me with a cup of tea to him in bed. As if you can blank it out. Of course, it stays with you. I can describe the rug on the floor. I can remember him in his stripy pyjamas, his newspaper lying there, so that he could cover his tracks well, and him forcing my head down. Even now, thirty years on, I remember this ghastly sensation of choking. You were petrified, but it wouldn't have been any use struggling. He had it all worked out.'

I went cold all over. He could have easily suffocated a young child, forcing her into such an act. Was this what had happened to Moira? I realized I had witnessed several occasions when tense young bodies had gone limp; I'd been at a loss to know why they were not fighting my father off. Now, with the insight of an adult, I could see why a child might adopt this strategy in a frightening situation. Hadn't I often transported myself mentally elsewhere when confronted with what I could not cope with? Hadn't I wished to be rescued by one of my comic heroines? It also struck me that my cousins were correct that my dad's behaviour was premeditated: it had not, as I'd been trying to convince myself, been a result of uncontrollable urges. What had happened to them had been every bit as carefully planned as the afternoon he had packed my mother, my brothers and me off to a film so that he could lure a tiny child into our home.

# Chapter Nineteen

I drove from my cousin's home that dark wintry night, reeling. My father's lifelong hobby had been depravity; he had the classic profile of the paedophile, whose goal is always to be in close proximity to his prey.

Before the evening ended, my cousins asked why my father had spared me. I could only repeat what I'd told the police – I had been an articulate child, and perhaps he had not been able to judge whether I would remain silent or not. He might have been reluctant to touch his own daughter, and, in fact, statistics show that girls are more likely to be molested by stepfathers rather than their own father. I felt incredibly lucky: physical and emotional abuse, yes. Mental torture, yes. But sexual abuse, no.

I described the strategies I had devised as a teenager to keep out of my father's way, because I had seen what he had done to my friends. They could all recall the amount of time I had spent in my grandmother's downstairs, and how I would call in every day after school, to make her tea and chat. I would not go upstairs if my father was alone, not even into the bedroom I could lock. My granny must have worked out why I did this. She had been my staunchest ally, often deflecting criticism my father targeted at me.

A said, 'If there's four of us here that he managed to molest before he left in 1965, there are many we played with in Ashgrove he must have approached. We'd not be the only ones.' They suggested names to me, including my friends from high school, Ellen and Barbara, and the immediate next-door neighbour's daughter, who had played at some point with every one of my cousins as well as me. I would have to have a word with them all, we agreed, and hope they would understand why.

Suddenly E burst into tears. I was horrified. She would not even have been at school when my father disappeared. She had been so young that, although she knew she had been abused, she could not be certain of who had done it. She only had one clear memory of her parents carrying her to see Dr Simpson, their GP, at his home. She knew she had seen him because of the pain she had been having on passing urine. It struck me as significant that the doctor had not been asked to make a home visit. Had she ever asked her parents why?

When she first regained the memory, E had been told that she had had a kidney problem, and a recurring infection had caused her to scream, so it was to do with getting help quickly. We asked what else she could remember.

'I know without a doubt that it happened to me. We moved into your old home at Partick Street, Sandra. I was terrified of the old man who lived below us who had tropical fish. I felt such relief when he died.'

'His name was McLaren,' I said with certainty, for I could remember disliking him too.

'All I know is I couldn't pass his door I was so terrified of him.'

He and my father had been friendly when we lived there, I knew that. 'What about my dad?'

'I just remember he was so tall, and his bus uniform,' she whispered, 'and him being friendly. But I know I hate tropical fish – and these sweeties you get wrapped in purple and gold stripy twists of paper, I forget what you call them . . .'

'They're toffee eclairs,' I said. 'My father's favourites, which he gave often to kiddies, and he and the neighbour knew each other because they were two of a kind.'

I was shaken by the things I learned that evening. It was hard to take in that of six women present, aged in their thirties and early forties, not one had had a childhood free of abuse; and I was stunned to have to absorb the certainty that my father had approached at least four, if not five, of my six cousins. They agreed that for Moira's sake they would make statements to the police.

Now, as I neared Edinburgh on my way home, I knew I wouldn't be able to keep my mother in the dark much longer. I had to tell her of everything I had done before someone else did.

E's description of pain when she passed urine niggled at me. I realized that I had once had a similar pain. I had to concentrate hard, but finally, there it was, just as I was about to drop off to sleep. I sat up with a jump. I was three or four years old and I was in the back bedroom of the house in Partick Street. I was angry because it was sunny outside but I was not allowed out to play. I was also furious at having to use an old china soup tureen with red roses on it to peepee in, rather than being allowed to go to the outside toilet. My mother referred to it as the 'chantey pot', and insisted on perching me there. An independent spirit and unwillingness to resume my toileting on something reminiscent of a toddler's potty led to a confrontation, with her using force to hold me there and me screaming my head off, partly through pain and partly through displeasure at being thwarted. The urine scalded my skin, which was nipping with the most awful burning sensation, and it felt as if a red-hot poker had pierced my abdomen. I was tucked back into my parents' big double bed and my tears were calmed with a favourite Rupert Bear story.

We were interrupted by a knock at the door, far off along the hall lobby. 'That'll be Dr Goldie.' My mother rushed through to greet him.

But it wasn't Dr Goldie, who knew every single Frew and who had brought many of my cousins into the world. Nor was it his partner, Dr Simpson. It was my mother's cousin, Victor Smith, who was training to be a doctor and of whom she was inordinately proud.

'Look who's come to see you!' She led him in. 'It's your Uncle Vicky, Sandra.'

I eyed him, standing there with his important medical bag.

'Are you going to look at my wee sore bottom?' I asked. 'It hurts when I go.'

My mother told him that she had noticed that my stools were an odd colour which perplexed me.

'I wonder where she's picked it up,' Victor said. 'It's possibly a bad chill in the bladder, which will need to be flushed out.'

Had I really suffered only a chill that had severely inflamed my bladder? Was my inability to pass urine for several days a result of an infection, or had it been more sinister? I closed my eyes, as I thought of the words the police had used. 'When we come across someone like your dad, Sandra, we don't normally have to go very far out of the family. It seems surprising he never got to you.'

I gulped. What if my dad *had* abused me as a child, despite my protests to Jim McEwan? I had now come across so many people unwilling to confront my father's behaviour for fear of upsetting my mother that I began to think it was entirely possible for someone mentally to avoid brutal truths to protect their own sanity.

I resolved to find out how my mother's recollection of this incident compared with my own. It was hard to find the right moment but I knew I had to take the bull by the horns some time. I had not intended to blurt everything out all at once to her, but after I had asked her about my childhood recollection of Dr Vicky's visit, she asked why on earth I needed to know exactly what had been wrong with me. 'You had a chill in the bladder,' she said. 'What on earth are you getting all worked up for? What's this all about?'

I looked at her, sitting at her fireside, Christmas cards strung round her living room. The floodgates opened.

My uncle Bobby was with us and clapped his hand to his mouth as I told my mother what my father had told me. Before I had finished, he said, 'I don't want to hear any more. Anything to do with that man is of a sexual nature – he's brought your mum nothing but pain, Sandra. Stop there.'

But I could not. I told my mother that I had gone to the police, and that an investigation was under way regarding Moira Anderson's disappearance in 1957.

Her face froze. Then she threw back her head into the

wings of the armchair and, screwing her eyes tightly shut, shook it violently from side to side. 'He had *nothing* to do with that!' she screamed. 'He was interviewed and he was cleared. Just ask our Margaret!'

'I have, and she was under that impression too,' I said. 'But he lied, Mum, to both of you, to his parents, and then in February, thirty-five years on, to me as well. The police say he was never interviewed at the time. He's responsible for that child's disappearance, believe me. There's things I know about him I've never been able to tell you, but I've told the police now, and it seems they'll have to speak to you before they go to Leeds to see him.' Then I told her about my cousins.

'Lies, lies,' she muttered, her hands fluttering helplessly at her ears to shut it out.

I was worried that breaking such news would destroy the relationship between my mother and myself – we had always been so close. She was subdued for several days and would not speak to me. I was desperate to patch things up, and continued to call daily. Finally, this strategy paid off, and I was heartily relieved the following week when she said suddenly, in mid-conversation, 'I don't want to discuss anything about your dad just now, Sandra, but I want you to know nothing's going to split *us* up. I know you did what you thought was right.'

December 1992 brought its usual whirlwind of activity, through which Jim and I kept in touch. He planned to interview my father in the new year. Four cousins had now made statements and Jim told me that my father was now liable to answer charges for his crimes against them.

When I returned to college for the start of the new term in January 1993 I felt tired and ill. Strange tingling pains developed in my chest, which I tried to ignore. I joked with colleagues about needles from our Christmas tree, which I'd cleared out of our lounge. The sensations got worse, and Sheena, the chief clerical officer, noticed my expression. A first-aider, she said she could not ignore inexplicable chest pains that worsened as I drove. Perhaps I had pulled some muscles lugging the tree outside.

Red blisters appeared on my abdomen, sprinkled round to my armpit, and a doctor found I had a severe attack of shingles. Had I been in contact with chicken pox? I recalled dropping off some late Christmas presents for E's children, who had been going down with something. But the underlying cause was the stress of what I had been going through over my father. The body soon lets us know its limits of tolerance.

# Chapter Twenty

The shingles left me at a low ebb, and I had never felt so down. Jim told me that he was planning to go in late March to Australia to visit his wife's relatives and celebrate her fortieth birthday. He would interview my father before he left.

Things were now very strained between me and my family, and my brothers were questioning the allegations made by my cousins.

I had explained to my children what their grandfather had done and that he was now facing prison, but Norman refused to tell his children. I thought this was wrong, because they might find out about it, as I had, from a stranger. I told him it would be dreadful for them to see it on a news-stand and then find out our family was involved: Lauren and Ross had accepted what I had told them without any ill effects, but Norman understandably wanted to shield his children from it until the issue could no longer be avoided.

When Jim and his then superior Detective Chief Inspector Ricky Gray were interviewing my father in Leeds, on 17 and 18 March 1993, I was staying at the Station Hotel in Inverness before speaking at a conference.

I tossed and turned all night and wondered if my father was in his own bed or in police cells.

Waiting to find out what had happened in Leeds was dreadful. Somehow I got through the events of that day at Inverness College. I couldn't stop worrying that Jim would return to tell me I had made a ghastly mistake, and I had wasted everyone's time. He had promised to phone when he got back, so all I could do was wait, something I am not good at.

Finally, he called me from his home and we agreed to meet up at Airdrie police station on 22 March. Then he'd fill me in, he said.

I braced myself for the meeting, when I now expected him to tell me that they'd got nowhere with my dad, who had probably accused me of being a scheming liar. I'd show Jim that I could take it on the chin.

Jim was remarkably perky. He cleared his throat, then picked up a photograph of Moira. 'Well, Sandra, I have to tell you that you're absolutely correct in your view that your dad *is* responsible for what happened to this young girl. I have come back convinced that we have our man. He holds the key to her disappearance.'

My legs turned to jelly and my heart dropped to the soles of my shoes. There were so many reasons why I hadn't wanted to be right. I asked, 'What did he say that convinced you?'

Jim handed me the photograph of Moira. 'As well as my own gut intuition, your dad's reaction to this. If I had lived down south for the amount of time he has, no way am I going to recognize after thirty years a school snap of a child to whom I've got no connection. When we showed him it, and asked if he knew who it was, he stammered out, "Moira!", and he started to shake. Then he said a very odd thing. "She looks a lot older there." '

I demanded to know what had been my father's first words to Jim when they arrived at his flat, and Jim's impression of his mental state.

He grinned. 'First, let me say you're right about your dad being on the ball. He told me, quite categorically, that everything you reported of your conversation with him in your gran's house was true. He didn't argue with the accuracy of the account you gave us. In fact, he *agreed* with you.'

I was astonished. I'd expected vehement denial.

'We took your dad to police headquarters in Leeds and interviewed him there, Sandra. There are quite a few hours of tape, which right now are all being typed into transcript,' he continued. 'The other person we thought we'd speak to was his estranged wife, Pat. We decided not to hold your dad at that stage, and took him home, then waited to see what he would do. He made a beeline to her home, where he spent a great deal of time, presumably filling her in on the events of his interview with us. He emerged in the small hours, and we picked her up in the morning. Hers was an interesting statement.'

I looked at him expectantly, reminding myself that although I'd never seen this woman, she was only a little older than me and she was now living with another man.

'Patricia told us two things I found hard to accept,' Jim sounded cynical. 'When we asked if she had ever heard your dad mention the name Moira Anderson, without a flicker, she said we of course were referring to the child who'd gone missing in the fifties in her home town. She said she could clearly recall him discussing Moira when the chum of Christine Keeler's was thought to be her in London in 1963. Just like that. We had no need to prompt her memory. This answer came out slick as you like. At the end of the session, we asked if she kept in contact with her ex-husband. She said only rarely. It tended to be of an accidental nature, such as running into him at the shopping centre. When I asked when she'd last seen him, she was adamant that it had been "some months" since they'd last met.'

Here was another of my father's ex-partners willing to protect him from the law.

I asked Jim if I could listen to the tapes. Not at the moment, he replied, perhaps later. He knew that many of the things my father had referred to could be checked out with me. And while he would not normally allow a witness access to them, he felt in this case it might aid the inquiry. 'Your dad is cunning, Sandra, and all my experience of handling suspects tells me he feels he can play cat and mouse with us. "You could check this out with so and so," then two minutes later, "but they're dead, unfortunately." That's the type of thing he's trotting out. He's damn sure that because I'm in a different age group, and not from the burgh itself, he can talk of routes and buses and crews, and we haven't got his inside knowledge. We've interviewed a number of his ex-colleagues, and I'm hoping the flurry of publicity will reap rewards.'

It didn't surprise me that my father was toying with the policemen. It had all happened so long ago that he had convinced himself that he had got away with it. I asked how his health appeared.

'He's pleading prostate trouble,' said Jim. 'His lawyer's ensuring that every time your dad feels the need to relieve his bladder, we have to let him go out. It's significant that when your dad finds the quizzing is making him go hot under the collar, it grinds to a halt so he can go off to take a leak.'

I asked if my dad would get legal aid, unsure why it mattered to me that he got some support. Jim paused for a moment. Instead of answering my question he said, 'Sandra, you asked what your dad's first words to me were. When we arrived, he said, "Someone's let the cat out of the bag up there. I'm not going to say anything that will commit me until I see my lawyer." He's trying to say now that you're orchestrating some kind of vendetta in your family against him because you've not forgiven him for abandoning your family and your mother.'

'Well, that's true, I haven't ever forgiven him for that,' I agreed. 'But it's hardly likely that I'd wait almost thirty years to seek revenge, and in such a manner. He knew he'd said too much to me that night and that was why he left with his son right after the funeral. It's also why I got that letter. And although what you've said today justifies me in talking to you, I didn't want it to be true. I don't hate *him*, just what he's done.'

Jim understood exactly what I meant. Whatever my father had done, he was still, and always would be, my father.


The news broke in the local papers that detectives had interviewed a man in his seventies in the north of England because of 'information that been given by someone who used to live in the Coatbridge area'. I saw the story first on our door mat low down on the front page of the

*Scotsman*. But the huge front-page headline of the *Airdrie and Coatbridge Advertiser* of 26 March 1993 grabbed local attention: 'DETECTIVES QUIZ MAN IN NORTH OF ENGLAND: Police probe case of Coatbridge girl who disappeared thirty-six years ago ... following a definite new line of inquiry.' Two revealing statements caught my eye which the reporter, Eileen McAuley, had ensured were given front-page prominence: 'The man police spoke to last week is not thought to have been questioned by the detectives who carried out the original investigation', and

> Contrary to official information released at the time, Moira did not vanish without trace from her grand-mother's home in Muiryhall Street. She was apparently spotted AFTER she left on an errand to pick up a packet of butter from a shop just three hundred yards from her own doorstep in Eglinton Street. Four eye witnesses claimed to have seen the youngster after she left her grandmother's. All four gave statements in 1957, and although three are now dead, their state-ments are still of great value to the police.

Moira's picture was also on the front. Inside was a massive two-page spread, headlined, 'THE LITTLE GIRL WHO DIS-APPEARED ON HER WAY TO THE SHOP', and a feature urging those who thought they could help to telephone Airdrie police station. It went on to say that although senior Monklands detectives felt they were on the verge of a major breakthrough, they were still anxious for fresh information.

Locally the story was on every other person's lips. Lunchtime reports were shown on television, and in the early and late evening bulletins, with a reporter pacing out part of the short journey Moira had made from her grandmother's house in Muiryhall Street, curious neighbours all around him. Details given were extremely sparse and neither Jim nor his men were interviewed. Naturally he was playing it low key. There was huge speculation in my home town about the identity of the pensioner being questioned.

# Chapter Twenty-One

Meanwhile I was still trying to trace down old friends who my cousins and I felt might have been other victims. Some were impossible to trace. Perhaps they did not wish to be found. Others had moved away from Coatbridge, but I found my ex-next-door neighbour Jan in Airdrie. She remembered my father locking her in his car, only releasing her when my brothers interrupted him, and told me she dreaded her widowed mother sending her to lend my father gardening tools.

Jan agreed reluctantly to be interviewed by the police but clearly would have preferred the past to stay in the past.

Another chum, I'll call Marie, had lived in Newlands Street, just round the corner from me. We had started high school together, aged twelve, but our friendship had suddenly foundered. I had never been able to work out why. I knew I had never left her alone with my father, and had always tended to visit her house rather than the other way round.

I found her in Glasgow. It had been so many years since we'd met that I barely recognized her at first. We chatted briefly for a few minutes of how our lives had changed and then Marie said, 'I think I can guess why you're making contact after all this time. My mum still sends me the local paper and I've put two and two together. You're the one who's gone to the polis in Coatbridge about why your old boy should be investigated about Moira Anderson, aren't you? Am I right?'

I told her she was spot on, and asked her if anything had happened to her, saying I always had wondered about why she broke off our friendship. Her eyes watered.

'Two horrible things happened to me, which I was never able to tell my mammy. Do you remember your dad taking quite a few of us one hot day in the summer over to Bothwell Bridge, you know, by Hamilton, to a place down by the river?'

I did.

'I only ever went with you the once,' she said. 'It was a boiling day. We took those long poles with fishing nets on the end of them, and you brought jelly jars, so we could look for minnows and sticklebacks. I don't know how he'd the nerve to do it, in a public place like that. He let us play for a while on our own. Then, after rounders, he took us all for a walk down to a bit of the river where kids could wade into wee pools, or lie on the bank to see if we could catch anything. Some went in paddling, and you were dipping in the water with the jars we brought. The next thing I knew your dad was lying right next to me with no space for me to shift away from him, because there was a log or something right there by me on the bank. We were all laughing and shouting, then I don't know why, but I felt uncomfortable. It was this hand going right up my dress. He wouldn't stop, and he was sort of pressing me into the ground, his weight almost on top of me, so I thought I'd be crushed to death. I was just frozen there. Can you believe he would do that in broad daylight?'

She was silent for a moment. 'I just couldn't believe it had happened. But I knew it had when I saw him smiling at me in his driving mirror on the way home. The worst part was feeling that because I hadn't shouted or screamed out for him to get off me, somehow I deserved what happened. I could've maybe stopped it, but I didn't, and that gave me the creeps for weeks on end. I hated myself for it. After that, I avoided him. I wouldn't even go on a Baxter's bus in case I ran into him.'

Worse was to come.

'One day after that I went to ask if you could come to the pictures with me and you weren't in, but your dad said, "Come on in, Marie, she won't be long," and I trooped up the stairs on to your landing. You'd a glass door at the top, just at the bend of the stairs, and he was standing right next to it. As soon as he had me through that door, your old boy clicked it shut, and snibbed it. He pushed me into the first bedroom and shoved me over the end of the bed, and I just knew what was coming next. He did what he'd done before, but this time he was moving his whole body into me. Then he shoved this half-crown in my hand, laughing away, and he said maybe I'd like to come back another time nobody else was in, and earn some more pocket money for being nice to him. I felt sick and I ran all the way home. The one sister I told wouldn't believe me at first, then said I was a little whore 'cos I'd accepted money from your dad, and then she said she'd never speak to me again, which she hasn't to this day.'

Marie had been in all sorts of trouble since those days. Recently she had had counselling and it was only through that that she had come to understand that my father's actions had been responsible for her alcohol and drug problems, and the failure of her relationships. Now she was sorting herself out: she had a new partner, she was happy and she didn't want to be involved again with the police. I understood why she refused to make a formal statement.

# Chapter Twenty-Two

During the week when the story broke in the media, I felt exposed and self-conscious. It would have been easy to sink into further depression but I reminded myself that I had to go and meet Jim's sidekick, Gus Paterson.

He was a friendly bear of a guy, who chatted away, putting me at ease. Over a coffee, he asked me the question I was now becoming used to: was I sure nothing had happened to me?

I sighed and said I really did not think so, though I could not be a hundred per cent sure. I told him I had thought of having regression hypnosis through a practitioner to whom my GP could refer me. That might put my mind at ease.

Gus told me that the team had had a good response to the publicity Jim had generated, and was following up a number of calls. 'One of Baxter's ex-employees actually phoned from down south after someone sent him the local paper with the headline, and the first thing he said was he wanted to travel north, stay with his sister here in Airdrie, and make a statement if he was correct about the identity of the man being questioned. We would not, of course, comment on your dad's name over the telephone, but the guy actually said he'd suspected a man whose initials were

A.G. for many years, and he wanted us to say yes or no to that. We've arranged for him to travel north.'

Finally a Baxter's employee was prepared to spill the beans.

My mother and Aunt Margaret made their statements on Friday 26 March 1993. Both were nearly hysterical, petrified of neighbours spotting police cars at the gate. Finally I quietened Mary by reminding her of the Biblical quotation about how we should confront evil. 'You're right,' she agreed. 'Where there is evil, cast it out.' Detective Chief Inspector Ricky Gray decided to interview my mother himself, while Aunt Margaret spoke to the WPC, Audrey. Before he began Ricky Gray told me that Jim McEwan, in Australia, had discovered by sheer chance that he was just a few miles from Janet Anderson Hart, Moira's elder sister. She had contacted Scottish police when a relative had told her of the mounting interest in the media about the reopened investigation. Jim visited her Sydney home on the same day my mother made her statement.

'So you're not the only one we are speaking to, Mrs Gartshore, about painful past events,' Ricky Gray said gently. 'I know you're divorced from him now, but you need to tell us all about Alex – how you met, what you learned about him, and what he was like as a husband, how he was at his job—'

'He was teetotal, wouldn't touch a drop all the years he was on the buses,' my mother declared. The DCI commented wryly that drinking was certainly one vice that caused his team headaches but there were worse offences.

If I had thought that my memories emerged like an old tank being sluiced out, in sudden rushes then slow trickles, my mother's resembled a torrent that had been dammed for years. The flow, however, spelt out a clear message to everyone in the room. She described the decent hardworking people my father was from, his excellent war record, how he had, it was said, rescued civilians from a burning building in Holland – she had even had a Delft plate from the couple on her wall for years – and how she was sure that Alexander had witnessed scenes in the war which had psychologically damaged him.

As she rattled on about his timekeeping and good attendance at work, and his bread-winning abilities, I began to see that she was attempting to justify her choice of him as a life partner. My mother had made a decision she had lived to regret, but felt unable to expose the man who had given her the three children she adored.

She explained the circumstances in which they had met, and how she felt assured that he was of the same Christian background as herself when Alex mentioned that he knew her minister. 'I've been in the manse and had tea and sandwiches with him,' he'd said, which had pleased her.

'I felt he was a kindred spirit – it wasn't till much later I discovered he'd been in the manse for reasons all of his own. By that time his family had welcomed me, I had got to know and like his mother, and the war was coming to an end, so it seemed logical to marry in October 1945. But after that came all the problems . . . all these other women. I blame the buses.'

'Ah,' said Ricky Gray, finally managing to get a word in edgeways. 'Womanizers. They're hard to live with. Baxter's Buses, too, we're finding, seems to have been a hotbed of affairs in the fifties, I agree. We need to talk to you, however, of what you can recall of the actual day of Saturday 23 February 1957, when Moira Anderson went missing. Can you remember what you and Alex were doing that day at all?'

Still as scrupulously fair to my father as it was possible to be, my mother recalled what she could of that winter weekend when her aunt from Australia was arriving, and she had been annoyed with her husband for failing to swap with a colleague for the evening. She talked about his late arrival home and his shift the following day for which she had prepared his sandwiches. Asked how she remembered hearing of Moira's disappearance, she was as clear as I was that this news had been given to us by my aunt Betty, her sister-in-law, on the Sunday afternoon. She could recall the circumstances of that weekend just as I could – it stood out from others because of its surprising events. Questioned closely, she was positive the news had not been broken by my father. She also described how after a week had passed with no sign of the child, my father had come in and said that he 'had been asked to go round to the station to be interviewed'. She gave the policemen in her living room the same version of events that I had given Jim McEwan, the tale of mistaken identity with the child called Moira Liddell, also from Cliftonville, who was well known for giving sweets to all the drivers.

'He was *definitely* interviewed at the time,' my mother said emphatically, although I had told her there was no written record of this. She looked at us all in bewilderment. 'Why would he say he was if he wasn't?'

There was a silence. I already knew from Jim that not only had no interview taken place, but the voters' roll for 1957 showed that while there were families named Liddell in the Cliftonville area, none had had a female child in the correct age group named Moira or anything similar. The child that Mrs Chalmers, the policeman's wife, had spotted talking to the bus driver that day *had* been Moira Anderson.

Jim had told me that Betty the babysitter, whose views had not figured at the time, had said that, despite numerous warnings from her parents, she had been drawn to my father's bus like a magnet. She had even been a passenger on his vehicle at some point during the afternoon of 23 February 1957 and had had a conversation with him about his plans for that evening. He had implied that he was off duty, but wouldn't require anyone to babysit: they wouldn't be going out on such a bad night. So, he had intended going out for the evening, but not with my mother, or herself. He had had other plans.

My father's version of how he had heard of Moira's disappearance and the events of that Saturday evening varies considerably from what is contained in my mother's statement, and that of Betty. He had insisted, when he was seen in Leeds, that he had heard the news on the night Moira had gone missing. There were, he stated, 'plenty of people mentioning it on the bus during the evening'. This must have been untrue because the child's father did not report it until at least midnight. My dad had finished work slightly late, he claimed, bought fish and chips on the way home, and had told my mother about the wee girl's disappearance at 11.45 that night. Moira's name had been mentioned by passengers, he claimed, but he didn't know who she was.

My father's view of how well he had known the Andersons changed subtly over the months he was interviewed.

Originally, in March 1993, he stuck to the line that he recalled Moira as just one more child who got on and off his bus regularly, even though he was visibly shaken when confronted with her photograph.

He insisted during his taped conversations that there had been no friendship between them: 'Ah never had much dealings with her . . . Ah never had any dealings except for on the bus.' He could not have chatted to her or anyone else, he maintained, as his cab was separate from the passengers.

Of her parents and sisters he pleaded ignorance, too, although my mother told me later that she recalled a conversation with my father *after* his release from prison when he returned to Coatbridge and to his old bus route. He had mentioned to her how sorry he was for 'that nice Mrs Anderson, whose kid had run off'. He had seen her from his bus sweeping the pavement outside her home and she had glanced up and waved to him. When my mother told me this, she had been trying to convince both of us that there was a caring side to my father's nature. 'I can assure you he was shaken to see that poor woman, still not knowing what had happened to her daughter,' she quavered. 'I hadn't realized he knew her. And how could he have come back here, if what you're saying is right? Nobody could do something like that, and go back.'

I reminded her that by the time the police had realized that Moira had not run away, my dad had been in prison. Because he was away, he'd been forgotten in the inquiry so when he came out he could slip quietly back into his family and his job.

But the truth was too much for my mother, who sobbed for hours after the visit by the CID, hoping still it was a nightmare from which she would awake.

# Chapter Twenty-Three

The second time Jim and his team grilled my father, his story changed.

The detectives told him they had interviewed two people still living in the area, who not only were able to say which bus he had been driving that day, but also who had a photograph of the very one, calling it EVA 26. The two bus spotters recalled it easily, for it had some features that distinguished it from the rest of Baxter's fleet, including a bull nose. They had kept a note over the years of every bus bought by the firm, and knew that it had been used between 1951 and 1958 in the Monklands, mainly on the Cliftonville to Kirkwood route, a journey of some twenty-five minutes, where crews maintained a half-hour service, with five-minute breaks and a longer lunch-hour. Built in 1939, they knew its model number, T58, and registration, CWY 219, and the fact that it was a hybrid, a Maudsley, which had been adapted with a Massey body. The driver was not completely isolated from his thirty-five passengers, and the vehicle had a capacious boot, the key for which was hung up in a special pouch in the cabin. Unusually, the boot could also be utilized from *inside* the vehicle, by lifting the rear passenger seats above, and operating a concealed lever.

My father recognized it instantly when Jim produced the photograph.

'It's a Maudsley. It has a Massey body.'

'Was that the one you were driving?'

'Similar. Don't know if it was the exact one.'

'That was the exact one, I assure you, Alex,' Jim replied. 'I can assure you that this *is* the bus that was on that route on that day.'

'You couldnae get intae them without the T-key,' my father said, when Jim asked him about access into the boot. 'We never got supplied wi' them.'

'I am assured by reliable sources that a driver would not take a bus out without taking what they called the budgie key with them, because it was part of the bus's equipment.'

'I worked in Baxter's for years, and never had one – only in the luxury coaches.'

'You were not aware,' said Jim in ironic tones, 'there was a passengers' luggage compartment under the rear seat of this bus?'

'Naw.'

He tried to insist there could be little contact with anyone, because of a partition between cab and vehicle, with only room in the compartment for one. When told that a witness had stated that Betty, the babysitter, had been observed sitting on his knee in the cab, he had protested: 'Naw, never. That was against the rules.'

'But we have drivers and conductresses telling us this.'

'Ah never took any lass intae the cab.'

'You were noted for having young girls on your bus at the terminus.'

'Me?'

'You.'

'Naw, Ah never had time. Naw, ye've got it all wrong.'

The detectives did not tell him then that a former conductress had recalled that horseplay had gone on among bus crews when they were taking breaks at a terminus, and she had a vivid memory of being bundled by Alex Gartshore into the boot of his bus.

When they told him that many of his former workmates had been seen by the police, my father demanded to know who had been interviewed. They included Cliff Harper, a man of similar height to my father, with a tiny moustache; George McArdle, an old buddy who had joined him on the buses from Allison's the butcher's – he had said that Alex Gartshore was very mannerly and plausible, and renowned 'for picking up girls who'd just left school' and that he had been invited by my dad to go into Glasgow to rendezvous with two fifteen-year-olds; Willie Brown, known as Tashie because of his large RAF-style moustache; and Pat O'Rourke the one I disliked intensely. My father was full of self-righteous indignation and denied their allegations that he had given young girls money to visit his cab, and George McArdle's claim that Betty had been one of many. Jeannette Mitchell Speirs, one of my father's regular conductresses, however, had agreed that it happened frequently.

My father also denied all knowledge of what three of his male colleagues and a conductress called Nan Laird claimed was common practice – for drivers to 'cover' for a friend. Being relieved on a Saturday to go off without your spouse having any inkling of your whereabouts had been apparently nothing out of the ordinary. George McArdle pointed out that a great deal of fiddling went on with ticket money, never mind subtle rearrangements of shifts, and wholesale deception of spouses. He said that he had always been suspicious of Alexander, about whom rumours were rife at the time of the child's disappearance. It seemed that as long as buses ran on schedule the inspectors were happy.

Two drivers who knew my father well in the fifties and sixties made particularly revealing remarks about his behaviour. Cliff Harper said, 'I knew he was a bit of a ladies' man. However, he was also the type of man who encouraged young girls to frequent the bus at the terminus.'

Tashie Brown agreed. 'Alex was attracted to wee lassies, schoolgirls, not older ones. They were always on his bus, and he was known to be interfering with them sexually.' He was also clear that, at the time of Moira's disappearance, speculation had spread throughout the bus company that Alex Gartshore had killed Moira.

Pat O'Rourke said, 'He would interfere with boys and girls. He wasn't too fussy.'

On his affair with Betty, the babysitter, my father refuted her statement, which described many meetings between them in Dunbeth Park, intercourse taking place by mutual consent after the first occasion some twenty to thirty times. She'd indicated the affair had lasted some six months, and that he had given her pocket money. This, she imagined, he had fiddled from the fares so that his wife would not suspect.

'I was with her once,' he declared, and denied ever having been near the park.

But Jim told him that the police had a statement from a woman who had walked into our house and caught him naked with Betty on the couch having full sexual intercourse.

In fact, *two* of my relatives, an aunt and a cousin, had described stumbling, as I had, into sexual encounters at 51 Dunbeth Road, over the winter of 1956 and 1957, and being unsure at the time of how to cope with their discovery.

One witness, an aunt who was pregnant over the winter of 1956/57, called to see my mother unexpectedly after a visit to the ante-natal clinic at the foot of our street. She was disappointed to find my mother out and had been about to leave when the back door opened suddenly. My father made an excuse, and seemed agitated when she pushed past him. She spotted a fair-haired girl rushing about in an attempt to dress. My aunt shouted, 'What the hell is going on here?'

She did not believe the tale he spun her, and she threatened to tell my mother if she ever came across him and this girl again. She was still upset when she reached her own home, but she and her husband agreed that my mother should never know anything of the matter. She also told Jim's team that she'd spotted my father in the back seat of his car, again with a fair-haired girl of twelve or thirteen when she was taking a short-cut over some wasteground. She knew he had seen her: their eyes had met before she had looked away hurriedly. She could not be sure if the child was the same one she had seen in our living room.

The cousin had often called to see my mother during the school lunch hour. On one particular day, there was no answer at our back door, and she found it was locked. Surprised, as she thought she'd heard voices, my cousin walked through our close and, on impulse, jumped up to look through the windows of my parents' bedroom near the front door.

She saw my father and a blonde girl of around her own age, thirteen, whom she thought she recognized as Betty, a fellow school pupil, naked in bed.

She also thought there had even been talk of an anonymous letter sent to my mother linking my father to Moira. A former neighbour might be able to confirm it, she said. Ella Brown Copeland agreed that this had happened just after Moira's disappearance. She told detectives that, even after all this time, she was not surprised that my father was being investigated.

When I asked my mother about the letter, she admitted it readily. She *had* received a cruel note, pasted with assembled letters cut from newspapers, immediately after my father was sentenced. 'It said I should take myself and my weans away to Australia with my aunt, and disappear from town,' she sighed slowly, 'and it said that the lassie Betty wasn't the only one – there were a dozen others he didn't get caught with. At the bottom they put: "Why don't you go, if you know what's good for you – you think you know what he's done, but you don't know the half of it. He won't stop with the lassie Anderson." ' Your grandfather insisted I took it round to the police station, and I did.'

'The police *saw* the anonymous letter?'

'Yes,' my mother answered dully. 'I handed it in to them at the desk, and told nobody else that I'd got it, except for my own mother. She told me I should ignore it.'

'And no police officer came to see you to discuss it?'

'No, I was terrified for days, waiting for them to come and ask questions, but I heard no more about it. After a while, I took the advice to put it out of my mind.'

I was stunned by what appeared another example from 1957 of staggeringly inept police work. My mother had given someone in John F. MacDonald's team a résumé of what was on many people's lips at the time and, like everything else to do with my father, the details of the note had not even been regarded as suspicious.

I decided my father had had a charmed life. But everyone's luck dries up at some point.

On Wednesday 17 March 1993, Alexander Gartshore was asked directly by Jim McEwan about his involvement in the missing girl's movements that day.

'Ah never had much dealings wi' her . . . Ah never had any dealings except for on the bus.'

'Are you responsible for the disappearance of Moira Anderson?'

'No, Ah'm not, Ah promise you that. Ah'm no used to sayin' Ah swear tae God . . . my right hand's up tae God. Ah swear on ma kids lives down here and up there as well . . . Ah had nothin' at all to do with it, nothing. If Ah could help ye, Ah would help ye.'

But eventually, he shifted his position on this issue too. He admitted to Jim that he had known the family; he knew them from coming on and off his vehicle. In particular, he had known Mrs Anderson and her middle daughter. When he was reminded that his cab had had open access and that the policeman's wife, Mrs Chalmers, had made a statement about Moira and herself exchanging smiles and then the child sitting at the front and speaking to the driver, he backtracked. He also denied all knowledge of 'Moira Liddell'.

'For thirty-seven years, the world was under the impression Moira vanished at four-ten p.m.,' Jim said, 'when she left her gran's and was never seen again. It's only since last year that *you* have come into the picture by saying to your daughter at the funeral what you said to her. You have made admissions that she *was* on your bus over an hour *after* the last official sighting.'

Still my dad maintained he had said all this in an interview at the time, which Jim knew to be untrue. Grilling him, however, paid dividends, as holes began to appear in his story.

'Where did Moira Anderson get on your bus?'

'At the stop just outside her door.'

Jim established that this was where Moira had been spotted by the old lady noticing the increasing severity of the storm.

'Ah seen her comin' in,' my father agreed. 'Front door bus.'

'Who else got on at that stop?'

'Don't know. Ah think her sister, I'm not sure, there was another lass with her . . . Ah can't mind if there was anybody, any adults or that.'

'Did you say anything to her?'

'Ah couldn't because the window was shut.'

'But your wife told us you said, "Hello, Moira," and the police wanted to speak to you about it.'

'Nut.'

'You left to go, allegedly, to tell the police about that a few days later.'

'Ah never said such a thing.'

'You told your wife you had to go and speak to the police.'

'Ah can't mind if Ah went because they interviewed me at the garage – Ah think it wis the next day.'

'Well, why did you tell your wife, "Hold my supper – the police want to speak to me and I'm going round to speak to them." '

'Ah said that?'

'Uh-huh. That is what your wife is saying.'

'Naw.'

Then came the breakthrough they needed. Having tried to insist that he and Moira had not chatted, my father finally crumbled on this part of his story too. From him, after so many years, the police learned why Moira, having found the Co-op closed, decided to take a bus into town alone, ignoring the arrangement to go to the cinema with her cousins. She had had a secret plan, which she revealed to no one except my father.

He had been the last person in Moira's company. In their conversation, she had told him that she was going to Woolworths near the Fountain, to buy a special surprise birthday card for her mother. No one else knew of her important task, not even her sisters or cousins.

Jim McEwan's men were stunned by this piece of information and checked. Jim discovered that Maisie Anderson's headstone proved that she had spent Sunday 24 February 1957, her fortieth birthday, searching for her daughter. This was proof not only that my father was the last person to have spoken to the little girl and hear what her intentions were, but that he had known her well. She would have been unlikely to share her secret during a casual encounter with a stranger.

My father did his utmost to distance himself from the inside knowledge of the card. He said that he had heard it later on the same shift.

'Ah learned that frae other people on the bus at the same time.'

'Who was that?'

'A young woman and a lass.'

'Names?'

'Naw, Ah don't know their names, but they said it was terrible . . . this Moira Anderson business.'

'When?'

'The following Monday.'

'But you said you told the police about this card on the Sunday when spoken to at the bus depot.'

'People came on the bus,' my father said eventually, 'on the Saturday night. A woman came on wi' a kiddie, and she told us about seven-thirty that night . . . "Isn't it just terrible, and she was going for a birthday card." '

'Nobody in the original enquiry knew that that was where Moira Anderson was going. There's no record of it at all,' replied Jim. 'She was never reported missing till well after eleven-thirty p.m. It's not until we dug really deeply that we found it was Moira's mum's birthday the next day.' He said nothing to my father of John F. Mac-Donald's admission that he had been unaware of the mother's birthday.

Ignoring this, my father would not budge from his tale of telling my mother the news of the child's disappearance between eleven and midnight on 23 February: 'There were plenty of people mentioning it on my bus, about nine o'clock, then ten o'clock, plenty of them.'

He had plainly forgotten the fact that all the buses had gone off the road with the bad weather.

Jim and his men were sure of the exact time at which Andrew Anderson had arrived, distraught, at the station in Dunbeth Road to report his child missing. Both Moira's parents were now dead but Janice Anderson Mathieson, mother of Moira's cousins, remembered that she had gone on the hospital visit to the family's grandfather with others, returning to Coatbridge after 5 p.m. Andrew had appeared at her home, 37c Laird Street, where they lived over the Co-op, at 10.30 p.m. She said that they had searched locally until it was felt that Andrew had to inform the police just prior to midnight. The news did not leak out to the general public until the next day. Only the immediate family and a handful of neighbours had known that something had befallen Moira late on the Saturday night. A tiny number of people and her killer.

My father said that Moira disembarked from his bus at Woolworths in Main Street, although that would have been an unofficial stop, and had waved goodbye. He had worked on, despite the bad road conditions, till 11.45 p.m. He had bought fish and chips on his way home, arrived before midnight, and he had told my mother the shocking news of a child being missing.

My father's black car would either have been sitting at Baxter's bus garage in Gartlea, Airdrie, that night, or it would have been parked outside our back door in the yard. One former bus driver, George McNeil, had handed over his bus that day to my dad. He said the crews had changed over at 2 p.m. at Jackson Street. From his statement, it would appear that my father, probably because of the blizzard, had left his car at home, and walked a couple of hundred yards from our home in Dunbeth Road to start his shift. This type of arrangement was also apparently common, to save crews going to the depot. At least one conductress told detectives that when she worked with my father on late shifts she rarely clocked off at the depot, which was the rule, but left him alone on the bus with the last few passengers, arranging that he handed in time sheets and collected fares, which allowed her to catch the last bus to her own outlying area.

I was interested in George McNeil's comment about my father being on foot that day. It had stuck in his mind, the association of such a tall man in such a small car being somewhat incongruous. If he was correct and my mother's recollection about 'listening for Alex's car arriving back' later that evening was also accurate, then it suggested to me that he had returned to Dunbeth Road at some point and taken out his car.

Some may question the idea of a man enticing away an intelligent girl like Moira, but I can see how she would have trusted this man in uniform, particularly if he had replaced money she had lost – for which the old lady had seen her searching in the snow – to purchase the birthday card. My father was equally capable of persuading her to stay on his bus, or of having her accompany him on some pretext to his car.

Once that had been achieved, whether it was in a large vehicle taken to a deserted terminus, or in his black Baby Austin which would cope better with treacherous road conditions, the victim would have been at his mercy.

# Chapter Twenty-Four

It was Easter 1993 and at last I remembered why I personally could be so sure that my father and Moira had known each other.

It had been a warm summer's day in 1956, in Dunbeth Park, and I had gone there from Aunt Margaret's house at the Red Bridge, pushing her eldest, Albert, who was sitting up in his pram. When we reached the park we found Marilyn Twycross, with a cousin called Marion, and one or two others; Marjorie Orr, who was from a big house, and Marjorie Anderson. We were all the same age.

We all ran to get on the swings. Several of us doubled up, one child standing, the other sitting, as the play area was busy.

There had been another group of four slightly older girls. My partner panted, propelling us higher, that two of them were Marjorie's big sister, Moira, and her pal, Beth. We wondered if they'd let us into their skipping game. Then my attention was diverted to the roundabout and we pounced on it, making it go faster and faster, accompanied by frenzied yells as we all felt sick. I noticed regretfully that the older ones had melted away, taking their ropes with them.

Suddenly, there was an accident at the swings. Some

kiddie had run beneath one, which had split his head open. I ran for help – the park-keeper's house was just at the entrance and I hammered at his door, shouting, 'Come quick, Mister, there's been an accident at the swings!'

For a few seconds, there was no response, and I looked behind me for him in his uniform. Instead, I spotted my dad's little black Baby Austin through the gates. What was he doing there? He seemed to be waving out of his window to some passers-by. I was still trying to figure this out, when the park-keeper opened his door, and I had to tell him what had happened. I pointed to the little knot of children still gathered round the casualty, then turned back towards the gates as he went to deal with the emergency.

As I walked towards our car, I saw that my father was deep in conversation with the older Anderson girl and her chum. I wondered what on earth he could possibly want with them. He seemed to be showing something to them, for their heads were close together as they gazed down into the interior of his car. Perhaps, I told myself, he had come looking for me. Various possibilities went through my head as I marched closer to the vehicle, as my dad chatted to both girls, who were in fits of giggles. Just as I got to the car Moira, in a short-sleeved blue dress, and her friend who was wearing culottes, ran off towards Dunbeth Avenue.

I looked at my father. Although he had seemed angry when he first caught sight of me, now he was smirking and fumbling about in the pockets of his bus uniform. He produced sweeties, and when I asked what he had been doing there with those girls, he wouldn't answer me. He asked if I wanted a lift but I told him of my task for the afternoon, grabbed the sweets out of his hand, and ran back to the path.

I was convinced that he would have persuaded the girls to go with him if I had not unexpectedly appeared. I had had no idea then what my father had been demonstrating to those two girls that had caused them to go into near hysterics. I only knew that something was wrong.

I wrote a summary of the incident and put it with the other half-dozen foolscap pages I had completed for the police. The one thing I could not force myself to write of, however, was the aftermath: when I had attempted to tell my mother she had turned on me, which was entirely unlike her. She had even hit me hard, and had made me promise never to tell anyone else. I had remained silent for nearly four decades.

Thinking that my sleepless nights might improve after this last flashback, I found instead that they worsened, to the point that I telephoned for an appointment with Brian Venters. He asked me what was disturbing me. I explained that I had now had the same dream for the past three nights, where I had got so upset I had had to get up and make tea, and there was no possibility of going back to sleep. Each time, I was woken by a blinding light, reminiscent of a lightning flash. In the dream the figure of a child was at the foot of my bed. The child was not Lauren, but was of her age, and as she drew nearer I recognized Moira. I sat up in bewilderment, leaning forward as she beckoned as if to tell me something. As the gap between us lessened, her smile widened and she nodded encouragingly. It was as if she was indicating that I should keep faith. No words were spoken but somehow I knew what the message was.

Then the image would blur, the light blue eyes turned into Lauren's deep brown ones, and the hair was no longer short and fair but long and curly. The mischievous grin became a puzzled look on my own child's face. Then the image would fade and shrivel. When I leapt out of bed, I imagined was standing among the bones of a small skeleton, the fragments disintegrating under my bare feet, the crackling sound only too real in my mind.

I looked at Brian Venters anxiously. He told me reassuringly that this was just my mind's way of adjusting to the enormity of my father's crimes. I was glad of his no-nonsense yet kindly approach.

That Easter, articles appeared in the *Airdrie and Coatbridge Advertiser* that caused a stir.

The Monklands front page headline on 2 April read: POLICE FIT ANOTHER PIECE IN THE MOIRA JIGSAW, and the article revealed 'the vital, new information that she might have gone to buy a birthday card for a member of her family'. Former staff of Woolworths were being traced, and one of the theories being followed up now was 'that Moira's killer persuaded her to stay on the bus she had used and return home with him because of the blizzard'. DCI Ricky Gray had spoken to Moira's sisters, Janet, now fifty, and Marjorie, forty-three, in Australia and England, respectively: 'Both said they were "very anxious" to see the mystery finally solved. Their eighty-five-year-old father Andrew died broken-hearted last July without ever knowing what became of the middle of his three daughters.'

Moira's description was given once more, and DCI Gray stressed that he wanted to trace anyone who had been at the abandoned football match between Airdrie and

Ayr United that day, and anyone who thought they had spotted a little girl fitting that description getting on or off the bus, 'possibly in the company of a man in his late thirties'.

The following week's local headline was MAJOR SETBACK IN MOIRA ANDERSON INQUIRY. This broke the frustrating news that police thought the bus conductress on duty that day had died six years before. Gus Paterson was quoted as saying, 'No one else has come forward. It is a disappointment and typical of the type of setbacks we are encountering. Nine people we wanted to speak to, who could have been important witnesses, are deceased.'

# Chapter Twenty-Five

Jim was back from his trip. To my surprise, he did not laugh when I told him that my cousins and I had decided to visit a medium. D had been at a meeting in Glasgow, and the medium on the stage had mentioned her name because he had a 'message' for her. When she met him afterwards she was astonished when he told her to ignore her doctor who had diagnosed her as having ME and to stick with the treatment she was receiving from her homeopath. She had arranged for him and the other five of us to come to her home. We decided beforehand to say nothing about the situation we were in with the police and see if he picked up that we were related and deeply involved in the investigation. His name was William and he was younger than any of us, which meant that the events of 1957 would be of little interest to him – if he even knew about them. For so far, all the media attention had focused on the Monklands and he was a Glaswegian. We planned to record what he said.

D had asked us all to gather at seven or so when her husband would fetch William from the station. He would do six individual consultations in her spare bedroom. I was late and didn't arrive until after nine.

I am not sure what I expected William O'Connor to

look like but he seemed innocuous, in jeans, a white T-shirt, and a casual jacket. He looked about thirty. As D changed the tape, she said, 'This is the last one, William. This is Sandra from Edinburgh.' He gave me an appraising look. I took a seat nearby, and felt silly, as before he even started I had begun to panic a little.

'Now, just relax, all I'm going to do is speak to you and I want you to calm down,' said William. 'All right? All you have to do is answer yes or no. You've come a distance to be here tonight.'

'Edinburgh.'

'And I feel it was a bit of a hassle during the day for you to get here.'

'It certainly was.'

I reflected ruefully that he was quite right about that – because of a chain of disasters I had almost not come at all. William stared at me searchingly.

'And also, as well as that, you have had an awful lot on your mind for the last couple of weeks or so.'

'Months.'

'It's actually not sorted out yet at all. And it's more on a personal level. You've had an awful lot of upset inside your own home. Are you OK?'

I nodded, though by now I'd dissolved.

'What they're telling me is,' said William, slowly and carefully, 'that you've had an *awful* lot to endure and nobody really knows the half of it yet. But your grandmother has been around the home and she's been giving you an awful lot of help and support.'

I was amazed at William's ability to tune into my feelings. He had no knowledge that everything had been set in motion with Granny Jenny's death a year before.

'What she's telling me here is that it's your strength of character that's keeping you going more than anything else. She's telling me here that you've to try not to worry so much because she's trying to help you sort it out. Do you understand? And there's someone round about you very stubborn – too stubborn, actually – it's like knocking on a brick wall and not getting through. It's as if the conversation's falling on deaf ears . . .

'Don't waste your energy any more.' William looked at me sharply. 'Let it materialize the way it's to go, because your emotions have been *wrecked* and you can't allow them to do it any longer. You've put everybody before you, you know, and you've got to put *you* first now. And you've not got a lot of support about you that you can run to . . . and you're distanced away from your family as well. What they're saying is – what the lady in the world of spirits is telling me is don't worry too much. Try not to blame yourself for everything, because you are not responsible.'

'I'm not responsible.' I repeated William's words like a talisman.

'D'you understand that? You are *not* to take the blame though there's some who would like to pass it. They should be looking in,' here William pointed to his heart, 'before they look out. Because their criticisms are just coming off their tongue like that, and the simple reason is, it's easier to blame others rather than themselves. I've got to be honest with you, they don't seem to feel they *are* at fault. The lady's saying that the most important thing here at the moment is you, right? Where is there a child?'

I wondered if William was using telepathy. I'd thought of Moira, and he had mentioned a child. Wordlessly, I extracted from my bag a nameless head-and-shoulders photo of Moira.

I pushed the photo towards him.

'This is the child,' I said.

'I know.' William glanced at the photograph briefly. 'All I keep getting is – I'm not getting a link on the other side . . . All I keep getting told is that there's a *lady* in the world of spirits who is trying to help.'

'I've had nightmares for ages about this child,' I interrupted him. There was a silence, then William regarded me with great compassion in his eyes. He concentrated hard, as if listening to a conversation to which I was not attuned.

'What I'm being told is . . . there's somebody connected to that child – family? – who has taken her away.'

'Yes.'

'They actually lured her into a false sense of security – and then took her away, miles from where she lived. And also it is not totally sorted out yet.'

'It's not, no.'

'Right. The child is now grown-up and doesn't know the half of it.'

'I was a child when this happened, and I don't, but *this* child,' I pointed to Moira's picture, 'is she on the other side? Can you say that?'

'Yes, I've got to be honest. I'm sorry, I feel that.'

'Yes, I think she is,' I agreed sadly.

'She's there, yes. She *is* there.'

'She's not a member of my family, but I feel—' I broke down at this point. 'I feel my father's responsible for this child not being here any more.'

William stared into the corner of the room, beyond me, but I could see nothing.

'I feel that now this child could be late thirties or early forties, maybe forty-three? And not long after she disappeared, she went.' He snapped his fingers quickly, and the sound made me jump. 'But you've had her several times in your material life back to you.'

My own eyes widened. There was only one thing he could be referring to.

'She – I've been having nightmares about this wee girl,' I croaked.

'Because she's visited you three times in dream form.'

'Yes.' The word was just a whisper. It can just be heard on the tape recording.

'It's to let you know—'

'She's told me the truth.'

'That's what's breaking you apart. All I keep seeing is that she's forgiven him.'

There was a silence.

'But I can't forgive him,' I said.

'That's what I mean. What I've been told to tell you is that if it's getting opened up, watch. Right? Because *you'll* feel the pain.'

'I'm feeling it now,' I said, and it was true.

'I feel as if you don't know who to turn to, and all she's saying is that she's – calm down, calm down.' William attempted to comfort me. Then he sat up, and seemed to become another person altogether. 'She was very chatty and very cheerful, and very, you know, as a child . . .' William tossed his head as a young girl would, and his voice altered to that of a child: ' "Yes, let's go here." She's got a wee bit of properness in her voice. And she's showing me a playground . . . where I'm near . . . a playground.'

Where I'm near. It could only be Dunbeth Park, so close to her home.

'A park with chutes?' I asked William quietly. He was still being her, I could see.

'Yes. I'm actually getting somebody playing with skipping ropes as well. There seem to be some trees, and a main road behind me – d'you understand? – and I seem to have a blue-coloured dress on, some kind of blue colouring. I have to make sure I know that whom I'm giving this to, it's correct – my guide tells me that it's taken a lot of strength and power to bring her here. But she *is* on the other side of life, she's *not* here on the material. OK?'

'I understand,' I said. 'I've known that, I think, for a year now.'

'She's passed away.' William's voice was his own now, which relieved me as the last few moments had been spooky, and the back of my neck was prickling. Moira had managed, through this young man, to confirm for me the one memory I had of seeing her which I had written down so recently. 'And I wouldn't say it was natural causes. I have to be honest, I feel the child has seen too much. She's deluding, and she's not showing me – but then again, sometimes there's things I'm not allowed to see – but I feel *you*'ve seen some of it.'

William looked at me hard.

'I've definitely seen some of it.'

'I feel that you couldn't believe it when you were seeing it. And it is not your imagination at all. Because,' added William, snapping his fingers once more, 'your life just went like that, overnight. I feel that what I've been told to tell you is you've got to let things go the way they are just now. What I'm getting here is that the child – she trusted the person that had taken her away. *She trusted the person.* All I'm getting is that she's come to you – you must've been close at some point? – and she's only been able to contact you in the recent past . . .'

'Very recently, only the last few weeks.'

'Because the simple reason is, she didn't want your material life disturbed earlier, because it would have damaged your life,' William explained, 'and, in spirit, we're not allowed to interfere in people's lives until it comes to a stage where something must be done. That's why the guides wouldn't allow her to come to you before, but she seems to be coming through now. You had to get on with your own life, and plus when your children were coming you would have been over-protective, and you would've gone over everything, and you'd have been going out of your mind. But now they're up, and they've got their independence.'

'They have.' I was staggered at how much William seemed to know about a woman he'd never encountered before, and when he only knew my first name. Certainly, you could tell from the diamond ring and the wedding band on my left hand that I was married, but there were no clues to my children or their ages.

'They've got independence,' he repeated, 'they're finding their own level, and they're going out into the world. So they're now able to let the contact come through.'

'Contact come through?'

'Don't forget that she's not a child any more. We're looking at a grown woman, and you'll probably see her in a grown form.'

'No, I've actually seen her as she is here,' I said, tapping on the photograph, 'but in my dreams, she's turned into my own wee girl.'

'Is that right? That's probably because of the innocence of it. Do you understand what I mean? Also, she could be trying to warn you as well.'

'Warn me?'

'Like, watch what you're doing. Be careful with your emotions. Do you know what I mean? That type of situation. Also, she's probably walked with your own wee girl in her life – she's been there to protect her and make sure nobody harmed her. But you haven't seen her in a grown-up form, though you'll probably be aware of her maturity at one point, when she comes back to you. The dreams have stopped slightly – right? – just to ease your mind a bit. Because you've *got* to ease your mind at the moment or you'll go out of it. And I've to say this, she's more worried about *you* than anything else and you've to try and accept that she *is* away.'

I noticed beads of sweat on William's brow now. He looked exhausted. But there was one thing I felt I had to ask before the session stopped.

'But, I've got to try and find out where he put this wee lassie. Her family never knew what happened to her.'

'It seems to be near a quarry or where there's a lot of land.' William was tense, straining his ears. 'But I'm being told by my guide that it will be almost impossible to find the remains of that child, where her body is.' Then he added, 'They'll probably reveal *something* to you. But it will be difficult to obtain it, because there are a lot of changes in the area that it happened in. Sorry I couldn't give you anything else, but *this* is what's dominating your life. You would never have turned against a man you felt respect and love for if you didn't feel it was so important. But I feel as if your family probably won't accept it.'

'My mother won't accept it.'

'For anything,' agreed William. 'If anything, she probably thinks you're going out of your mind, and she really won't accept it – but she knows things about your father that nobody knows. She will probably defend him—'

'Right to the end!' we said in unison.

William reassured me again that Moira's spirit was fine and added that both her parents were now with her. I asked if he thought the body might have been dumped in water.

'All I'm getting's a quarry, so it could be water, I'm not sure. When you get sites like that, there's usually water round about it. But I don't see her being flung in the sea.'

'You know how you said she was taken away? I'm sure she was,' I mused, 'but I can't see it being *far*.'

'It's not far but it's definitely near a quarry,' said William, getting up and heading for the door. 'Now she didn't tell me what happened. I'll see what I can do for you. Stay here and I'll get you a glass of water.' He was visibly shaken.

When C took him to the station, he told her not to take the car she was driving north next day. Then he said, 'How close are you to that last girl I saw there?'

'Actually, we're all related,' said C. 'I'm her cousin. What is it?'

'I couldn't tell her that what we were getting . . . It was a murder. Tell her if she wants me to help the police I will. Good night. Don't take this car on your trip.'

C stared at him as he got out and went into the station.

The following day, she took her car in for a service. A number of faults came to light.

# Chapter Twenty-Six

There are those, I am sure, who will be cynical about the events that occurred in Coatbridge that evening of 23 April 1993, and of what passed between a young man from Glasgow and a woman he had never set eyes on before, from Edinburgh, and who will question both sincerity and authenticity. All I can say is that Jim McEwan was not one of them.

D's brother-in-law taped a copy of the recording of our consultations and Ronnie listened to it carefully. He said, 'Give it to the police team, tell them he's willing to help, and leave it to them to decide on whether this man is some kind of fraudster or the genuine article.'

While the tape made its way to Airdrie police station, I got William's full name and address from D and telephoned him to let him know the police might contact him. He did not sound surprised. 'I'll do all I can to help,' he said simply. 'Something similar has happened before.'

He told me a little of his background, and I realized he took his gift very seriously.

'So, anyway,' I said, 'you're quite happy for me to pass on your name to the police?'

'Absolutely,' said William. 'What you should be aware of is that your gran told me she couldn't rest in peace, knowing she had covered up for your dad all these years. Now she's in spirit, she knows he's responsible. This is why something is being done to try and balance the scales of justice now.'

I was silent. I thought of Granny Jenny and the cryptic remarks she had made to me, always retracting them or changing the subject.

'I've had her back,' said William, as if describing someone he'd bumped into in the street.

'So is she still worried about me?' I asked with interest.

His answer was forthright. 'Oh, no, I don't think so. She's just very upset that he has the same name as his father, who she tells me was a very respectable ambulance man.'

'Did she say his name to you?' I held my breath.

'Yes, she did,' he answered cheerfully, 'and I can see you're called after him, too – it's Sandy, or Sanny or something like that, short for—'

'Alexander.'

'That's right. She was worried about the surname too, because it was unusual.'


Jim McEwan and Gus Paterson arranged to interview William a week or so later. They assured me it was not preposterous to involve him and Jim spoke of a recent murder investigation where the killer of a Rutherglen woman taxi driver had been traced through the help of a clairvoyant. Jim's view was that, with a murder case as complex and long ago as Moira's, he was willing to meet William and form his own opinion. The two policemen picked up William, escorted him to Coatbridge and drove him around the area to see what he picked up in the way of vibes.

I spoke to Gus the day after. He said that he had been almost as staggered as I was by William. 'It was uncanny,' he said. 'Jim and I were determined to give the guy as few clues as possible, so we just drove him around to see what he would say and do. We headed through the Cliftonville area, and it was as if the guy came to life. He recognized her street and murmured something about it "not looking right". The Andersons' home was knocked down years ago. He said, "It isn't there any more," though all the rest of the houses are exactly as they were. He talked about the park being nearby, and directed us to Dunbeth Park. Then, at the gates, he asked us outright if it was an ex-cop we were interviewing. He seemed confused, then stressed the man we have to speak to wore a uniform. He kept repeating, "She says she trusted him because of his uniform, so I guess it must be a cop." Then, a moment later, he was saying, "Where is a bus involved in all this? I'm clearly picking up she got on a bus." On the way back from the Townhead area, he made us turn off a side road. We went up Gartgill Road, into quite a desolate area. It takes you up towards abandoned pits and quarries, but he got us to stop at the large pond that's round that way, near the old signal box. He seemed to be looking for three big brick chimneys near railway lines. There *were* old brick works round there, years ago, but they were demolished in the sixties.'

'I lived in Coatbridge all through my childhood,' I said, 'and I've never wondered where that little road goes or used it.'

'It's a real backwater although it's only a mile from the

town centre,' Gus agreed, 'and few people seem to notice it. The pond is hardly any distance from the bus terminus in Townhead. All the drivers would probably know that a pond was screened by the wood near their turning circle. Now you can't see it for high flats. William got out of the car and indicated to us that he felt Moira all around. It's marshland and you're sinking up to your knees in bog, but though he couldn't pinpoint an exact spot, he said he was certain he was being directed to the general location. Then he looked pale, and started choking and being sick. He threw up, and told us he wanted to leave.'

I recalled William's pallor when I'd last seen him, and decided it would be difficult to vomit unless it was the real thing.

'He talked about people being burned and drowned and said it was a tragic spot. He was in a state, so we decided to take him up to the station in Airdrie and let him get cleaned up.

'We checked the map of the whole burgh on the wall here,' Gus added. 'I'd been trying to remember the local name for the pond, when some guy said he'd lived in a police house round that area of Townhead. Told us the tower block's called Witchwood Court, and the pond's been called that too for donkey's years.'

'Witchwood Pond,' I repeated.

'Yeah,' agreed Gus. 'You'd need to check it out with the local historian.'

I had few problems finding my way round the familiar haunts of the Carnegie Library, where John White, an expert on the folklore of the Monklands area, has built up a formidable archive. I discovered that while there is only fragile historical evidence for witch-hunting having taken place in that part of Coatbridge several hundred years ago, no one has ever been able to explain why those woods and that pond carry the name they do. I resolved that I would visit the spot when I could.

On my first free afternoon, I set off to explore an area of my childhood home that we kids had never gone near. I parked my car by the signal box, climbed over some wire, then set off towards Witchwood Pond, with its spread of bright marsh marigolds.

I had worried that I, too, would pick up horrible feelings in this lush green place so incongruously set in an industrial sprawl, but this did not happen. I did not feel nervous, although I was alone for half an hour without seeing another soul. Perhaps dreadful events *had* happened here, but I could not detect the malevolence that had so upset William. I placed the bunch of red carnations I'd brought on the soft moss before I rose to leave.

# Chapter Twenty-Seven

I knew Jim had arrested my father on suspicion of the murder of Moira Anderson on his visit to Leeds on 18 May, then had to release him on bail until 11 August. He planned to use divers to search the pond at Witchwood in the autumn when the undergrowth could be cut back, but it began to look more and more likely that things would go public in a much more national way in the summer.

His months of work, contained in seven large boxes of documentation, were all with the Depute Procurator Fiscal, a Mr Griffiths, who Jim thought would wish to see A and B. We would have to wait for his decision on the next move. His recommendations would be considered higher up in Edinburgh's Crown Office.

The days slipped past, but my cousins heard nothing from the Fiscal's Office at Airdrie and I went south for my university summer school at Nottingham. When I returned, Ronnie said Jim wanted me to call him.

The next morning, 29 July, I went down to the police station and Jim showed me the letter he had received from the Crown Office. At the top, my father's full name and address were given, under it the words 'Investigation into the Disappearance of Mary McCall Anderson (known as Moira) from Coatbridge, Lanarkshire, on February 23rd,

1957', then: 'The Scottish Crown Office notes with interest the stage reached by the present inquiry, and advises this matter should continue to be investigated. Further evidence will continue to be examined. You are instructed to proceed with such till further notice.' Below this were the names of my four cousins. My father was also named, in connection with five charges of lewd and libidinous behaviour against them on various occasions. I read the concluding sentence with disbelief: 'On the above matters, it is advised that there be no further proceedings.'

I knew my father had admitted the abuse of A, and he had made another incriminating statement on tape, which indicated that B's allegations were also correct. What more did they need? I demanded angrily.

'I have spoken to the Fiscal and he won't reveal reasons,' explained Jim. 'It may seem odd, but they don't have to tell you or me why. I told David Griffiths that you'd be at a loss to understand this decision, Sandra. I was sure you'd want answers from him, so I've arranged for a car to take you to his office shortly.'

Jim and I walked to where a driver was waiting. Jim slid into the back seat beside me, saying he would make the formal introductions. Seconds later we arrived at the large, airy offices of the Procurator Fiscal, and Jim escorted me upstairs to a seat, where I waited. When Mr Griffiths came in Jim made formal introductions and departed. He had to be as neutral as possible, but I felt uneasy as he left and I was shown, with no obvious cordiality, into an office.

The man sat down behind a huge desk and I asked why such a puzzling decision had been taken regarding my father and my relatives. He told me, rather as though he were delivering a lecture, that it was a long-standing

WHERE THERE IS EVIL

tradition for the Crown Office never to give any reasons. 'The documentation I sent to Chambers in Edinburgh went to a very senior level for consensus, Mrs Brown,' he answered stiffly. 'They have obviously reached the unanimous conclusion that what happened to your cousins is not to be proceeded with because it is not in the public interest. In other words, in their view it is not worth pursuing this case.'

Not worth pursuing! I began to argue that abusers don't stop, and my father had continued to add to his victims over the years. How could they have reached this crazy decision to do nothing about my cousins and the trauma they'd endured, when if they charged him, and brought him north, they would, in all probability, gain a confession for murder?

'There is no murder without a body, let me remind you,' said Mr Griffiths. 'The Moira Anderson case is still officially a missing person's inquiry, pure and simple.' He went on to say there had, of course, been one or two examples in British courts of a murder trial without a body, but it was rare; that, in such cases, there would always be other evidence to go on. Everything he had read in Jim's documentation, he said, was of an overwhelmingly circumstantial nature, and there was no proof that Moira Anderson had met her death at my father's hands. 'I know your father has said some extremely incriminating and suspicious things, but they have not enlightened us. In my view, the police aren't much further forward than in 1957.'

This was nonsense, and we both knew it.

'My father has lied to other people as well as myself, about not knowing Moira, about saying he was interviewed at the time when he wasn't, and the tape recordings made with his co-operation in Leeds are full of inconsistencies.'

'That may be so, but just because someone lies about something doesn't mean to say the converse is true,' Mr Griffiths said. 'Inconsistencies aren't enough to go on. While your father's made a number of very suspicious admissions, we take the line that an admission is not the same as a confession.'

Then he added, 'I have never understood – what do you hope to gain from all of this coming out? Why would these women want to go on a witness stand and testify to sordid acts your father committed long ago? What possible satisfaction would your cousins gain from sitting in a witness box here in Airdrie, in front of the local yobs and describing what your father did all those years ago?'

'Justice, perhaps.' I felt my cheeks glow with anger. 'Justice for what happened to them and all his other victims including those who can't speak up. Like Moira, who was murdered.'

'You can't call this a murder inquiry, it's a missing person's,' Mr Griffiths said again. 'May I remind you that your father *has* served his sentence.'

I regarded him with incredulity. 'Mr Griffiths, these offences happened to my cousins *after* my father had served his sentence at Saughton prison. I was unaware of what he had put them through till this investigation brought it to light. What do I tell them now?'

'Sordid things happened to all of us,' he replied. He went on to describe some of the things he was presently coming across in child-abuse cases, and said that what had happened to my family was long ago and relatively less severe.

Shaking with anger, I made a mistake that would return to haunt me later. 'If you'd taken the time to interview my relatives, you would know that all have suffered long-term emotional damage, and you cannot possibly be in a position to judge the effects of it unless you have been a victim of sexual abuse yourself. He is still a danger to children in my view. What about his recent prison sentence?'

Mr Griffiths answered, 'I know nothing of that.'

I went on, emphasizing that because of my own field of expertise, teaching child development and child protection, I felt qualified to judge whether my family was still suffering. He rose. My persistence annoyed him. I could see he had reached the end of his tether and was relieved when I got up. I told him that I would be writing to the Crown Office to complain. He handed me a note of their address. 'No one is disbelieving you or your relatives,' he repeated several times, 'but I assure you it just isn't in the public interest to pursue these matters.'

Before going home, I saw Jim briefly and related to him my conversation with Mr Griffiths. I left him saying that I would not, however, let the matter rest there. 'Didn't think you would,' he replied with a grin.

Next day I dashed off a letter of complaint to the Crown Office, and a few days later I received a brief formal reply, which politely fobbed me off. It pointed out that it was a long-standing tradition of the Scottish Crown Office not to disclose to anyone its reasons for arriving at decisions. I did not need to be told.

It was a polite brush off, which I related to Jim in some disbelief.

'Maybe,' he said, 'it would be an idea to get yourself a good lawyer.'

'A lawyer! But I've done nothing!' I protested. 'Why on earth should I need one?'

'It's just a thought,' he replied. 'I think you need to get some good independent advice from the best you and your cousins can afford. If you're not giving up at this point, then you should. You're sailing into deep waters, Sandra.'

'I'm not giving up. I've discussed it with my cousins, and neither are they giving up on this,' I answered. 'If it will help, I'll seek some expert advice.'

'Do it. You'll need it.' Jim's voice was resigned. 'You're up against it. Good luck.'

Later, I discovered that rarely does anyone in Scotland quibble over the decisions of the Crown Office, particularly not an ordinary member of the public. Only two alternatives were open to me: either to publicize this unbelievable decision, or to pursue a private prosecution.

# Chapter Twenty-Eight

Nowhere in Scotland does an independent body exist, chaired by a lay person, to investigate a complaint against the legal system, which can duck behind its get-out protection clause by saying that it is not accountable for any decisions and need not reveal why they were taken. At present the support mechanisms favour the offender, rather than the victim. I was being ignored by the legal authorities, I told Jim, who agreed to my next request. I wanted to meet with Eileen McAuley, the local reporter who had given massive local coverage to the re-investigation. Jim knew her well and respected her.

That August, media interest in Moira and my dad had not died down. Speculation continued to hit the headlines, but even now, no link could be made between the man being questioned repeatedly in Leeds about the disappearance of Moira Anderson in 1957 and the man being accused by a group of women in Coatbridge of sexual abuse. Those south of the border were also unaware of this connection, according to Ann Inglis, assistant minister at my church. She had been on holiday with her family in Yorkshire, and had been astonished to hear details I had told her in confidence reported as the main item on the local television news.

'I was flabbergasted,' she said to me later. 'They clearly

stated that a local pensioner was being investigated by Scottish police who had visited Leeds three times in connection with Moira's case, and they showed a picture of the little girl who was from his home town in Lanarkshire. They said he was presently on bail while a decision is being reached by the Scottish Crown Office as to whether they will press charges. The whole thing was headline news down there.'

Such a splash in my father's own territory unnerved me. Despite her reassurances that I would make a credible witness, based on her experience as a barrister, I still dreaded a huge court case with all its accompanying publicity. I did not relish 'celebrity' status as the woman who had accused her own father of a murder that had taken place when she was an eight-year-old child.

Eileen McAuley and I met in a small café, close to the office of the *Airdrie and Coatbridge Advertiser*. We talked of William's unexpected involvement, about how devastated my cousins and I were at the latest events, and the possibility of employing a lawyer who could take on the establishment. I mentioned that I had thought of approaching John Smith, the local MP. Two of my cousins were in his constituency.

Eileen frowned. 'He might help. He's honour bound to do all he can to help them, if not you. He can't have missed the developments on this case.'

We spoke for an hour, but I was careful not to mention either my father's or my cousins' full names. We shook hands and agreed to keep in touch. I felt reluctant to speak to any other journalist, and somehow the link with Jim helped. I had a positive feeling about Eileen and knew she would respect confidentiality. I wrote to John Smith.

On 11 September, as I stretched out in bed with the Saturday morning paper and a breakfast tray, he rang me. The voice at the other end of the phone was brisk but kindly. 'I understand from your résumé of events that two victims are my constituents?'

'Yes, and they would be happy to meet with you. They are entitled to have their day in court, and have people listen and believe in them. Not like before, years ago, when nobody wanted to know.'

'Well, that attitude is changing, but I agree there are still those who prefer to look the other way,' he commented. 'There has been a spate of these cases in Scotland over the past five years or so, which date back thirty years or more. It is indeed a feature of these that the victims were unable to come forward at the time, and one hopes today they are treated more sensitively than in the past.'

We discussed my meeting with Mr Griffiths, and how my father had linked himself to Moira. 'But it must be terribly difficult for your family,' Mr Smith said, after a brief pause. He revealed he could remember the original case without difficulty, such was its impact. 'Although your brothers were just very small children in 1957, nevertheless, they share his name, and in a place the size of Coatbridge, they are bound to feel everyone will know if it comes out who is responsible. They must be very concerned about being identified, and I can understand that perfectly. I know you feel your principles are the correct ones, but there are times when you have to choose between your family and your own integrity. You run the risk of damaging family relationships.'

I murmured agreement, but pointed out that another family in his constituency would never know the truth about their child. I went on, 'Everyone has the right to tell the truth about her childhood, her upbringing, her life. Keeping silent about painful memories is in the interests of the abuser. Silence doesn't help anyone, and little girls are still at risk from him.'

Mr Smith said he would do his best to help: he would write to Lord Rodger, the Lord Advocate, personally and request a meeting. He wished me well, and indicated he would be in touch shortly.

I reflected on what he had said about family relationships. I didn't wish the rift between my brothers and me to widen, but there was no going back. I thought of the last time we'd met up, when Norman had insisted I drop everything and stop supporting my cousins. 'I don't know how you're going to feel, Sandra, at the end of all this,' he'd declared angrily, 'when that lassie turns up.'

'What lassie?'

'Moira Anderson. When she turns up safe and well, how will you feel then?'

I was dumbfounded. He had still not come to terms with the truth about our father.

Two or three weeks after our meeting, Eileen published a piece in her newspaper about the latest developments in our case, but took care to make no link to the Moira Anderson investigation. Her headline of 3 September said: WOMAN IN PRIVATE PROSECUTION BID.

A woman is poised to take out a private prosecution against her father in respect of child abuse allegations dating back 30 years. The former Coatbridge woman, who cannot be named for legal reasons, is furious the authorities have decided not to prosecute. Mrs X claims her 73-year-old father – who no longer lives in the area – sexually abused four female members of her family during the early 1960s.

Monklands detectives, who investigated the claims, submitted a report detailing a series of Lewd and Libidinous allegations to the Procurator Fiscal in Airdrie. But the Fiscal's Office, acting on Crown Office advice, ruled it was not 'in the public interest' to proceed with the case. Mr A. Taylor Wilson, the P.F., this week refused to discuss the case, stating he had 'no comment to make'.

Mrs X maintains the justice system has failed her family and stressed there was no 'statute of limitations' on sex offences. 'I am extremely disturbed by the Fiscal's decision, backed by the Crown Office, not to proceed with charges against my father,' she said. 'Because of this situation we are being forced to seriously consider taking out a private prosecution against him. It is intolerable for the Fiscal to say it is not in the public interest to proceed.'

Mrs X also claimed the Fiscal's office 'minimised' the alleged offences against her four cousins. She stated: 'I pointed out the long term effects were still evident. One victim has required regular psychiatric treatment over the years because of childhood events and another has experienced great difficulties with relationships because of the abuse. The type of attitude taken by the Fiscal's office sends out the wrong signals about child abuse. During the '60s people simply did not discuss it, it was a strict taboo, especially among families. Now that members of my family have had the courage to make an official complaint, they have been slapped in the face by the justice system. I understood the prevailing attitude nowadays to be more enlightened than that displayed by the Fiscal's office in Airdrie.'

The article ended by indicating that the police felt it inappropriate to comment. Privately, however, Jim McEwan and Billy McCloy were both supportive.

Jim phoned. He had been studying aerial photographs from the fifties that showed the pond at Townhead. Glasgow University experts had told him the topography of the land there had changed dramatically over the years, particularly following the hot summer of 1959. He told me how important any find by divers would be that made a link between Moira and her killer ... a heavy tool from a bus, or a wheel that would have acted as a weight. I reminded him that the leather bucket bag and the wax cloth Co-op book she had had would not have been bio-degradable either.

'You should've been a cop,' Jim laughed.

My cousins A and B had been worrying that should a trial go ahead it would be their word against my father's, given that there had been no other witnesses to the abuse. Billy phoned and reassured me that, in Scots law, a factor called the Moorov Doctrine comes into play where allegations of a pattern of behaviour emerge. Named after a Glasgow case from years back, in which a shopkeeper had molested his assistants on evenings when he asked them to work late, its thrust is that when a group of independent witnesses come forward with similar complaints about an abuser their statements are treated as corroborative.

# Chapter Twenty-Nine

On 13 September 1993, I received a formal reply from John Smith, with the green portcullis logo of the House of Commons.

*Dear Mrs Brown,*

*I refer to our telephone conversation, and to the letter you sent to me which very fully sets out your concerns. As I suggested, the best thing for me is to take up the matter with the Lord Advocate which I have now done. I will let you know when I get a response.*

*I mentioned the complication that you are one of Lord James Douglas-Hamilton's constituents. I have written to him explaining why I have taken up the issue with the Lord Advocate, but it might be appropriate for you to approach him also. Kindest regards.*

I did not particularly wish to write to my own MP to set out all the facts – so difficult to condense in a few lines – but as John Smith was concerned about parliamentary protocol, I did so.

My letter ran to four pages, and took me almost as long to compose as my latest Open University essay. I glanced through the last section, for which I had had to do some research in one of the Edinburgh libraries, on what the Sexual Offences (Scotland) Act 1976 involved. This was the one my father had contravened, and I had been keen to check it out, highlighting the part that mentioned the main crime he had perpetrated against my cousins:

**Sexual Offences (Scotland) Section V:**
Lewd (i.e. lustful), indecent or libidinous (lustful desire for sexual indulgence) practices or behaviour towards a girl less than twelve years of age.

I had read the footnotes concerning Presentation of Abuse, and recognized the hallmark of my dad clearly defined over a paragraph or two.

The sexual encounter between the child and the adult may be of a single episode which may be very violent and traumatic, particularly if the abuser is a chance acquaintance, or a stranger. It may be the motive for the murder of a child. Much more often the sexual contacts and encounters are multiple with the initial advances made towards the child being relatively minor, but as days, months, and years pass by, the advances become more involved often coming to a stage where sexual intercourse or sodomy is occurring with the child. A crescendo type history is typical of such complaints.

If the sexual encounter has been violent, the child will often present with severe injuries to the body or genitals as an emergency; on occasions this encounter may also result in death of the child. The victim has been restrained, strangled or throttled in the process, or sharp or blunt force trauma has been perpetrated against the child to ensure that the child succumbs to the sexual demands being made of it, or as part of the sadistic nature of the assault. The very act of penetration of a child by an adult can 'per se' result in death of the child as a result of vagal reflex cardiac inhibition. The body of a young child on occasions may show no other evidence of violence other than features of sexual penetration.

Very often, presentation is non-acute, and may even be delayed, and frequently is, until adult life when the presentation is to psychologists, psychiatrists, and marriage counsellors – indeed, under-reporting is a feature of childhood abuse.

I had photocopied this information, and read it several times in a grim attempt to try to understand what had occurred on that February night so long ago. I came up with several theories and succeeded in reawakening my wish to be regressed back to my troubled childhood, to eliminate any shred of suspicion about my dad's relationship with me. I decided to go to an expert in hypnosis regression, recommended by my GP, Brian Venters and with the knowledge of Ashley, who was still counselling me.

Hypnotherapy is a powerful tool, which, in the correct hands, can provide the key to deeply rooted emotional problems; it taps into the subconscious, where the experiences we meet early, and how we deal with them, lay down our behaviour for a lifetime. I had never been hypnotized, had never witnessed any kind of stage show, and had only read articles on the subject. Everything learned or seen is stored in the brain, and using hypnotherapy to reach what is present in the deeper recesses means you can re-evaluate with adult eyes what took place in the past and cut through the child's confusion. Often the subconscious reveals events repressed by the conscious mind because they were too distressing for the child to cope with at the time.

It is important that the hypnotherapist is able to deal professionally not only with helping the client access the subconscious, but also with any revealed trauma. I had every faith in the woman with whom Brian Venters put me in contact, a Glasgow GP named Hetty McKinnon, and visited her home one Friday evening.

Hetty showed me into a charming study, lined with antiques, and soon had me installed in a comfortable winged armchair with a little footstool in front of me. She set up the tape recorder I had remembered to bring, and tested its volume. Recordings could be passed on to Jim if they proved useful.

'Now, you've absolutely nothing to worry about.' She beamed at me. 'When we start to regress you, just let me show you what to do should there be anything that worries you, so that I know you're concerned about it.' She demonstrated how I should move my finger to alert her.

Reassured, I felt tension slip out of my body. I concentrated on her framed watercolours, then closed my eyes and let myself drift as she suggested, while her gentle voice washed over me. She made it clear that I could stop what was happening at any time simply by opening my eyes. It was just like entering the lightest of afternoon naps.

Hetty described my arm, which I had to extend straight in front of me; it would be as heavy as one of the huge iron bars which were manufactured in the foundries of Coatbridge many years ago. Within a second, I could not budge it when asked to move it, neither could I curl my fingers. It was the strangest of sensations.

'I want to take you back, Sandra, maybe to think of happy occasions first from your past, then others. Go back to when you were a little girl. Imagine you've got a book in front of you and each year will be on a page so we'll have to turn back a few, and more and more, till we can reach 1962, when you'd be thirteen. Then 1961, when you'd be twelve. If there's anything on the page to worry you, just show me by giving the signal which I have shown you.'

# Chapter Thirty

Slowly we drifted backwards from 1993. Images were flashing through my brain, some happy, some disturbing, but nothing to make me feel I wanted to pause and talk of the memory. Fragments passed me as if I were in a long tunnel like a kaleidoscope of visions.

I frowned. One vivid picture came from Ashgrove, not long after we had moved there. I was twelve. I was wearing my best dress, a bright sunshine yellow one with some fancy embroidery and a little matching bolero, originally bought for my uncle Bobby's wedding.

I examined the memory more closely.

I'm terribly proud of my outfit, but now it hurts under my arms, and there's a faint line you can see where the hem has been let down, so it's no longer just for Sundays any more, and I'm playing out in the street. Then I go reluctantly to Allison's van that has stopped at my granny's gate. My mother's shouted at me to get items from the butcher for her and Katie, but I always look warily into the sawdust interior at the back. Dead carcasses swing about, still swaying from the vehicle's momentum, as do dark brown sticky fly papers; and the white trays are clogged with bits of minced meat, attracting large bluebottles which make me feel sick. Clutching my wares in their hastily wrapped brown paper, I run up the path to Katie's door, then stop dead as I feel the blood soak through the cotton material of my dress. I scream as a gory ox tongue rolls out of the package and right down the front of my frock, marking it so that I can never wear it again. The crimson splashes are everywhere, the rivulet down my leg and in my sock a dreadful reminder from the past. I end up yelling like a banshee and now all the linked sausages are scattered about on Katie's red Cardinal-waxed steps. My father, running from his garage to see what has occurred, curses me for the needless fuss I am making over some blood-stains, and wallops me for stupidity at dropping what will be his tea all over the path. My granny Katie also clatters me across the head to silence the shrieking, which I cannot stop for a good minute, particularly when I see her pick up the huge dripping tongue. 'What a stushie to make about a frock!' she declares as she shoves me in the door. 'God bless us, stop drawing attention to yerself!'

I let the memory drift away. I had been terribly ashamed at the time: to draw all eyes to you was the worst of offences and against my granny's code. Then, I had not been able to cope with it. As an adult, it makes perfect sense to me why the sight of all the spilt blood had had such an effect: it had brought the sexual attack I'd suffered from my unknown assailant in Dunbeth Road three years previously straight into my mind with no warning.

I did not make any signal to Hetty, and let her turn another page back, then another.

The early 1960s . . . Davy Crockett hats . . . crocodiles of children bouncing jauntily to the baths with wee string bags stuffed with ancient family towels and our elasticated, horribly ruched swimsuits.

1960, 1959 . . . wonderful memories here, of splashing in and out of tubs in back yards, skipping about through sprays of water hosed into groups of kids by adults enjoying amazing summer weather. Lurid-coloured plastic hula hoops.

1958, 1957 . . . I am absolutely fine till 1957.

'Is there something on that page worrying you?'

Hetty has spotted my finger trembling. I have still not spoken so far on the tape.

When I do, it is a childish little voice that speaks, and it astonishes me. I find myself listening to what this wee girl is saying. I'm quite detached from her, yet she is *me*.

'It's very hot. I've got flu. Lots of people have it –
my two little brothers, they're usually in my bed here,
but I'm on my own. They might get it, in the bed in
the wall, where I am, with flu . . . but it's OK, Mum's
here . . .'

Hetty tried to establish when this had taken place, and asked some questions about winter, and took me back a little to Christmas in the same period.

'My dad's not here. He's not, and we have to go on
Christmas Day to my aunt Bessie's. I've asked for the

*Girl's Crystal* annual – but he's not going to be there. We're not allowed to visit him.'

Hetty asked me about missing my father, and how I had enjoyed Christmas.

'I think the tangerines in my stockin' – he put them there, with the gold coins. He must have remembered about me, he knows the gold chocolate coins are my favourites. Children aren't allowed in the big hospital where he is ... The gold coins, I know they're from *him*. The other children at school, they said: "Your dad's been sent away to a bad place," and I said, "No, he hasn't! He's in hospital, he's hurt his back," an' they said "He's forgotten all about you," but he's not forgotten about us ... I wish there was a real Santa.'

How strange, I think to myself. This child is devastated to be without him.

We went further back, and I gave an involuntary signal to Hetty.

'Is there anything else on this page which worries you, little Sandra, aged seven?'

Loud sobbing can be heard on the tape.

'He wants me to get my friends ... There's Joy, the Elizabeths an' the others and he keeps wanting to play our games. It's horrible.'

'What's horrible about it?'

231

'Because we jus' want to play our own games, but he – he keeps *doing* these things . . .'

'Is he touching you when he plays these games?'

'He's touching my friends an' he won't stop.'

'What is he doing to them?'

'He's puttin' his hands under their clothes and he's ticklin' them, and makin' them laugh – but I don't think it's very funny.'

'You don't laugh. Does he do it to you?'

'No, but he doesn't want me to tell.'

'Does he speak about this?'

'He gives me money and ice cream, he can be so nice. He says there are some things you shouldn't say . . .'

'Some things should be secret?'

'Uh-huh. But I went to play with Elizabeth an' she came to the door and said: "I can't play with you any more, your dad does funny things," an' she's going to tell people at school.'

'And you start crying?'

'Yes, he gives me sweeties, and he gives them to my friends, and money as well. I *tried* to tell my mummy about it – I saw him. I saw him trying to take girls into his car at the park. My mum wouldn't believe me.'

'You did try to say to her, but she doesn't believe you?'

'She says he went into Molly Gardiner's shop for cigarettes for his clippie because he was going to work, an' she says how could he be talking to people at the park if he was on his way to work? He wouldn't have had time. I told her an' said why was he there? He was talkin' to them and I think he was wantin' them to go with him. I wasn't there, this time. I wasn't meant to see him, it was jist an accident that I saw him with them.'

'And did he say anything to you, Sandra?'

' "Keep yer mouth shut, in future." And he burnt me with the spoon. After I'd been trying to tell my mum, he put the teaspoon in his tea, no milk in it, an' then he put the teaspoon in my face.'

'And it's sore.'

'Yes. It's sore.'

The furthest back we went that day was 1953, when I was just four years old. I had had no recollection of this memory in my normal day-to-day living; I described the panic of my brother Norman having a fit, and the terror of going along what seemed miles and miles of great long corridors at Yorkhill, the hospital for sick children in Glasgow, which I revealed in some detail. Then:

> 'My mummy's giving me such a row! It's because I'm so . . . she keeps saying, "You're so crabbit. Why are you so crabbit?" An' then the doctor comes, an' the doctor says – the doctor's *black* – an' he says: "Can you not see that this child has chicken pox coming out? No wonder she's upset," an' there is red itchies comin' up, m'm. I'm kept in hospital too.'

Hetty explained afterwards that a number of things from this memory had caught her attention. My description of the hospital was very much as she remembered it when she had worked there years before, and my child's reaction to an ethnic face had not surprised her: immigrant doctors were rare in the early fifties. (I discovered later from my mother that the incident had indeed taken place, although she, too, had forgotten all about it. She confirmed that Norman had had a fit aged eighteen months, which had involved a short spell in hospital. And yes, I *had* ended up covered in a rash there.)

Hetty remembered flu sweeping Scotland the weekend Moira vanished. Then she said I would need one more session with her. We set a date for an October evening before my Open University examinations.

After my session with Hetty, I received a message at work, asking me to meet Lord James Douglas-Hamilton at his local surgery in Davidson's Mains, another suburb of Edinburgh, on Friday 24 September, at 5 p.m. All he could do, he said, was add his voice to John Smith's and ask the Lord Advocate why no one would meet my family or myself to enlighten us. The whole business seemed to strike him as distasteful.

My cousins asked about the hypnotherapy. Had I been a victim too?

'We haven't finished, but I don't *think* so,' I said slowly. 'Much of what has come up are the same memories I've given the police in my witness statements, but the details are just that bit sharper. We went pretty far back, but not as far as the memory with Doctor Vicky. It must have been even earlier, so I've not dealt with that nightmare.'

Not yet.

# Chapter Thirty-One

I had a meeting over tea at the Sheraton Hotel with Irene, my oldest friend, and her cousin, Sheila, who'd known me for years too. Sheila's husband, Bill, had grown up beside A and B and knew of my father. He'd told me that he did not doubt for one minute what my cousins were saying: my father's predilection for young girls was 'well known'. Bill had a colleague, Richard Kinsey, who Sheila felt could give me the best advice and recommend a top lawyer who might help our cause.

I telephoned Richard. He was a well-known expert in criminology at a Scottish university. He was generous not only with his advice, but also with his time: our chat lasted some two hours.

He told me to think carefully before launching a private prosecution, and cautioned me on its inherent difficulties. He was keen to know what my motives were. Did I realize I would be placed under the spotlight? He warned me of the personal scrutiny I would receive from the media. A private prosecution would hit the headlines, the journalists would have a field day with the daughter who wanted to see her father in court, and my husband and I could court financial ruin, if none of my cousins or myself qualified for legal aid. 'You and your family run the risk of losing your home,' he pointed out, 'and even if it doesn't come to that, how will you feel if your kids are perhaps pointed out at school – others would certainly gossip about their mum and what's in all the papers – or what if you have reporters hanging round your gate? Have you thought all this through? Because some will view your desire to see your father behind bars as a revenge trip. A moment ago you called him an evil bastard. How would that sort of vilification come across in a high court setting? You would find it incredibly hard to separate off your emotional relationship with this man when sitting in a witness box.' He reckoned that the only person who could help me, if I was determined to bring my father to court, was the top Scottish lawyer Alistair Duff.

I had also contacted Robert Reap, from Falkirk, who had spearheaded the formation of an abuse survivors' group. C had shown me a *Daily Record* article on his work, and thought he might have advice on how to lauch a private prosecution. He advised me to talk to Maggie Barry, who had written the article on him. I had never heard of her, but filed her name for reference. If she was anything like Eileen McAuley, there would be no problem, I thought.

Over the next few days, events occurred that undermined my self-confidence. I had rung Jim to have a word with him about the second of my meetings with Lord James Douglas-Hamilton, but he was out and could not be contacted. I gave Eileen a quick call instead, and was put through to her. She asked if I had heard anything more from John Smith. I had had a note from him, I told her, and then mentioned in passing that I hadn't been able to get hold of Jim. There was a short silence. 'Has he mentioned to you he's about to be moved from Airdrie CID? It's a sideways shift to Clydebank on the other side of Glasgow. It's come out of the blue.'

This was a blow, but I was getting used to taking one step forward and three back. However, I had been looking over Eileen's story on Moira's friend, Elizabeth Taylor Nimmo, which had appeared in the spring, and I felt compelled to contact her. I had told the police in my original statements about a girl I had seen with Moira and my father by his car at the park and I wanted to ask Elizabeth Taylor if it had been her. I asked Eileen how to get in touch with her. Eileen checked her notes to make sure that Mrs Nimmo would not object to her passing on the address, then gave it to me. 'She was very helpful,' she said. 'She wants to see justice done as much as you do – though I doubt if she will have made the connection that the man interviewed three times in Leeds who's prime suspect for Moira is *also* the same pensioner from Monklands whose nieces are claiming sexual abuse.'

'I don't see why the public can't be told of that link,' I said.

'There's no way we can publish that. If we did the Procurator Fiscal would be down on us like a ton of bricks. It's highly prejudicial.'

On the last Saturday in September, Jim, Billy and their wives came to dinner at our home. We had a pleasant evening, with our friends Janet and John also among the gathering. Although Jim insisted he would still be technically in charge of the case, I feared he would find it almost impossible to keep control from another police division. Also, everything was being shifted from Airdrie back to Coatbridge. We'd gone full circle.

# Chapter Thirty-Two

The blow of Jim McEwan's sudden move to Clydebank was quickly followed by a second, even more upsetting, event.

One crisp October morning, I went to pick up the mail and found my heart jumping into my throat. A plain brown envelope was lying on the floor, and unfamiliar assertive dark blue handwriting leaped out at me. My knees buckled and I almost keeled over. Someone with a bold, heavy, backhand style had scrawled in large script a name followed by our address.

I laid it on our dining table, and sat down. I couldn't bring myself to open it.

Ronnie asked what was wrong.

I pointed to the letter. 'I think it's hate mail.'

Horrified, he grabbed it and stared in puzzlement at the name.

It was addressed to Moira Anderson, care of our home.

The letter contained one page with about fifteen lines of the same firm script.

*Dear Moira,*

*    I understand you may be launching a private prosecution against your father and I would like to speak to you about*

*this. I enclose an article I wrote recently which has prompted a lot of feedback and I am now in the process of putting a second one together.*

*I would appreciate you getting in touch with me either at the office or my home. Bob Reap gave me your address because I have been doing some work on children who have been sexually abused, and I wondered if I could have a word with you. I look forward to hearing from you.*

The letter, signed 'Maggie Barry', and dated 29 September 1993, was headed with the logo of the *Evening Times* and *Glasgow Herald*.

I felt anger rise in me. How dare this woman not get her facts right? The telephone rang. I grabbed it and a voice at the other end said, 'Maggie Barry here. May I speak to Moira?'

I gasped. 'This is Sandra Brown. I have just received and read your letter.' I chose my words carefully. 'Perhaps it's just as well you rang. I'm so angry, I was thinking of ringing you to complain.'

'To complain?' she sounded bewildered. 'Isn't Moira Anderson there?'

'No. She hasn't been for almost forty years either,' I spoke through gritted teeth, 'and if you're wondering who I am, I am the woman who has accused her father of abducting Moira from Coatbridge in 1957. You've got your information all wrong. I don't think any newspaper editor would be thrilled at the way you've managed to upset me, trying to contact the child I have claimed my father is responsible for murdering. I've just had a huge shock.'

There was a brief silence. She offered to come and apologise and we agreed to meet a few evenings hence.

A day or two later Lord James Douglas-Hamilton's secretary contacted me. He had received a reply from Crown Office and had sent me a copy of it. Lord Rodger had written to him with assurances that both enquiries reported by the Procurator Fiscal's office at Airdrie had been given 'careful consideration'.

The Lord Advocate added:

*I have had an opportunity to consider the papers and am satisfied that the decision in relation to the allegations of sexual misconduct against Mrs Brown's father represented a proper exercise of the Crown's discretion. As you are aware, the Crown's reasons for its decisions are not disclosed.*

Within hours, however, this letter was followed by a copy of the reply John Smith had received from the Lord Advocate. Although both documents carried the same date, 5 October 1993, John Smith had received much more information, even if it was negative.

A paragraph in the middle leaped out at me.

*In relation to the disappearance of Moira Anderson there has been an active investigation by Strathclyde Police notwithstanding the length of time which has elapsed since the girl's disappearance and the difficulties which that has inevitably caused. Crown Counsel have had the benefit of full reports of the outcome of the various police enquiries, some of which they have directed. While recent enquiries have still not explained Moira Anderson's disappearance, Crown Counsel have noted the results and instructed the*

*Procurator Fiscal to report any further evidence or
information which comes to light. I would only add that
while Mrs Brown appears to have some knowledge of the
enquiries, some of the information which she appears to have
provided to you is inaccurate and some incorrect.*

I reread the last sentence in astonishment.

*The police also investigated allegations against Mrs Brown's
father, and interviewed him in connexion with 5 allegations
of lewd and libidinous conduct involving four girls. The
results of these enquiries were also seen by Crown Counsel
and after careful consideration they instructed that there
were to be no criminal proceedings against him in these
matters. As you are aware, the Crown's reasons for its
decisions are not disclosed and remain confidential.
However, I have had an opportunity to consider the papers
and am satisfied that the decision represented a proper exercise
of their discretion. Again, I must comment that some of the
information which Mrs Brown appears to have provided is
incorrect.*

*I was concerned to note that she had commented to you
on the approach and attitude of David Griffiths, the Senior
Procurator Fiscal Depute at Airdrie. He has been involved
in these enquiries from their outset and has been the author
of a number of reports to Crown Counsel. I have read his
reports which are informative, thorough, helpful and
prepared in the professional manner I would expect from a
senior member of staff.*

*Following Crown Counsel's decision in relation to the
allegations against her father, Dr Griffiths agreed to meet
Mrs Brown as the spokesperson for her family. I understand*

*that he spent some two hours with her when he
endeavoured to discuss the matter rationally and sensitively
with her. In the circumstances I am saddened that Mrs
Brown has seen fit to criticize Dr Griffiths in the way she
has.*

   *Yours,*
   *Alan (Rodger of Earlsferry)*

What incorrect information had I given? I searched out
my original letter to them, and the letter I had written to
John Smith, seeking ambiguities or anything that could be
misconstrued, to no avail. I could not fathom from their
reply to John Smith to which sections of information they
were referring.

I was furious. The inference to the Labour leader was
that I was not a credible person as I had fed him false
data. The reiteration of this point reinforced a question
mark over my integrity. I also noted how I was subtly
undermined in the parting shots at the end, with the
emphasis on the 'rational and sensitive' Depute attempting
to discuss the issue with me. The iciness of our meeting
came back to me: there had been no hysterical raised
voices, but I had broken a cardinal rule. I had said I would
complain and I had done so, daring to voice my criticism
of him as an individual and them as an organization. The
Lord Advocate was simply closing ranks. Lord Rodger
had turned a complaint about one of his staff and lack of
information on a decision into a query about my trust-
worthiness and a complaint about my attitude.

I was still upset when Ronnie appeared for our evening
meal. I showed him the letter. 'If you read between the
lines they're saying I'm a crackpot. I don't know what

they find inaccurate. I'll have to show it to Jim and ask his advice.'

He read it, and shook his head in stunned silence. 'Damn right.'


Over the following week three meetings were scheduled. I was returning to Hetty McKinnon's home for our second session, and two nights later, on 12 October, Maggie Barry was visiting me. Also, I had organized a rendezvous with Jim at the main Strathclyde police HQ in Pitt Street, Glasgow.

'Don't forget, Sandra,' my husband pointed cheerily at the calendar we keep on the wall with four columns for the family's various commitments, 'I've booked theatre tickets for the Lyceum for our anniversary on the 16th.' We were still attempting to juggle an otherwise normal life through this period.

I was pleased to see Hetty again, and in no time at all, I was venturing back through that kaleidoscopic tunnel of flashbacks.

A gallery of faces paraded before me: Miss Mack, my formidable teacher in Primary 7, with her Jackie Kennedy-style pillar-box red suit. She was marking my essay on the Matthew Arnold poem, 'The Forsaken Merman', debating with me the comment I had made about how much easier life was for men, and how I wished I was a boy. Her shocked face had stencilled arches of eyebrows shooting upwards into a midnight black razor-cut hair-style. She was making a cutting aside to a teaching student about such decidedly unfeminine views, but the younger woman spoke to me quietly later, and when she questioned why

I had written it, I did not hesitate to tell her the truth: 'Ye kin do anything ye like, Miss, when ye're a man.'

Hetty took me to 1957 once again. The tape was running on, but only Hetty's tranquil voice was recording. Then came the familiar echo of my voice, with its strong Scots accent, from childhood when we lived at Dunbeth Road.

> 'There's a lady visiting my mum, and I'm helping with the san'wiches. I'm pressin' the banana on them for the lady an' she's askin' 'bout ma dad. I'm listenin' in the kitchen 'cos he's away. My mum's whisperin'. I've not to hear. An' the other san'wiches, with the brown bread, the stuff on the meat is kind of – like glass. I've taken it off, it's jelly stuff an' it looks horrible. Don't think Ah'm gonna get a row fur doin' it. They call it gammon. The lady's sayin' why dontcha go out and play? She wants to speak to my mummy. I've not to be there . . .'

'And that's upsetting you. Do you know who this lady is?'

> 'She's someone who's got a baby in 'er tummy, I think – but I got a row for askin' about that too. An' my dad's not here, and they don't wanna tell me where he is, I've gotta go out and play . . . My mum's angry 'cos I've asked what "pregnant" means. She says I'm only eight an' I'm too wee to know about that.'

'And do you go outside to play?'

'M'm, but the lady doesn't have any children with her. There's nobody outside except me playin'. Her tummy's fat. I know that's what happens, but my mum's upset with me askin'. I'm jus' goin' to go in and get my Enid Blyton diary and put my writing in there . . .'

'What happens then?'
There is silence, then:

'I went intae the cupboard. I wis lookin' for the Christmas presents an' I wis wonderin' about Santa – an' there's these books my daddy has about, *Exchange 'n' Mart* it's called. An' there's horrible magazines 'n' comics and things that belong to my daddy. It's horrible the things they're doin' to these ladies, an' I'll jis' put them back an' cover them up, an' not say anything . . .'

'You're scared. And you're going to put them all out of sight?'

'I know that he'd some of these pictures he showed to my friend.'

Here the child named one of my buddies from Dunbeth Road. Here was an incident I had not previously recalled.

'He made her kiss him and he gave us all sweeties.'

'When did he show them to Elizabeth?'

'He did things – in the back of the car. Her mummy says that she's not to go back in the car because Elizabeth's got oil on her good dress. So they've not to go back in the car. It's because their mum's very angry about the stains on their clothes an' he's – you know – he keeps givin' sweets to my friends and me. An' I *told* my mummy 'bout the other girls he gave sweeties to, as well, at the park. But she didn't believe me about that. An' I think . . . he wanted them to go into his car, too, at Dunbeth Park.'

'Who were these other girls?'

'They were big girls, two big girls. They're not my friends, but they were going to go into his car till I went over to speak to them. It was Marjorie's big sister, an' her friend Beth. An' they *were* going to with 'im . . . but I told my mummy about that.'

'And what was Marjorie's big sister called?'

'Majorie's sister Moira an' her friend Beth. An' I was with Marilyn Twycross an' we were playin' at the park. I think he wanted . . . to go away with them, an' do things too. My mum – she wouldn't believe me. But he *wis* givin' them sweeties. He wis in his car.'

'And what did you say when you went up to him?'

'I saw him, through the park gates. I thought he'd come to get me. He's in his bus uniform, an' his hat an' his badge. The letters are MM 9507, an' he told me that's his PSV number, an' inside his pocket he's got his watch on a chain. An' when I went over, he said, "Whit are ye doin' here?" I thought, He's seen me comin'. An' they jist went away . . .'

'And what did you feel like then, when he was saying that to you?'

'He didn't want me to come along. He wanted me out of the road. But I'm really worried about them, because I think he wanted to take them away. An' not with me there.'

'And what do you think would have happened if he'd taken them away?'

'He would do bad things – again. An' I wouldn't be there to make him *stop*.'

'Did you make him stop before?'

'I banged on the glass, with the ice creams an' I said to him, "I'm gonna tell my mummy," but he was right 'cos she wouldn't believe me—'

'And what did you see him do through the glass? What was he doing, Sandra?'

'He was touchin' my friends. Under their pants. I think he wasn't in the front seat of the car when I came back, he was in the back, with them. An' I

can't see properly, but I look in . . . it's all misty, an'
I bang to make him . . .'

'Stop. What does he do then?'

'Wound the window down, an' took the ice creams,
an' told me to keep the money I had left. He's angry
with me, he's angry. He's shouting at me. Calling me
a liar . . .'

Hetty went further back. I could see myself walking to
school with Jim, my first boyfriend at age six, the two of
us arguing over conkers. Then came my memories of the
trip to Callander with Baxter's bus staff and the knickerbocker glory. Even further back I was jumping off dykes
and wash houses, thrilled with the baseball-style boots I
had pestered my mother to buy. And now I was very
young, way before school.

Hetty asked if I had sore bits on my body anywhere,
and there it was. The visit from Dr Vicky, trainee physician
in the family. I remembered the excruciating pain of
passing urine, the deep-seated cramping in my intestines,
and the relief of hugging a hot-water bottle tightly to my
abdomen. I held my breath, and the memory began to
fade; I was aware of no adult touching me anywhere it
was sore.

# Chapter Thirty-Three

The sense of relief was indescribable as I left Hetty's sandstone villa. We had discussed her amalgamated notes from the two sessions and she firmly pronounced that she did not believe me to have been a victim of incest in childhood, despite my father's paedophile behaviour which I had witnessed.

As I drove back to Edinburgh, a huge weight seemed to roll off my shoulders with each passing mile.

On Tuesday evening Maggie Barry turned up on our doorstep, looking apprehensive. She apologized profusely over the mistaken identity, then interviewed me in a fairly subdued way, asking the question I now expected. Quietly I declared I had not been a victim of my dad's sexual practices. She looked up. 'Let me get this right. There's been no link made so far between the man quizzed down south in recent months, about Moira Anderson's disappearance in 1957, and the pensioner whose relatives in the Monklands are accusing him of abuse from the sixties?'

'No, the general public aren't aware of that connection, and you can't link them.' I pointed out what Eileen had told me, that lawyers would say that he would not be able to secure a fair and unprejudiced trial, and the door would be slammed on any court case.

'We'll see.' Maggie Barry shrugged. When she had gone, I was left with a nagging feeling of uncertainty.

I met up with Jim at Pitt Street HQ, and we caught up with the news. He was enjoying his new post, but had arranged for a machine to filter the levels of silt in Witchwood Pond. This operation would take some weeks, he said, and a team of frogmen would eventually be able to explore the bottom with an unrestricted view.

He frowned when I passed him the letter Maggie Barry had sent. Then I showed him the letters from Lord James Douglas-Hamilton and John Smith. Jim read and reread them.

'Inaccuracies? About what?'

'Exactly. I haven't a clue what they find inaccurate,' I said indignantly. 'But here's the original letter I sent off. Plus all the correspondence I typed up to both the politicians. I've gone through it in detail. See if you can spot what isn't correct.'

Jim began to read, then groaned. 'I've just spotted it, and it's a cracker.' He glanced up. 'You report here that Griffiths didn't appear fully conversant with all the facts about your dad – including not knowing of his prison sentence in the mid-eighties down south.'

'But my dad *was* in jail then.' I looked at Jim in stupefaction. 'You'd his mug shot on the wall, with an ID number under it, in your office in Airdrie. You asked me to identify him for you the first time I went there.'

'I don't deny it,' said Jim, 'and I even remember telling you your dad *had been in trouble with the law* but I have the sinking feeling that you've picked up that information the wrong way. I don't recall a sentence, so maybe he got community service or a fine or something in Leeds, but not jail.'

'But his photograph, and number?' I was aghast now. 'Wasn't it taken in prison?'

Jim shook his head. 'It was certainly taken mid-eighties, when he was in trouble about obtaining a mortgage under false pretences and deception. But that's what they do to everyone who's in for questioning at the nick – they all get mug shots taken by a police photographer, and get given a number.'

I put my head in my hands. I had scored an own goal. Angrily, I reflected that I had given Crown Office the perfect opportunity to claim that I'd provided misinformation.

'Well, it's done now and there's no going back.' Jim passed me the letters. 'I can see how you came to that conclusion, given what I had said. It doesn't change the fact that Mr Griffiths alluded to your dad having served his sentence, without acknowledging that these crimes against your cousins followed it.'

'You're right, Jim,' I said. 'As far as they're concerned, he's done his time. But not for Moira, and not for my cousins.'

'I advise you to put what's a genuine misunderstanding to one side,' he said. 'Whatever happens, you can bounce back from it, and that's what to do now. Forget the murder investigation, and concentrate on your cousins. This is about getting justice for them – Moira's past all help. So acknowledge that, fight for compensation for them, and do it right. See it through for their sakes.'

But I knew I could never give up on Moira. It was Moira with whom everything had started, and she was the reason I had approached Billy in the first place, long before I had ever known about my own relatives. I said, 'I'll do all I can to secure a meeting with Lord Rodger. Even if he agrees purely for public relations, it'll do. But count on it – we won't give up.'

I felt strong, despite discovering the stupid error I had made, which had cost us dearly, but I had a feeling that for what lay ahead I would need incredible reserves of energy.

'Good luck with your exam!' Jim called as I drove off.

It loomed within days, and I needed peace to revise for it. Maggie Barry, however, had other ideas. She rang me out of the blue. 'Hi. It's just to let you know my paper will carry the story tomorrow evening. Lawyers are checking out the possibilities of us naming him, but we'll certainly highlight your dad *is* the same person involved in both the stories coming from the Monklands in recent weeks.'

'But what about repercussions?' I asked. 'What about Eileen's prediction that doing that could knock a court case on the head? Don't you need to get permission from anyone to do that?' I could not think straight.

Maggie Barry, however, was unequivocal. 'We don't need permission. My boss wants to run with it in tomorrow's edition.'

After she rang off my mind was still in turmoil. I had spoken freely to her, in my own home, and now she was to use what I had given her. She didn't need permission.

I contacted Eileen's office next day. 'I don't believe it!' she gasped. 'They can't identify him and link the two things without running the risk of libel. If they go ahead, the whole thing steps up a gear again, and it will go crazy. Look, if it's all going to blow, will you think about speaking to a national reporter, on my recommendation? Someone who'll treat this the way it should be handled, to give maximum publicity to the miscarriage of justice going on here.'

'I don't know. I've my exam on Thursday. Who are you thinking of?' I was wary.

'Melanie Reid. She's to be trusted, believe me,' said Eileen. '*Sunday Mail* columnist and one helluva reporter. Think about it. I'll ring you later.'

At work I tried to keep my mind off her words. As I left college, I ventured into the nearby Livingston shopping centre, and purchased a copy of the *Evening Times*. ABUSE PROBE POLICE IN MURDER MYSTERY was Maggie Barry's headline. I noticed that my father's name was not used throughout her half-page article, but that she had revealed that 'police have been talking to one man about the unsolved disappearance of Coatbridge girl Moira Anderson in 1957 *and* the sexual abuse of four young girls from the same area, now grown women'.

I told Ronnie that things were taking an explosive turn. 'Maybe when I've done the exam tomorrow we should go away for the weekend, right out of Scotland. It could all get nasty.' I rang Eileen and told her I would see Melanie Reid, then spoke to our friends Peter and Gillian, who lived in Wolverhampton. Surprised, but delighted to hear from us, they confirmed they had no plans for the coming weekend.

I felt relieved I had taken Thursday off. My exam was scheduled for the afternoon, but instead of being able to spend the morning calming myself and getting into the right frame of mind, I was visited by a *Sunday Mail* staff photographer, who introduced himself as Henry. He would take some photos, he explained, unpacking a battery of camera equipment, and Melanie would come to see me later in the evening. His portrait would be from the back, so that nobody would recognize me. 'Only your nearest and dearest.' He smiled, not realizing the irony of his words as he looked for a location. His eyes brightened as he spotted a small statue I have in our bedroom, of a young girl, hunched over her knees, whose face is hidden, but whose posture conveys sadness. Somewhat bemused, but wishing to indulge his enthusiasm, I obligingly perched on our bed and gazed out of the window, so that the statue and I were framed together.

After Henry had gone, I set off for the city centre. My heart thudded into my boots when I saw the sea of wooden desks inside the examination hall, but the hour of reckoning had arrived. If I did not know the course material by now, I never would.

The three hours passed in a flash, and then I headed home, where a tall, fair-haired journalist was speaking to my husband in our lounge. She smiled reassuringly as I kicked off my shoes, and poured us a drink. We discussed our respective jobs. I had read some of her columns, and we had similar views on several subjects. Then, delicately, she asked me about child abuse. I told her of my childhood, my father, Moira and my cousins. She only interrupted with an occasional question. She asked about William, the psychic, and I explained that Eileen could put her in contact with him. When she asked the location of the pond to which William had taken the police, I would say only that it was on the outskirts of Coatbridge.

More than two hours passed. I tucked my feet under

me, and pressed my knuckles into my eyelids, shattered by the long day. Melanie surveyed me. 'You're exhausted,' she declared, tucking her notes in her bag. 'Thanks for sharing such an amazing story. It's right the public should know what happened to Moira, and your family. It'll appear this Sunday. How will your mother take it?'

'It'll be devastating for her and my brothers,' I said quietly. 'We're going to go away for the weekend, with the children. To friends down in the English Midlands.'

# Chapter Thirty-Four

On our way back from our trip, stopping at a motorway service area on the M6, I had no doubt that I had certainly blown the whistle. My eyes widened as I saw rows of Sunday papers on full view, with a front-page picture of Moira on the *Sunday Mail* prominently placed, and the headline screaming beside it: MY DAD KILLED THIS GIRL.

People were discussing it in wonder, as I stood behind them in the checkout queue, surrounded by Hallowe'en merchandise. 'In't it queer,' a lady was saying, 'that such a thing should come out so long after?'

'Nowt surprises me these days, but it's hard to imagine it's his own lass saying such things about him. Likely she's doing it for the money.'

I wanted to tell the Lancashire couple who had said this that in this case no cheque-book journalism had been involved, but I didn't. When I returned to our car, I handed the newspaper to Ronnie. He glanced at the headline, the portrait of Moira, and the double-page spread inside. As well as Melanie's article, it featured a photograph of an old-fashioned Baxter's bus of the correct era, a less well-known faded snapshot of Moira in a cotton summer dress, a wide-angled view of the pond at Witchwood, with high flats shown in the distance, and, of course, Henry's picture of me by our window, gazing at the small portrait photograph he'd given me of Moira.

I did not utter another word all the way home.

We got back to an answering machine full of messages, some irate, some bewildered, others compassionate. My mother finally got through, and said my brothers had been hitting the roof. Where on earth had I been? To put all this sensational stuff in the Sunday papers was bad enough, but why disappear in the middle of it? 'I hope you know what people are saying about you,' she said. 'I heard the whispers when I was at the kirk this morning.' She repeated what the couple at the service area had said.

'And do you believe for one minute that I would do something like that for money?' I hated to hear her sound so upset, but I realized why she needed to go on the attack: my mother was full of the most awful guilt nowadays, acknowledging that there *had* been signs years ago that all was not well in our family, signs that she had been unable to bring herself to face.

'Well, no, of course I don't think you've accepted thousands of pounds from a paper. I'm just telling you that the gossips are having a field day and some will think that was your motive, Sandra, to get lots of money from a family catastrophe.'

I waited till her sobs had subsided a little. 'The main thing is that you and I know the truth, Mum,' I said. 'All my life people have said how like you I am. It happens to be right. *You* know why I've exposed it all, and so do I, and I don't give a toss what the gossips think. You ignore them, and they can think what they like. The truth is what matters, that's all.'

A few days later, a reporter named Marion Scott, a

colleague of Melanie Reid, rang me. She stunned me with the news that she was going to visit my father to give him the opportunity to reply to my allegations. 'It was some story Melanie did, and it's had the phone ringing non-stop,' she announced brightly, 'including, you'll be interested to hear, ex-cops who agree with you that the original investigation was cock-up of the year at the time. It's caused a real stushie. That's what you were after, right?'

'Yep, right,' I agreed miserably. 'That was the idea. You said you're going south?'

'We have to keep a balance here,' she replied. 'He's bound to have seen it, with Leeds having the high ex-Scots population it does, and our circulation figures down there. He should have the chance to put his views in print. So I'm off, to see if I can speak to him, and follow the story up. Melanie's gone down with flu.'

It was clear that Marion was thrilled to be given the assignment.

'You're going to face him alone, and confront him about the accusations?' My voice faltered. Marion's confidence amazed me.

'Nae problem. It's just a matter of keeping an element of surprise, then seeing if he passes the Daz doorstep challenge.'

I protested about her safety. He might go for her. Did she know he was still a big man? She could not go alone.

'Nah, I don't think I'll be at risk, but as I'm five feet nothing, they're insisting I have a heavy with me.' She laughed, then suddenly her voice became serious. 'Haven't you thought even once about going there to confront him about that horrendous conversation you had when your grandmother died?'

I was silent for a moment. Then I said, 'You're right, I have. I tried convincing my husband to let me go with the cops down south, but he put his foot down, and Jim McEwan wouldn't hear of it.'

'Well, there you are, then.' Marion's voice implied that I now had the perfect opportunity. 'Let's see,' she added, while I started to shake like a leaf, 'this is Monday, and the idea's to buy two tickets for Leeds from Glasgow early Thursday 4 November, on the first flight. Think it over and I'll phone you back. It isn't any problem to make it three of us going – you, me, and our escort for protection.'

She rang off abruptly.

Ronnie was reluctant to give his views one way or the other, but I could see he was perturbed. Clearly, he himself felt no fear of a pensioner in his seventies, albeit one of over six feet who had been an exceptionally strong man in his prime; his concerns were for me.

I had no time to ask my cousins what they thought about me visiting Leeds, and I knew Jim would advise me against it. I decided to consult William by phone.

He was encouraging, and predicted I was strong enough to cope. 'Seeing him again may not have the outcome you want, Sandra, because this man will do any-thing to save his own skin. He doesn't have a conscience, and will blame everyone else under the sun. He'll probably even try to pin it on a former buddy. Everyone except himself. But he knows in his heart he is responsible for all the things you have openly said.' He also foresaw that I'd come back more convinced than before, with my resolve strengthened.

On Wednesday evening, I jumped into my car and drove to Milngavie in Glasgow, where Marion Scott had arranged to meet me. She was tiny, with dark brown eyes in a pale, creamy face, and glossy jet black hair. She described the arrangements for an early-morning call at 4.30 a.m. It all felt surreal to me. 'Child abusers really piss me off,' she said, lighting a cigarette the moment she had stubbed one out. 'I can't wait to meet him.'

I had now met several types of journalist, but Marion was different. Her language was the saltiest I had heard in ages, but I couldn't help liking her. Perhaps her earthy sense of humour kept her sane in the tough world of journalism – that, or the fags she smoked non-stop.

We met, as planned, in the small hours. Our male escort, Marion announced, would be waiting to rendez-vous with us at Glasgow airport. I kept up with her tiny black figure as she pelted along the tarmac into the terminal.

My jaw dropped and I almost laughed when I recognized Henry, the photographer, standing bleary-eyed by the ticket desk, almost bent in two by the amount of equipment he was carrying. He smiled at me. 'Henry's our great big male protector, is he?' I hissed at Marion on our way to the departure lounge. 'I'm the biggest of the three of us and I'm less than five feet six!'

'Yeees, well.' Marion burst out laughing. 'Never mind. Safety in numbers, perhaps.'

Our Loganair flight was due to depart before 7 a.m. The fog outside, it was then announced, was delaying our departure. As we sat waiting for its call, I reflected wryly that if my father was aggressive, Henry was not going to be a deterrent. I grinned at him. He was keen, he said, to snap a photograph of my father for publication.

This worried me: any identifiable snapshot could jeopardize possible legal procedures. If a meeting was granted to me by Lord Rodger in Edinburgh, it might be possible to have the Crown Office rethink its decision and have my dad charged for the offences against my cousins . . . I did not want that chance to vaporize.

A voice announced over the tannoy that our flight was ready for take-off, but Leeds airport was fog-bound. We could expect further problems.

We trooped aboard, and as the small plane took off through the thick haar blanketing most of Glasgow, I told myself that, as usual, the fates were protecting Alexander Gartshore. It would be no easy journey to his home.

Sure enough, my fears were confirmed when we were diverted to Teesside airport, and placed on a coach that would take us, they said, to our original destination. Of course, what the announcement neglected to say was that this involved crossing the mist-shrouded Yorkshire moors.

The nightmare coach trip seemed never-ending. Eventually, though, we picked up a hired car, and sped towards the correct area of Leeds. It was fairly easy to locate the Burmantofts suburb of the city, its tower blocks visible from a distance. The one my father lived in was like any other grimy inner-city fortress, with broken glass strewn around an entry system installed by the main entrance. It reminded me of Alcatraz, but small kids were playing on the concrete.

Henry and Marion were as nonplussed as I was at the entry system, and I had not bargained for having to speak into a microphone. We all looked at each other in horror, then Marion indicated I would have to make an initial overture to get us in. I closed my eyes and gulped. To make it even more surreal, Marion pointed to her capacious bag and showed me a cassette recorder, hidden in its depths, as small as her mobile phone, but already running a cartridge.

'Don't worry.' She grinned. 'Whatever he says, we'll have him taped. Henry will hang about down here, and if anything happens that worries me, I'll give him the signal that we want help, and he's to come to the rescue.'

Henry smiled weakly at me, then trotted off, saying he hoped we'd be able to get my father to come out of the building so he could achieve a clear shot of him.

Marion's bravado was infectious, and I put my lips to the mike, terrified to hear a response, and yet acknowledging I would be despondent if we had come all this way only to find that my father was out. I buzzed the correct number, and felt my throat close as I heard a responding click. The voice at the other end sounded more Yorkshire than Scots. I said my name. There was silence, then, 'Is that you, love? Come on up.'

# Chapter Thirty-Five

'It's Sandra. I've come down from Edinburgh to see you.'

My father's tall figure wove towards Marion and me as we stepped out of the lift. He approached us, and I saw that he was smiling benignly. Would he say something that would lead us to the truth? He certainly did not look as if he expected trouble as he ushered us to his door.

As we entered a dingy hallway, I told myself that while a full confession was perhaps too much to hope for, I wanted to appeal to any shred of decency he had. Surely he would see that it was time for him to come clean, to sort things out before it was too late, and right a great wrong?

He surveyed us speculatively as he shut the door.

'I've not brought the boys in blue with me, Dad,' I said hesitantly, 'or even the girls for that matter, so you needn't worry. Ronnie didn't want me to come here at all, he would only agree if I brought a friend. This is Marion. We need to speak to you, Dad, and get some answers, for the sake of my sanity, and others.'

Marion smiled ingratiatingly while I scrutinized my father's expression as he gestured us through to the main room of his flat. So far he had not uttered a word.

His reaction to me was interesting. Daughters who

have accused their parent of murder and child abuse do not expect to be welcomed with open arms. I might have imagined I would be accused of being a lying bitch, who should go straight back to Scotland, or I thought he could have flared up in righteous anger about me daring to make such outrageous allegations about him. Neither happened.

He motioned us to sit down, and I glanced round briefly for the first time. There was so much junk we both had to move stuff to clear spaces on his furniture. The whole flat looked as if some gang had been in and smashed it up.

The room was flooded with good natural light from a large window, which gave an excellent view across the whole of Leeds, and helped to combat the violent tangerine wallpaper, patterned with wild swirls that could have induced migraine in minutes. The few pieces of furniture were meagre and basic.

As soon as we were seated, we began to grill him. I begged him to have some compassion and put people's minds at rest and Marion implored him to have some decency, to think of his daughter who'd been through hell for months now, and she asked him to describe just what did happen that day in February 1957.

My father reddened and blustered. If anyone had been going through hell, it had been him, he declared. We got all the details of his prostate problem. Smokescreen. Marion and I exchanged a look. It was poor-me stuff, designed to gain our sympathy. It would not wash.

In she came with direct questions about why he had said the things he had to me at Granny Jenny's funeral. Had he been attempting to shift a load of guilt off his chest? She reminded him that everyone in Scotland now knew he had been the driver on Moira's last journey, that his own father had searched for the child in his son's home and on his bus, and had died convinced that he was Moira's killer.

My dad became agitated.

I tried psychology, I tried tears, I tried appealing to his conscience, but I could see why the police had run out of strategies with my father. I was not making much headway, until he said how much he wanted things resolved. When Moira had alighted from his bus at Woolworths in Coatbridge all those years ago, she'd had a 'mystery friend' with her. If she could be traced, that would clear it all up. He had mentioned this unknown girl to Jim's team, he insisted. Yes, absolutely. He remembered her particularly because all three of them had got off *together*.

'You got off with them?' I brought my head up with a jerk. This had not been in the transcript I'd read. 'You told the police *Moira* got off, and you waved goodbye.'

Backtracking as he realized I knew the contents of the police tapes, my dad added, 'Well, yes. I telt the polis she got off, and I mind she looked back at me. I was in my cab, and she mouthed, "Cheerio," tae me, through the windae, then I'd to get out tae let on ma relief driver. Ah last saw her, wi' this other lass, going through the swing doors at Woolies, right as rain. Aye, Ah wis the last tae see her, like Ah said at the time I was interviewed, but she left me safe and sound, I know that.'

'You were never interviewed at the station,' I said flatly. 'So you got off with her?'

'Right after them,' he put in hastily. 'Ah went home, for Ah'd a break. An hour or so.'

I stared at him. I knew from my own experience that

it had not been my father's custom ever to take a break that involved going home for an hour between shifts. My mother could only ever recall him doing such a thing once, when toothache became so unbearable he had nipped home to put whisky on a plug of cotton wool; the event had stuck in her mind, because he had then taken himself off to Mr Downie's surgery in Whifflet to have the molar removed. He did not normally pop home for a short break, and she knew he had not done so that particular Saturday.

Marion spoke of the abuse to which he had subjected various children, while I sighed at his indifference. Names from the past, that was all they represented to him. She berated him about the effects on kiddies of such a tender age. She mentioned A's name at this point and, to my shock, he suddenly ventured a detached observation. 'Aye, ye're right about her.' He sighed. Yes, he had molested her, but it had happened just the once, when she was about fifteen. Marion's eyelids lowered, and I knew she was wondering if her tape was still running, because we had had two tiny breakthroughs in the past couple of minutes. We were wearing him down, seeing glimmers through the tissue of lies that he had spun for so long he half believed them. I held my breath.

'Aye, Ah admit that Ah did touch her, but it wis never the full thing,' my dad chipped in now quite briskly. 'Everythin' else, like, but she wis a relative, and I liked her ma and pa, so it wisnae the whole hog. And she was fifteen, like Ah said.'

'That's not what she says.' I stared at him. 'It wasn't just once and she wasn't fifteen at the time, Dad. She was eight the first time.'

He shot me a furious look. He insisted then, as anger

built up in him, that everyone was telling lies about him. All these children I had known when I was little, friends, neighbours I had played with, and my cousins – they were all making it up, these kids, he didn't know why. I pointed out that not all his accusers were children he had known. Some of his former colleagues had made some allegations to the police every bit as damning as mine. The only difference, I reflected wryly, was that the cops had had to go to them, whereas I'd gone to the police myself.

'They're all being paid,' he asserted. 'All of this comes from up there. It's a campaign, Ah tell ye, a vendetta goin' on against me by them . . .' He pointed towards a copy of the *Airdrie and Coatbridge Advertiser*. 'They'd no right to start it all up. Ah've gone through hell, wi' two strokes, ye know. And the doctor says Ah've got palpitations now, tae.'

'*You* started it yourself,' I pointed out, pleased that his anger was taking us forward a little, 'when you spoke to me the day Granny died. You were the one who linked yourself to Moira. You were the one who said you were last to speak to her. You had me cracking up with worry. Then it turned out all the stuff you gave me about going to help the cops at the time was garbage. Grandpa was right about you all along.'

'I'd a good relationship with my father.' He shot an indignant look at me. 'I don't know why he came to look in the house and insisted on searchin' ma bus. Ah took him and Ah opened that boot and Ah showed him. Ah telt him, "How could Ah do somethin' like that wi' all thae passengers around and a conductress tae? How could I possibly harm a wean like her?"'

I gazed at him as if hypnotized. I thought, These are

like the rhetorical questions you fed my mother, which made her feel terrible for even thinking them. It was quite a strategy, I had to agree.

'Naw, how could he think it? How could I do such a thing?'

Oh, you could, I thought, you could. Particularly if you managed to get rid of the passengers and your conductress, and achieved your goal, which was to be alone with that kiddie. Particularly if you can convince yourself my cousin A was seven years older than she actually was. Particularly if you've convinced yourself that whatever went wrong with Moira was all the child's fault.

I knew from Jim, too, that my father had insisted he had never had the T-key of EVA 56 to gain access to the boot, yet here he was telling Marion and me that he had used it to reassure his father that the boot contained no child's body.

'Oh, yes,' he smiled now at Marion, repeating, 'I'd a good relationship with my father. In fact, he forgave me on his deathbed for everything that had happened.'

Marion raised her eyebrow at this.

'Well, that's very interesting,' I put in, 'since I don't recall you being at his deathbed at all. You didn't show up till the day of the funeral.'

He recovered quickly, and added coolly, 'What Ah meant was my mother told me later he had forgiven me completely.'

So manipulative, so skilful.

He was angry again, now, that I'd dared to voice any doubts. He couldn't understand it, he said, pacing up and down, why everyone told lies about him, always painting him as a villain when it wasn't true. He said he was fed

SANDRA BROWN

up being questioned. Interviews, he ranted at us, it was
nothing but interviews, and the police just picked on him.
He was a fall guy, and over the years he'd got fed up with
it. They treated him like a black sheep too, always looking
for things to pin on him. All these kids, he argued, who'd
nothing better to do than tell lies about him, it was
pathetic. He'd kept count and over the years the figure
was over a hundred – in fact, they'd questioned him about
one hundred and twenty-two kids.

My eyes widened in disbelief.

Marion and I could not even look at each other. I knew
my jaw was agape. Had I misheard? But no. My dad
repeated the exact figure. 'One hundred and twenty-two,
Ah tell ye!'

He thought it ridiculous. Some kids he'd been questioned about he didn't even know properly, or he couldn't
remember their names after all these years, and some he'd
bought sweets for and had been friendly with, though now
he wished he hadn't bothered. He'd always liked kids,
always been pally with them, playful with them, and this
was the thanks he got.

Regaining her composure well, Marion took a breath
and started to flatter him subtly, saying she could see he
had been a fine figure of a man in his prime. He had
obviously been very noticeable, she simpered. He started
to chuckle and nod. 'Yes. Ah wis well liked.' He smirked.
'All the women liked me, and Ah liked them.'

I interrupted his reverie once more, with another home
truth. 'But it wasn't just women you wanted sex with,
Dad,' I said. 'You liked wee girls too – you still do. You
wanted away on your own with them. It's true, isn't it?'

I was amazed when, solemnly, he agreed. Marion,

seeing another chink in his armour, followed this line of thought. She smiled sympathetically, moving from the role of coquettish young vamp to serene-faced counsellor. 'Is it something – like an impulse? You know, like something you can't help?'

He nodded. His head lowered, and I thought, We've pushed a button somewhere. This has hit a raw nerve.

'Is it something you've done all your life?' Marion asked delicately. I noticed his eyes shift sideways, and his knuckles tighten on the couch.

'Aye.' He said it at last after what seemed like the longest silence. 'Ah regret it. It's been wi' me all ma life. It's just somethin' that comes over me. Ah cannae help it. Still happens, even now. And Ah regret leavin' my first family tae. Ah dae.'

His eyes were swimming and it was difficult not to feel pity. He was sad and sick. I could not hate him. It is so much easier to abhor the murderer and molester who looks like a monster. I recognized that it was the behaviour and crimes that repulsed me. The man was separate. Tears swamped me, but all my grief was for his victims. How terrible to contemplate the havoc he had wreaked, how ghastly to think of the lives he had ruined, when all his days he had needed help.

'Dad, you're really not ready for the truth to come out just yet,' I said. He looked at me with the eyes I would never forget, for their coldness, detachment and callousness. 'But you know you have to do it. Maybe not this week, or this month, but the time will come.'

We had been with my father almost two hours. Marion had gone into the loo at one point, I realized to change the tape and let Henry know we were both OK. It was a measure of my father's sharp hearing that he picked up the sound of her dialling.

'Is that your pal phonin' somebody?' he asked.

'Oh, yes. She'll just be phoning up north to let them know we got here safe and sound,' I agreed. 'She's got one of these mobiles.'

'Oh. One o' thae new mobile phones.' There was not a sign of suspicion on his face. When Marion returned, she tried to regain his confidence, but he deflected her attempts with different tactics. If we would just come with him to his ex-wife Pat's, she'd tell us what a good guy he was. She would tell us he had nothing to do with it all those years ago, and these bastards up north were just pinning it on him.

We had no intention of taking up his offer.

Marion asked him about Witchwood Pond, describing the area with some accuracy. My dad shrank back on the couch, hands clutching uncontrollably.

'What happened there, Alex?' she demanded. 'That's where you took her, isn't it?'

My father grabbed a Bible. He swore on it dramatically: 'Look, Ah swear on ma children's lives up there, and down here, Ah never touched that wee lassie Moira. This has come back tae haunt me, but honest Ah didn't.'

His body language told another story.

In the last fifteen minutes of our strange three-way meeting, my father tried to shift the blame on to another of Baxter's bus-driving staff. He mentioned one of the ex-colleagues interviewed by Jim's team, and said there had been others, on that route that day, who could be responsible for the girl's murder. And if he could just have a think about it, maybe he could come up with something to help us in the new inquiry. I scribbled my phone number on a piece of card, and he went through the ritual of saying if he managed to come up with new information he would contact me. It was almost laughable, the way he took the card, nodding sagely, and he emphasized his ex-colleague's possible involvement. William had been spot on again, I thought.

Immediately afterwards, I felt terrible as he came down in the lift with us to see us away. He accompanied us to where our hired car was parked, giving us directions to the ring road. As he waved his arms around, I could see Henry, who was beside the car, snapping happily.

My father caught sight of him, and I expected him to go purple, but still there was no recognition of the set-up. I felt ill. It wasn't fair. Why the heck did I care so much? He asked who was the guy taking all the pictures. Just a friend, I lied, although Henry was so loaded with equipment, he could have been David Bailey.

'He's our driver,' Marion said smartly, 'and he's taking us to the airport. OK?'

My father's jaw dropped. It was clear he had few visitors who followed our pattern.

Henry moved closer to my father so that he was now just feet away. My emotions were in turmoil as I attempted to get in the car. I could see him, smiling trustingly, as Marion said I wanted photos of him. It felt deceitful to me, though I was in no doubt that this same man in his life had laid some pretty devious traps for children. Tears of bitterness flowed unchecked, and I was ashamed of the huge sense of betrayal that swamped me.

He hovered beside the car, while Marion attempted to get me to come and embrace him. She looked from one of

273

us to the other, but then perceived that there was no way I would do it. Back came the memory of how as a child I'd had to be pushed forward to kiss him on his return from 'hospital'. I was unable to put one foot in front of the other. As my father stood grinning at us all, she pulled me into her chest and comforted me. Although a welcome gesture, which helped me hide my tear-stained face, it also seemed pretty manipulative. I dissolved, and Henry snapped this frozen trio.

# Chapter Thirty-Six

To her annoyance Marion's report on our visit to Leeds appeared on an inside page of the newspaper. She let rip a series of irritated epithets on the royal beauty whose troubled marriage was beginning publicly to founder. 'Our story was front page, till Di did her usual and hogged all the headlines.'

I was noncommittal. I felt uncomfortable about Henry's photograph of the three of us standing outside the tower block with Marion clutching me determinedly to her. I consoled her as best I could.

'Did the whole tape turn out?'

'Oh, yes. I've been able to transcribe the bulk of it. I'll give you a copy.'

'I did some notes on my return,' I replied, 'but it would be great if you would. Jim McEwan says he'd welcome a copy too, of any part which is incriminating.'

Marion snorted derisively. 'The whole effing conversation was incriminating! I'm as positive as I've ever been about anything in my life that your dad did that little kid in, Sandra. Did you see his face when I described that wee road that winds along to the pond under the old railway bridge? God, he was having kittens.'

After Marion's call, I gazed out of the window, absently

noticing the first decorated Christmas trees going up in the homes of neighbours. Did my father really feel a strong bond with me that had affected him deeply enough to disclose subjects he had avoided strenuously with the police? I could not be sure. I was reminded of the famous words Sir Thomas More wrote to his children: 'Brutal and unworthy to be called father is he who does not weep himself at the tears of his child; I love you with my whole heart, for being a father is not a tie which can be ignored.'

Marion and I had arranged to see Jim together in Glasgow. She had brought a large manila envelope for him, with several typed pages of manuscript. Unfortunately, when we arrived he was not around. We left the envelope with a note and Marion dashed off.

Soon afterwards, I met Alistair Duff, the lawyer recommended by Richard Kinsey. In recent weeks, I had seen him on the television news as Alistair had been interviewed by journalists after agreeing to represent the two Libyan nationals named as suspects in the Lockerbie air disaster of 1988, should Colonel Gaddafi ever allow them to come to Scotland to stand trial for the bombing. On television, he had seemed older, with a precise, formal manner. In the flesh, however, I realized he was about my own age and much less formidable.

'I know very little of the background to this matter, so go ahead and start from scratch. I've half an hour. Fire away,' he said.

He listened as I told the story. A deep cleft formed between his brows as every now and then he made a note or fired a question.

I glanced at my watch desperately. To attempt to explain in minutes such a complex web of events seemed like an impossible task. I groaned inwardly. To my relief, at 5.30, he agreed we should both go home and reconvene later at his house.

When I got to his rambling Victorian villa, we went into a room I supposed was his study to resume my story. My host put on a fire to take the chill off the room, but I could not help shivering. Talking about my father always had this effect on me, and so it remains.

At last I stopped. It came as a huge relief when he looked at me and said, 'I have never heard anything like this in my life. It is straight out of the stuff of nightmares – it is so surreal, it could make a film but I believe you. My personal reaction aside, what I have are enormous concerns *why* Crown Office, of which I have long experience, is doing precisely nothing about your father. Firstly, it seems very surprising that the PF at Airdrie is not willing to take up proceedings in relation to the allegations made by your cousins. It seems to me there's enough evidence there to justify them. Secondly, in the present climate, it is entirely in the public interest that such matters be addressed. Finally, even if the Crown took the view that for some reason these particular charges were not worth prosecuting alone, it would be only sensible to keep them live, so that if he *is* ever charged with the girl Anderson's murder, these other things could be dealt with at the same time, thus increasing the likelihood of a conviction. It seems illogical to dismiss them summarily.'

I described the correspondence stalemate that had gone on for months, and said I had concluded that the only strategy left to try was writing to John Major at Westminster.

'Right. It's worth a try,' he replied. 'Should that effort

run into a brick wall as well, there are two influential figures I know, one in the Commons, one in the Lords, who might help pressurize Crown Office to re-examine its decision or at least have some sort of meeting with you. Their clout might help following on from the representations by John Smith and Lord James. You write the letter to the PM and let me check it for you before sending it off, and we'll take it from there.'

I went straight home to compose it.

Alistair and I had briefly discussed John Smith's problems in the Monklands, with allegations rife of nepotism and religious discrimination, and I had not been surprised to have had no further news of him. So I was astonished when he telephoned me the next day. He apologized for his delay in getting back to me, and said he had seen the articles of October and November in the *Sunday Mail*. He imagined that the Crown Office would not be thrilled by them. What an understatement. I had to smile at his deliberately neutral tone. However, he went on to say that he felt, regretfully, that he had done all he could, and his involvement could not continue in our representation.

'Why?' I jumped in. 'The Moira Anderson case happened in the Monklands, my father molested and abused a number of children there, and my cousins – the two worst affected by all this – live there. And it is your constituency, Mr Smith.'

'Well, naturally I *am* concerned about everything that you have divulged about your father's pattern of behaviour, the fact that he appears to have been missed by the police in 1957 altogether, and the very worrying stories that your cousins have claimed happened to them.'

'If you're concerned, then why do you feel you can no longer support our case?'

After a brief pause, he explained.

'Let me just check what you are saying here, Mr Smith. You feel that as Leader of the Opposition, you cannot afford to become embroiled in this situation with Crown Office, and you really feel you have done all you can for myself and my cousins?'

'That is correct. I have every sympathy with your situation. Your public-spiritedness is to be commended, but unfortunately the outcome is the worst possible. The Crown's decision does seem somewhat inexplicable, but I have done what was asked and do not feel, as Leader of the next Labour government, that I can afford to become further involved in what could evolve into an explosive issue. I can't be involved in a campaign. I am sorry, but that is how I see it.'

I replied that I had taken legal advice, and would now have to go over Lord Rodger's head. Who, I asked, might be the Lord Advocate's line manager?

There was a great roar of laughter at the other end. 'That's a good one! He is totally independent. No one oversees his decisions.'

'I find it quite incredible, Mr Smith, that Lord Rodger's not accountable to anyone.'

'Well, yes, it's a unique feature of our Scottish legal system. I suppose, though, if he has to heed anyone, it would be John Major.'

I told him of my letter to the PM, and he wished me well warmly.

Mindful of my earlier costly mistake, I completed a three-page letter to Downing Street. Alistair suggested two

tiny changes, but otherwise declared it to be 'excellent'.
I posted it with a huge pile of Christmas mail on 10
December.

It was not, however, until after the holidays that a
note acknowledging receipt of it, from a Miss Gorman,
appeared, along with my Open University results. I had
passed – and reasonably comfortably too, to my delight.
Before I knew it, I was immersed in my next course, on
child psychology, for 1994.

Still there was nothing from Westminster.

College resumed around my birthday on 7 January,
and a piece of information came unexpectedly to me. One
of my colleagues, whose father had been taken ill and
died, had departed in a rush to Sydney, Australia, before
Christmas. Such was the frustration point I had reached
that I had decided to ignore my assurance to Jim
McEwan that I would not contact any of the witnesses
outside my own family circle. I could remember the
married name of Moira's sister, and the unusual name of
the wealthy suburb where she lived which, in passing, Jim
had mentioned. It was time, in my view, to join forces to
get something done. I asked my colleague to help and,
when she returned, she gave me a contact number. I calcu-
lated time differences and dialled.

My first call to Janet's home must have been shattering
for her, but she listened carefully and agreed we should
work together for justice. Both of us were in tears by the
end of it – she because she felt so frustrated at being on
the other side of the world and was desperate to meet me;
and myself through sheer relief that she had not rebuffed
me. We agreed that we would correspond immediately and
keep our link under wraps.

'I haven't heard anything from Jim McEwan for weeks now,' she said. 'Is he still on the case?'

'Technically, yes,' I replied, explaining the changed circumstances. 'When I last heard from him, divers were going down to search the pond this week despite freezing conditions. And obviously they've waited for the media interest to die down a bit.'

'What I find very worrying is that when my relatives, the Mathiesons, recently went to Airdrie police station, they were told that the case was now closed.'

'That isn't correct, Janet, so I don't know why they would be told that.' I explained, 'Everything has been moved to Coatbridge police station, according to Jim. They still have a set of family photographs and pictures of my father with other Baxter's bus staff which they have not returned. But it sounds like they want it all to disappear again.'

Finally she pleaded before hanging up that if I heard of *anything* being found where the divers were searching, I should let her know right away. 'Please,' she said. 'It's awful being thousands of miles away. If any remains are found, I'd fly direct to Scotland and never mind the cost. I owe it to my parents to ensure Moira is given a Christian burial.' Her voice cracked. 'That's been the worst thing of all. Not having a body, not having a grave to visit, all these years. It broke my parents' hearts. So cruel. If John Major actually reads your letter, I hope he'll have some compassion for my poor mother and father who both died not knowing. I least now I do. I know why you won't give me your dad's address, but I'll always be grateful to you for doing all this, and going to the police.'

Her words haunted me for hours after that first call.

What a tragedy. When there is no body, how do you *begin* grieving?

Anger flooded through me against my father, the Crown Office, and those too apathetic to do the right thing.

# Chapter Thirty-Seven

Only my husband and one or two friends knew of the call I had made to Australia. The conversation with Janet echoed in my head for days. The most terrifying aspect of it was her conviction that the tall man in overalls who had motioned her over to his car near her home and indecently assaulted her, as a young girl, had also been my father. Shaken to think that lightning could strike twice in one family, I had asked her to give me a brief description of her attacker. 'I told Jim McEwan all about it when he took my statement,' she had replied. 'A great tall fellow with a small dark car, that's all I can remember. That and what he said to me: "C'mere, come and help me hold this." When I went over to see what he was doing under the bonnet of his car, he grabbed me and said, "Hold this dip stick for me, would you?" I was mortified when I saw what I was to hold.'

I had hardly been able to answer her. An image of my father in his navy boiler suit with its buttons down the front, the clothes that had terrified A, surfaced. Not only was Janet's description accurate, the words the man had used mirrored the experience of my cousins C and D. 'We were warned, you know, that a bad man lived near the town hall,' she added. 'And now you say your folks did. Tell me what your father looked like, Sandra.'

'Very tall, and dark, with strange, light-coloured eyes. If you'd met my dad's gaze in the street, you'd remember him. I always felt uncomfortable with the way he looked at me, and any young female for that matter. And he had a black Baby Austin car.'

'It *has* to be him!' Janet had spat out the words with loathing, so I was not surprised when she answered the letter I sent her with a furious tirade against the police of 1957, who had made such empty promises to her parents. Not only had Andrew reported the assault on his eldest daughter, she herself had reported it to staff at Coatbridge High School. While noting that she was not the only victim of the man with the black car, the school had declined to take any action. It seems incredible to think that the local police would ignore an attack on a girl from a family who had hit the headlines in such a tragic case, but this appears to have been exactly what did happen. Andrew took to escorting both his remaining daughters to school, having lost all faith in the local cops.

In mid-February 1994, I finally met Moira's childhood friend Elizabeth Taylor, now Nimmo. I arrived without warning at her comfortable home in Glenmavis, which she took in her stride. We chatted about Moira for several hours. Elizabeth shook her head at the craziness of the legal system. I asked about her memories of Dunbeth Park. Was she the 'Beth' I had remembered as being with Moira? I described the girl I hazily recalled.

'She'd a rounder face than Moira, darker, different hair, and she was wearing something pink on top, with those sort of culottes that we called divided skirts then.'

To my disappointment, she shook her head. 'No, we were lookalikes, I wasn't noticeably darker than her, and we wore our hair in the same style – people sometimes confused us, in fact, so it doesn't sound like me.' She shrugged. 'We went there a lot, though, with my wee dog, which Moira loved, Lucky. Your memory doesn't ring a bell for me, but it could be that the Beth you're looking for is her cousin. I'll give you her number.'

I left her home, pleased that for once I'd not broken down speaking of what I had recently been through. Elizabeth had passed on Jeannette Mathieson Friar's number. I spoke to her at length, then she gave me a contact number for her sister, Beth. It seemed odd to be speaking to the grown versions of the two cousins who had been due to take Moira to the pictures so long ago, and who had been surprised when she failed to rendezvous with them at their grandmother's home. Once again, however, I drew a blank: despite a long, encouraging conversation about the whole affair, this Beth turned out not to be the one who had been Moira's companion that day. And yet I was sure she had not been a casual acquaintance of the little girl's, but someone she knew well. I gave up with a sigh.

I had still had no reply from Westminster.

A huge double-spread article on the saga of the reopened investigation was featured in the *Airdrie and Coatbridge Advertiser* of 25 February 1994, on the thirty-seventh anniversary of the disappearance. I noted with interest Eileen's comment:

> We can reveal police divers are this week expected to resume their search of a local pond where the youngster's body is thought to have been dumped.

Strathclyde's underwater search unit began scouring the little-known stretch of water in Coatbridge at the end of January. They have since made a number of searches but so far have found no traces ... Recent sub-zero temperatures have hampered the effort and forced last week's dive to be called off because the pond was frozen over. The search for Moira's body marks the culmination of an intensive police investigation relaunched two years ago. Despite the exhaustive probe, the youngster's remains have to date never been recovered or her killer brought to justice. It ranks as one of Scotland's most bizarre unsolved cases, which last year saw a woman brand her father a child-killer and launch a campaign to have him charged with Moira's murder. The renewed investigation may have failed to yield tangible results in terms of body or killer, but it did succeed in turning up several dramatic new leads which advanced the case beyond all reasonable expectation, given the passage of time. It is now accepted that she did not vanish on the way to the local shop for her grandmother, but instead took a bus ride to death, after embarking on a secret errand to buy her mother a birthday card ... The mother's prayers that one day her daughter would return safely were never answered. Moira's killer was aided and abetted by the atrocious weather conditions on that fateful Saturday in 1957. A blizzard provided a cloak for him to strike and dispose of the body without being spotted by a single witness. As the snow fell, and the temperatures plummeted, local people were understandably preoccupied with getting home out of the biting cold.

But the only certainty in a case littered with uncertainties is that Moira Anderson did NOT make it home safely that evening. And what became of her is a grisly secret only she and her killer share.

Alistair rang me early one morning to check if I'd heard anything from London. I read to him the reply I'd finally received, which had come from the Scottish Office in Edinburgh. It was from a civil servant named Elva Langwill, and apologized for the two-month delay. The PM had passed my letter to the Secretary of State for Scotland. She was replying for him:

*Although the Lord Advocate is a Government Minister, when he, or Crown Counsel on his behalf, take decisions in individual cases, they do so as independent prosecutors acting in the public interest. While the Lord Advocate is ultimately responsible to Parliament for his actions, he cannot allow himself to be influenced in individual cases by factors which do not arise from the merits of the cases themselves. It is therefore not open to the Secretary of State, or indeed the Prime Minister, to seek to influence the Lord Advocate in the decisions he makes as prosecutor, or to call him to explain the reasons which lie behind a decision taken in a particular case.*

*The independence of the Lord Advocate in matters of prosecution is a fundamental feature of the system of criminal justice in Scotland.*

The writer closed by saying that she was passing on my letter to Lord Rodger himself, and she appreciated this might not be the hoped-for response, but trusted it clarified things.

'For heaven's sake!' Alistair cried, in exasperation. 'You should not be getting replies from the Scottish Office, Sandra, when they've absolutely nothing to do with it. And it's ludicrous that they're passing on your correspondence to the Crown Office when that's the very body you're complaining about! It's totally outrageous. Time for you to write to the two others I suggested: John McFall in the House of Commons, and Donald Macauley who sits in the Lords. They're both the relevant spokespersons. Get off a résumé of the events to them, and I'll back it up with a supporting letter. Let's arrange an appointment.'

We met up in mid-March 1994, just after I had seen Jim, to whom I revealed that I had now made contact with Janet Hart in Australia. He was noncommittal on this and, to my disappointment, confirmed that the pond search had not revealed any remains or artifacts which could be linked to her sister. He could see I was as determined as ever, and rolled his eyes with amazement when I told him I was putting together the transcript of the William O'Connor tape so that I could send Janet details of the meeting that had led to police interest in the Witchwood area. I hoped it might bring Janet some comfort.

It was to be my last meeting with Jim, who hinted that he was busy tidying some loose ends in his post. It seemed that moves were afoot, and I was delighted for him when I heard in April that he had won promotion to Detective Chief Inspector. I bought a card to congratulate him and sent him my best wishes on his success, with a sense of relief that his involvement with me had not hurt his career.

I showed Alistair the documents I had prepared for

the two politicians. He gave me a copy of one of the covering letters he had written to accompany my request for meetings with them both: I wanted them to press my case in Westminster. I read it when I got home, and his words made me feel much better after the rebuffs I had received.

*Without going into all the details, having met her father again, Sandra became convinced he was responsible for the likely abduction and murder of a child called Moira Anderson in Coatbridge. This may all sound a trifle improbable, but I can say that, having heard the details, I am pretty sure that she is right and that the original police enquiry was a terrible botch . . .*

*As you have probably guessed, this document is very much a potted version of the whole saga, but what I can assure you of is that Sandra is not a crank. For what it is worth, I am firmly of the view that her suspicions are well-founded and that a major injustice will be done if this man is not brought to book for his wrongs. I hope you can help her, and would be quite happy to talk with you about it all in greater detail.*
*Alistair J. M. Duff.*

John McFall chose not to become involved, but Lord Macauley wrote to say that he would make some discreet inquiries first, before we met with Alistair at Parliament House. His initial reaction was of great disquiet. He requested copies of all the correspondence up to date, and a complete summary of events.

'What's the problem?' Sheena, the chief clerical officer, who was also working late one night, had spotted my haunted look over the paperwork I'd to do. I felt I could confide in her, given her connections to Coatbridge from childhood, and the discreet comments she had made as events in the media had unfolded. 'How can I help?' I was stunned when she took away the letters which all had to be copied, and a covering letter I'd drafted to type. Later, I discovered that Moira Anderson's was one of two child abductions in Coatbridge this century. The other, in the 1920s, turned out to have been of the brother of Sheena's grandfather. The murder of a child does not affect only one generation.

More unexpected help came in other forms. Alistair and I left Lord Macauley after a supportive meeting, with a book on the infamous 'Carol X' Glasgow rape case, in which Donald Macauley had been involved as a young man. He lent it to me to let me see what was involved in pursuing a private prosecution, and he waved away my thanks while indicating to us that as Shadow Lord Advocate he would continue to press the Crown Office on my behalf in an attempt to glean further information. So far, between them, he and Alistair had ascertained that no written notification had ever been sent by the Lord Advocate's office to Leeds to let my father or his English solicitors know of their decision in relation to possible future proceedings. They had been able to check that the Procurator Fiscal at Airdrie had never intimated to Mr Gartshore any word about their decisions. As far as my two advisers were concerned, this seemed to indicate that if and when we could pressure the Crown Office to re-examine its findings, the door was not firmly closed on a possible case against my dad.

Financially, however, I told Alistair, my cousins and I

had ruled out the idea of a private prosecution. It was too much of a risk, with too many folk and their families worried about maintaining a roof over their heads. Despite Lord Macauley's view that my cousins could be eligible for criminal compensation, we had dismissed it. None of us, I told him, were interested in gaining financially from a tragic situation. We just wanted justice, for Moira and ourselves.

'I suppose the only way forward is if you happen to know a millionaire, Sandra.'

Alistair's remark had been a joke, but after he dropped me off at home, I pondered over what he had said, and realized I *did* know of one multi-millionaire in the Monklands, who might help us.

# Chapter Thirty-Eight

Through Eileen, I arranged a meeting in the Georgian Hotel in Coatbridge with a local philanthropist, Vera Weisfeld, who had made a fortune with her second husband, Gerald, in the rag trade. I introduced myself to her and her son Michael, of Celtic football club. Close up, the girl from Coatbridge who had worked so hard to gain unbelievable wealth and status, and who was easily included in the top ten of Scotland's rich and famous, was unassuming and genuine. She chatted away to break the ice, but a sharp business brain was at work. Her smile was warm, her interest in my story genuine, as she asked her son to fetch us both a sherry. 'Of course I recall the whole saga of Moira Anderson's disappearance vividly.' She proceeded to do what every contemporary who remembered the event did – she recalled her exact movements on Saturday 23 February 1957. Then she and her son listened to my story.

'Michael, how can we help?' Vera was decisive. She wanted to consult with lawyers, see how feasible financing a private prosecution would be and get back to me. Meanwhile, I had to give her a copy of the correspondence that had passed between all the parties concerned, and she would think it through. Her decision would not be made overnight, she said, but she'd be in touch. We left the hotel to the sound of electioneering, and discussed the forthcoming by-election caused by John Smith's death. We both felt sure Helen Liddell would succeed him, and I mentioned that Janet in Australia had gone out with Alastair Liddell years before. His family had been friendly with Moira's, and still lived in Cliftonville.

'Scotland is really a very small country.' Vera Weisfeld smiled.

Meanwhile, I received a call out of the blue from Elizabeth Taylor Nimmo, up north visiting her daughter. I was surprised to hear from her: she sounded upset. It transpired that her family had had a new baby, and her daughter had asked her to bring all the old family albums to have a look through before they inserted the new ones.

'I couldn't believe it, Sandra. I hadn't seen them for years. Pictures that my parents took at St Andrews when I was a kiddie – it was such a shock when I saw myself on the beach in this pink sloppy joe T-shirt and the grey divided skirts. It was just as you described, and I'd forgotten that in the summer of 1956, my mum had got my hair permed. It does look different, and darker in those snaps. My daughter said something when I was just gazing at it, and it must have triggered something. It was horrible.'

'You've remembered,' I said softly. 'It *was* you. You're Beth.'

She sobbed for a few moments, then I heard her agree quietly.

'I've told my daughter, though it was so painful. The photo brought it all back, because we're there, all of us on the beach, the family, my big sister and her boyfriend, who'd been allowed to come with us. They were the ones who got married the same week as Moira disappeared the next February, and their anniversary always coincides. Well, when he was changing, the towel slipped and, of course, there was a lot of hilarity, mainly at my expense because they thought I'd never seen a man undressed at my age. My parents were very fair people, but strict, and they would've died rather than discuss sex with my sister and me. They thought I was pure as the driven snow. I was mortified. But I couldn't tell my folks that I *had* actually seen a man's sexual organ that summer.'

I felt a sweeping sense of relief. Here was the final piece in my own personal jigsaw of memory slipping into its appointed place, from the heat wave of 1956.

'I've been so upset discussing it with my own daughter, but she insisted I phone you to let you know you were right about the flashback you had all these years ago. It was Moira and your dad and me that you saw, though why I should've repressed it all this time, I don't know. I genuinely had no recollection of the man Moira knew who called us over to his car that day at Dunbeth Park, till I saw that picture of me on the sands at St Andrews and realized it was the same outfit you'd described. Suddenly, there I was, back with her, and laughing like a couple of drains at what he was doing in his little black car.'

'What was he doing, Elizabeth?' I asked, already knowing.

'He was exposing himself, wanting us to come and touch him and get sweets.'

'You're sure she knew him?'

'Yes, I'm sure she called him by name. She definitely knew him, but when he spoke to her, that's when you appeared, and we ran off in fits.'

I told Elizabeth how grateful I was that she'd shared this recollection with me.

She contacted me later to tell me she had called at the police station, where she had hoped to see Gus Patterson, whom she knew, but it had turned out there was only desultory interest in the additional statement she gave. It seemed to her, she said, that the case, as Janet, my cousins and myself had feared, was being quietly put to rest once more in the recesses of Coatbridge police station.

Now, I told my cousins, our only hope seemed to lie with Vera Weisfeld.

But it was clear when I met her again that she has decided reluctantly that a private prosecution was not the way forward. On advice from her lawyers, she felt she did not want to take on the Lord Advocate. Then she said, 'Have you considered writing down what has happened to you at all?' She asked if I'd heard of Eddie Bell, a local guy of my own age, who, like herself, had surpassed the aspirations of many. He had risen to great heights at Collins, the publishers in Glasgow. I remembered him as a bouncer on the door of the youth fellowship at Gibson's church from my teenage years, when they ran discos, a fair-haired square-set chap, who had sold greeting cards for a living.

'Sure, I know who he is.' I smiled at her. 'Local boy done good, as they say! Now a real star in the publishing world, I understand.'

'More than a star. He's executive chairman these days of HarperCollins, and his reputation's formidable, but like myself, he's never forgotten his roots, and I imagine the events of 1957 would be included in his memories of this town.'

Vera described how she was working on a book for him, and said she would be happy to arrange a meeting on my behalf. On the way home, however, I reflected on what she had suggested and I realized that, for all sorts of reasons, I should consider her idea. I left it for some weeks, to mull things over, then contacted her again. 'Right. I think I could do it. Tell Eddie I'll see him when he's next north of the border.'

And so, through the millionairess, I met Eddie Bell, whose face seemed the same but whose shape had expanded since our teenage years. After a long lunch at Glasgow's Devonshire Gardens, when he'd heard of the ordeal we had all been through, he said simply, 'This story has to be told. No question.'

I informed Alistair and Lord Macauley that the last resort, it seemed, would be a book. They were in broad agreement that it was perhaps the only real avenue remaining to me, though the latter continued to fire off letters to the Crown Office. In November, he also accompanied me to meet Helen Liddell, now settling in as MP in John Smith's constituency. As I had expected, she showed great sensitivity and promised to do all she could, and met A and B to assure them of her support.

I took a short break after my second lot of autumn exams and started to write down all the events of the past few years, which seemed far too outlandish to be true but every one of which had happened to me.

Only one thing worried me, and that was my mother's reaction to what I was doing, but as 1995 dawned, and she wished me a happy birthday, I spoke to her of my intentions to see it through. I waited fearfully but there was no outburst from her, just a deep, heartfelt sigh and a nod.

'I know there's no point asking you not to do it. You're driven, I can see that,' she said slowly. 'And I know why it's important for you that the truth comes out, but I just hope it isn't in my lifetime, Sandra. I hope I'm not around to see it.'

I noticed with a wry smile that the sepia photograph of the long-lost fiancé who had drowned had emerged from her box into pride of place on her sideboard. It was her way of letting me know that she no longer held any allegiance to my father. 'He saw me as an opportunity, I think,' she said. 'His life was in a mess when I came along. He'd got a girl into trouble, and her baby had to be adopted, but I didn't know that at the time. The baby was the reason he'd met our minister, which lulled me into a false sense of security. I found out about her later on – you could tell when you saw them that there had been an affair. But they couldn't marry.'

'Why not?' I asked curiously.

'She was his aunt – his own mother's sister. They hushed it all up at the time.'

My mother got her fervent wish. She lived only six weeks or so after having said that she would not wish to witness a book by her own flesh and blood based on the tragic events that had happened in her life and then in mine.

Many ministers will tell you that it is a common phenomenon for those on the point of death to believe they can see someone dear to them who has already passed on. When my mother died unexpectedly in March 1995, only a few hours after collapsing without warning, she regained consciousness for long enough to tell my brothers, their wives, and my uncle who stayed with her what she had been doing that day, what she had eaten for her lunch at her club for the blind in Coatbridge, and she heard that one sister-in-law was doing her best to contact me in Edinburgh. The staff at the Monklands Hospital were just making arrangements to transfer my mother from the casualty department to a ward, when she had a cardiac arrest. Despite all efforts, the staff could not resuscitate her, and when I arrived, she had been dead an hour.

While I was upset that I had not been there, the family told me that seconds before the chest pains took hold of her, my mother looked towards the end of the bed and said very clearly, 'Daddy. There's my daddy.'

She repeated it, so that they were in no doubt that she was seeing her own father. Knowing how deep their relationship was, those words have given me comfort. It seems entirely appropriate to me that the one man in her life in whom my mother had implicit trust was there for her at the very end.

# Epilogue

Many people will question why I felt it necessary to take up my pen after all other avenues of attempting to obtain justice for Moira and my cousins had failed. It is a duty, as far as I can see, that I should alert others to look into the darkness that surrounds the world of the abuser, to probe and question how he gets away with such behaviour, and to demand answers even when it may be easier to shy away from what may be sickening to hear.

It is important to realize that the inquiry I sparked off in the 1990s ran parallel with an even more depraved situation that was investigated in a small English city. Sadly, it will now be for ever associated with the horror of sex abuse, sudden disappearances, and the murders of young women. In Gloucester, it quickly became obvious to those who followed the trial of Rosemary West, which followed the suicide of her partner, that over the preceding decades there had not been nearly enough co-operation between all the relevant agencies with whom the family had contact. Warning bells, we are told, would be heard immediately today. But would they?

Their plausibility and adept deceit helped Fred and Rosemary West evade detection for years, but the couple were aided and abetted by official records being lost, destroyed, never kept or never passed on, with no one agency being blameless. Not only were children not observed independently or listened to, but the rape and torture of an early victim, Caroline Owens, then seventeen, in 1972, turned into a meaningless farce, where the Wests found rape charges dropped and each was fined £50. Information from surviving victims did not lead to investigations, and women who were attacked by the two at the roadside in enticement attempts gave descriptions that went nowhere.

There is no such thing as a typical paedophile, but from childhood, both my father and Fred West showed a precocious interest in sex and a love of pornography that grew as they matured. Their lives followed separate paths, but both became sexual psychopaths. This is a lifelong problem, which in my view only ceases with infirmity or death. My father will be a threat to young women and children until he is overcome by one or the other.

Both men's first offences were recorded on police files as sexual assaults on thirteen-year-old girls who lived in their local area. Both were involved in incest within their own family. Fred West's sister was taken into care as a pregnant youngster, and there is little doubt that he was the father of her child. My father made his aunt, a woman older than himself, pregnant with a child who was then adopted.

Both men had a sadistic streak, and were able to hide a complete disregard for the feelings of others and a need to gratify their own sexual demands behind a façade of amiability. A deep-seated need in both meant presenting an air of hardworking respectability, and they sought token approval from others, whether through working long hours on building projects as West did, or as my father did, by stopping his bus for old ladies. When they were interviewed by police, neither man showed any desire to clear his conscience or give information that would help the families of victims.

How differently things might have turned out for my father, had he married a Rosemary, rather than my mother. Fred West used his wife as an ally: her presence in his car lulled young women into a false sense of security. Behind my mother's back I, too, was used unknowingly as bait by my father. I have had to confront the fact that I was an unwitting ally on a number of occasions for my father's depravity. It never crossed the minds of my friends that anything would happen to them if they played with me. Sexual assailants don't come with their daughters, do they?

Finally, both men evaded formal interviews when girls went missing at bus stops. Fred West's attack on Caroline Owens seems to have been overlooked when it bore similarities to the assaults other women reported, and there had been disappearances of several women in the area; in 1957 the police chose not to round up all the local suspects in Moira Anderson's case.

In the final analysis, it is significant that neither man *was* arrested through painstaking paperwork or strokes of insight by dedicated men. Fred West's undoing was that one of his children's statements about the disappearance of their sister, Heather, was finally taken seriously by a social worker, then followed up by a policewoman who checked out that her national insurance number and other personal identification details had never been used in the United Kingdom. In my father's case, it was his own startling statements to me after a twenty-seven-year absence that sowed the seeds of doubt. Detectives only then reopened forgotten files. In the end, the finger was pointed by the flesh and blood of both men.

I think there are other parallels. Like Fred West, I believe my father was able to build up a self-belief system that allowed him to go about his business normally. It has acted like a safety net, helping him to live with what he has done and enabling him to push aside any stray emotion he may feel from time to time. I cannot be sure what he has been doing over the years he has lived in Leeds, but all the evidence shows that paedophiles and abusers do not change their spots and in a lifetime may have more than a hundred victims. Retrospectively, Glasgow police are examining the files of those women and girls who disappeared when Fred West resided in the south side of the city in the 1960s, during his first marriage to Rena Costello.

Despite the open manner of the reporting of Rosemary West's trial, there would appear to be a conspiracy of silence going on post-Cromwell Street Gloucester. A hundred or so pornographic videos were mentioned in the 1992 trial in which she and her husband were involved that led to nothing. What happened to them? They could not possibly all have been made by the pair. A video-shop owner had reported that Fred West had openly offered him film of 'real murders'. It is fairly clear that the Wests were part of some ring, and although we cannot be sure that all the facts will emerge, others may have known the secrets of 25 Cromwell Street. Will these others be brought to justice?

The story of the Wests exposes non-intervention, non-pursued lines of inquiry and disregard for child-protection procedures. No one bothered to put the jigsaw together. Did Charmaine West's school never query where her records should be sent? Did the local hospital never query that a fifteen-year-old brought to them by her father with an ectopic pregnancy was under age? The Wests were able to get away with their catalogue of crime because as a society we refused to confront the possibility that such crimes *could* be occurring in the heart of a perfectly ordinary British community. This was no Stephen King-type *Texas Chainsaw Massacre* horror movie to thrill adolescents. This was real, and far more ghastly for it.

We cannot ignore the fact that everyone, from agencies to institutions to ordinary next-door neighbours, put their heads well below the sand while a large number of young women perished in their midst. The most chilling aspect is that nobody cared enough to notice. Not one person, despite a church being next door. But if professionals such as social workers, police personnel and childcare staff do not receive the resources or the training required to deal with the perpetrators of child sexual abuse, what chance have we that members of the public will be able to recognize the features such deviant people possess?

The wickedest sexual crimes are often carried out by those who look normal, but whose behaviour patterns are a give-away when we take time to observe them closely. We ignore these people at our peril, and we do our own children no favours by joining the conspiracy of silence on sexual abuse. If we study their behaviour and peer down into the darkness, a disease is revealed that goes so deep, we begin to realize that we are naïve if we assume it has not spread its roots through the entire fabric of our nation.

We are not alone.

It has come as a huge shock to the people of Belgium, two years on from Gloucester, that they have their counterparts of the Wests, with allies highly placed in the police forces who covered for them. For those who would suggest that I exaggerate, and insist that Britain is no worse than any other civilized country in its attitudes to child sexual abuse, I would ask if they are aware of the slow response our government made to the worldwide campaign to end the abuse of children in Asia, created by the demand for child prostitution by Western tourists. We show our true colours by being out of step with a remarkable number of other world powers who took early action to ensure that their nationals who abuse children in other countries will be pursued, prosecuted, and dealt with accordingly, despite international crime syndicates who aid and abet paedophiles with information and pornography peddled through the Internet.

We have a choice.

To tolerate such a malignant blight on our society is not the answer. These people – the paedophiles, the abusers, and the Mr Bigs who feed from their unhealthy tastes – must be exposed for what they are. A positive step would be to listen to what our children are saying. Perhaps the most surprising element in the West case was that someone finally listened to their children, which our culture does not encourage. Too often, what children say is swept aside as fantasy.

Even professional people accept ancient myths about offenders that are quite untrue; that they are sexually inadequate, disturbed individuals whose behaviour will be noticeably bizarre. Little is circulated about them being powerful, clever, manipulative and in control, with a system of carefully planned strategies to avoid being caught. There is little about them instilling such deep fear in their victims that disclosure *can* only surface years later. So thorough has the disparaging of children's evidence against abusers been, it is no wonder that the typical pattern shows itself as initial denial, then disclosure, followed by terrified retraction as the possible consequences set in, then reaffirmation when support is given. If there are fears by children that accusations of malicious fantasy will be aimed at them, it is understandable how adults such as my cousins, who finally summon the courage to reveal childhood abuse and who then find the legal authorities totally uninterested in doing anything about it, feel as if they have been kicked in the teeth.

Infection spreads when it goes unchecked. All cancers start with an insidious if minor change, but the progress of the disease can be halted if it is treated early. When I look back to the events I have described that took place in 1957, it is easy to diagnose that something began to go askew in that community. I ask myself why, given all the signs that foul play had occurred and hints that something was seriously amiss, the investigation was never scaled up from a missing-persons inquiry to a full-scale murder case. The responsibility for that seriously flawed judgement rests on someone's conscience.

Repeated deception by the paedophile Thomas Hamilton, the executioner of sixteen five-year-olds and their teacher in Dunblane in March 1996, in retaliation against worried parents who helped close down his dubiously run boys' clubs, went unnoticed and unchecked over years. Sloppy police work did not follow up his claims in the mid-eighties that he was a top marksman who competed throughout the UK. Internal police records (made available, but not brought to attention at the ensuing Cullen Inquiry) show that no effort was ever made to check out to which gun clubs he was supposed to belong. Negligence is nothing new when it comes to catastrophic outcomes regarding the safety of our children.

All those people I have come across down the years who muse about what befell Moira in 1957 and pontificate, 'Of course, it would never happen nowadays,' need to have their complacency shaken to its foundations. Not only was it *allowed* to happen then, the same thing was equally condoned in Gloucester: the luring of young women or children, none of whom suspected the harm she would meet, to satisfy the vilest of sexual appetites. Tenfold, or more. The final tally of victims may never be complete, but in the end, they met the same fate as Moira: in many cases, missed by their immediate families, but consigned to public oblivion. Some were never reported as missing, such as Rena and her child, because out of sight seemed to mean out of mind. They had simply gone, and not enough questions were asked.

There are never enough questions asked by those whose job it is to seek information or by ourselves. As ordinary human beings, we should care about the loss of one person, never mind twelve. I find myself staggered by the view of some people I have encountered who find it hard to fathom why I should wish to fight for justice for a child to whom I was not related. Whether or not it belongs to you and yours, or is part of me and mine, the loss of a child should be mutually mourned.

I vowed that I would not stop campaigning on behalf

of Moira, and would continue to fight to see justice done for both herself and my cousins, and all other victims of sexual abuse. Even when shutters descended, and rebuffs came consistently from the Scottish Crown Office, with refusals to answer any of my questions regarding my father's non-prosecution, I decided I would not stop asking: 'Why?'

A book that set down the events I have met, the people who have given support, and those who have presented obstacles to justice inevitably raises questions that cannot be ignored. I also saw it as a way of keeping faith with Moira and ensuring that what happened to her will not be forgotten or covered up.

'Perhaps,' I told myself, 'when I have written the last page, and typed the last sentence of such a record, then maybe I shall finally feel I have redressed the balance, even a little. I will have done all in my power to draw attention to the attitudes we must change when we deal with abusers. *They* are not going to change, so it is up to us to look at our strategies for dealing with offenders and the way we treat the victims of abuse.'

The legal system in Scotland is woefully lacking at present in its communications to victims and shows remarkable inconsistencies in the way that it deals with sexual offences going back years. Some victims abused in childhood receive compensation, others do not. Other pensioners in their seventies have appeared in court over the period in which I have written this book, and often there have been parallels. Some have received sentences of several years, others generous spells of community service. What is so special about my father that he remains at large in the cover of a big city where he can so easily continue his lifelong habits? The Scottish Crown Office doesn't see him as its problem. Again, out of sight, out of mind. But if it was relatives of *theirs* who happened to move into his stamping ground, I feel certain that they would ensure that people were alerted.

There is no question of my cousins or myself seeking financial compensation for what my father put us through, although his behaviour continues to affect our lives. My motivation in writing down what happened to them, to my friends, to Moira and to me, is to let the public have the opportunity to hear the facts. This is in direct defiance of the Procurator Fiscal in Airdrie who shepherded me from his office saying that it was not in the public interest that our story was heard. He could not have known that his attitude would only strengthen my resolve. Clearly the last thing he expected was that the ordinary Scottish woman he brushed off with excuses would go on to bombard the people he represented at the Crown Office in Edinburgh with letters questioning his decision and theirs, which undermined months of painstaking police work.

It is my hope that, on reading this text, questions will continue to be asked by others, which cannot go away as they hope I have. It has been enormously important to me to write these words alone and without the help of a third party who might have influenced what I say here. The memories set down are mine and mine alone. I am prepared to accept the responsibility which accompanies this, and stand by every word written, and I can withstand any attack after what I have already had to bear. Anyone who teaches child-protection courses to others cannot be hypocritical and walk away from what has occurred.

What is also painfully clear to people like my cousins and myself, to Kate and Joe Duffy of Hamilton, who have campaigned long and hard for the Scottish 'Not Proven' verdict to be scrapped in the aftermath of the acquittal of Frances Auld, who stood trial for the murder of their daughter, Amanda Duffy, is that the Scottish legal authorities rebuke criticism, do not recognize any accountability to citizens, and see no need to change the way they handle a system that clearly lets down many ordinary people. Despite its worldwide high regard, our legal system is far from perfect, and needs fixing – now.

It is significant that none of my cousins or myself would have qualified for legal aid, had we tried to launch a private prosecution. South of the border, these are much more common. We own our homes, which would have had to be remortgaged. There was no way we could contemplate that. Yet Robert Maxwell's sons got legal aid for their court appearance. Again, it seems it is the little people who fall through the gaps in our legal system.

Sometimes, however, even the littlest, most insignificant person will not take no for an answer. Sometimes the questions are just too important to be dismissed. Support to keep asking them came to me from the unlikeliest sources. Strength came from the knowledge that my unease at the way in which all charges against my father were dropped without explanation was shared by several of the keenest legal brains in Scotland and many of the police élite involved throughout.

I am not the same person I was when events turned my life upside down over five years ago. It's direction changed irrevocably with what came to light in 1992, and I have had to find my way back, through a valley of shadows and horror, where what had been only imagined previously, became all too hellishly apparent. I had to absorb hostility on this journey, which came in the form of attack, verbal abuse and rejection, as I groped for the truth.

At the worst moments, when I was sinking under the sheer weariness of it all, someone would appear and carry some of the weight with me for part of the way. I find that my store of faith in my fellow human beings has not been eroded. Small acts of kindness boosted me. Amazing links happened which I do not now dismiss as coincidences.

A sense of having restored the balance a little came when Janet Anderson Hart allowed two of her children to come and stay in my home, to help convey memories of their aunt that could be added to this book; then finally, my family and myself travelled to Australia and met Moira's namesake.

'For there is nothing hid which shall not be uncovered,' Mark's gospel tells us, and I have emerged from the darkness with my faith renewed. I know that everything that has happened since 1992 was meant to happen, and I believe that I was guided spiritually.

The road was terrifying, but I was able to make sense of the events of my childhood, and what really happened in 1957, to myself and to Moira. If I do not warn others, however, of the lessons learned and the knowledge imparted, then the nightmare can and will descend on all of us. For the sake of our children, we can never let it settle again on unsuspecting innocents.

Where there is evil, we must cast it out.

# Endpiece

Since this book was completed in 1997, Alexander Gartshore, although continuing to reside in Leeds, moved out
of his home temporarily after a shooting incident. It
occurred outside the block of flats where he lives, while
he was standing at a bus stop. It is believed that
although he was taken to hospital to have a number of
pellets – thought to have been fired from the tower block
– removed from his head and neck, he was not seriously
injured. He chose, however, not to involve the police in
any investigation on this matter.

Following this incident which took place in February,
a Coatbridge man was arrested on the eve of the General
Election, in May, after a young girl was molested in a tower
block lift in the Whifflet area of the town. A pensioner, and
a respected church elder, he was later charged for carrying
out a series of harrowing sexual assaults against two sets
of sisters over two decades.

At the High Court in Glasgow, in August 1997, this
man received ten years imprisonment for his paedophile
behaviour from Lord Cameron. Although his photograph,
which was splashed across the national papers, showed a
retired male of sixty-six, the author had little trouble in
recognizing him as Jim, one of Alexander Gartshore's

colleagues from their days together on Baxter's Buses in Coatbridge. As a young man, she had seen him visit her Dunbeth Road home; her mother had commented that despite an age gap, they seemed to have struck up a firm friendship, but she could not work out what they had in common.

The author now finds it horrifyingly clear what their mutual interests were, for Jim was the man who engineered the situation where he persuaded Betty, the thirteen year old, to come to Alexander's home regularly, and which led to prison for the older paedophile. Betty the babysitter was Jim's young sister.

He is now in Peterhead Prison within the secure unit for his protection and at his own request. Detective Chief Inspector Jim McEwan confirmed his connection to Alexander and indicated to a Glasgow newspaper that the two men *had* worked for the same local bus firm at the same time when Moira disappeared. He said, 'We will have the opportunity of speaking to him further in prison, and we will take it from there. It is too early to say if he will be of assistance to our inquiries into the case of Moira Anderson, which remains open.'